Roraima and Brit

With a Glance at Bermuda, t ˷˷ ˷˷˷ᴜ˷ɪes, and the Spanish Main

J. W. Boddam-Whetham

Alpha Editions

This edition published in 2023

ISBN : 9789357947770

Design and Setting By
Alpha Editions
www.alphaedis.com
Email - info@alphaedis.com

Contents

CHAPTER I.

OUTWARD BOUND—THE 'CANIMA'—A ROUGH VOYAGE—
FIRST VIEW OF BERMUDA—COASTING—IRELAND ISLE—
COMMISSIONERS' HOUSE—THE SOUND—HAMILTON—
LANDING—AN INDIA-RUBBER TREE—A BILL OF FARE—THE
REGISTER—HAMILTON HOTEL—PAPAWS—A SUGGESTION.

"Under the eaves of a southern sky,

Where the cloud roof bends to the ocean floor

Hid in lonely seas, the Bermoothes lie—

An emerald cluster that Neptune bore

Away from the covetous earth god's sight,

And placed in a setting of sapphire light."

"Well, if we are going to a warmer temperature than this, few of us will return," was the remark made by one of the passengers on board the little steamer 'Canima,' which was rolling heavily in a perfectly smooth sea, past Staten Island on her way from New York to Bermuda. It was the month of November, but the sun was as hot and the sky as brassy as though it had been August. On shore we could see preparations being made for cricket, lawn-tennis, and archery; and there were we bound for a semi-tropical climate. It was one of those days with which the clerk of the weather favours New York in early spring, and sometimes even when the Indian summer is supposed to have ended.

I have said that the vessel rolled heavily, even in a smooth sea, and we were naturally anxious to know what she would do in rough weather; some thought that she would turn over altogether, others, that she would regain her equilibrium and keep it, but this latter idea was soon proved to be a fallacy, as the wretched ship had no more centre of gravity than a cherub.

Hardly had we entered the open sea when a change in the weather occurred. The sky was overcast, the waves assumed a threatening aspect, a cold drizzle set in, and general discomfort prevailed.

How gay and lively the scene on deck was when we started! how dull and quiet it suddenly became! just as I was imitating the example of the rest of the passengers by retreating to my cabin, an old gentleman who had made the passage to Bermuda thirty-two times spoke to me of

"The old green glamour of the glancing sea."

As I did not feel much inclined to listen to poetry, I merely remarked that I thought Lucretius was right when he declared that "the sea was meant to be looked at from shore," and then withdrew.

A less enjoyable voyage could not be imagined, and what with a head wind, rainy weather, the gulf-stream in a state of extra-roughness, and French-Canadian stewards, whose dirty appearance made the greasy food less appetising, if possible, than it otherwise would have been, a more ghostly, half-starved lot of travellers never arrived at their destination. How many lines of steamers there are whose owners trade on the old Sanscrit proverb which they might adopt as their motto, "The river is crossed, and the bridge is forgotten."

Fortunately the passage only lasted four days, the advertised time being seventy-two hours; and glad indeed were we when we had passed through the narrow reef-channel, and were coasting along the western side of the main island of the Bermudas, and within the formidable chain of breakers which surrounds them.

The first view of the island is disappointing, as the low hills have a barren and desolate appearance, and the plain white cottages which are dotted about here and there stand in bare, uncultivated spots. Lower down, however, as we approach the central portion, the face of the island brightens. Old acquaintances of Bermuda point out the position of Harrington Sound, which they declare—and rightly as we afterwards thought—to be the most lovely part of the island; but from the vessel all we can see is a narrow inlet which one could almost jump across. The long lines of roofs which sparkle so in the sun on the hill yonder are the barracks, and the red coats of the soldiers make pleasant bits of colour, which contrast well with the gleaming sand and the deep green cedar-nooks in which the white houses nestle.

Farther on we pass Government House and the signal station, from which the arrival of the steamer has long been signalled; then Clarence Hill—Admiralty House—is left behind, and we round Spanish Point, with Ireland and other islands forming a semi-circle on our right. On Ireland Island is to be seen as everybody knows, the famous floating dock which was towed from England in 1869. At another time, this would probably have been the centre of attraction, but the eyes of our sea-worn passengers were directed to a fine large building well situated at the extremity of that island. "What a splendid hotel!" said one, and "How delightfully cool it must be there!" said another. It proved to be the "Commissioner's House," now used as military quarters.

The history of this building is rather singular. A certain Treasury clerk was appointed "Commissioner" in charge of the dockyard, and, not being satisfied with the house given him to occupy, received permission from the Home Government to spend £12,000 in building a new one. This concession appears to have turned his head, for the house gradually assumed the dimensions of a palace; marble chimney-pieces were erected, and stabling built for a dozen horses, and this in a country where fire-places were hardly necessary, and where, at that time, horses were useless. Marble baths and other trifles ran up the bill to over £60,000. The gentleman for whom this expense was incurred never occupied the house, as he went mad, and the office of "Commissioner" was soon dispensed with.

Whilst an old resident was telling us this story, we had entered the Great Sound, and we found ourselves in a pretty land-locked harbour, on whose wonderfully clear blue water floated numerous fairy islets—a scene which reminded us of the words of Moore:

"The morn was lovely, every wave was still

When the first perfume of a cedar-hill

Sweetly awakened us, and with smiling charms

The fairy harbour wooed us to its arms."

Through these green islands we wound our way carefully, one channel being particularly narrow and dangerous. Beneath its transparent waters we could distinguish an old cannon; and then a sudden turn brought us into the pretty port of Hamilton, where we dropped anchor close to the shore. But being on shore and only near it are very different things, and it seemed hours to us hungry mortals before the vessel was gradually dragged to within forty feet of the quay. Nearer we could not get, on account of a shallow.

Now to land in boats appeared too ridiculous for such a short distance, but no other means were visible. A bridge lowered by a crane would have landed us all in a few minutes, but there was no appearance of such a thing. Old-fashioned Bermuda wanted no new-fangled notions, so we had to abide our time and wait until a bridge had been manufactured in the following way: Ropes were thrown from the vessel and fastened to the outer ends of long beams, which were hauled on board, their other extremities resting on shore. Then a number of grinning darkies strided these beams, and lashed cross-bars to them; planks were laid on the frame, and over these we walked on to the quay.

There were only two passengers besides myself for the Hamilton Hotel, and these were a very charming old lady and her son—a young physician from Boston—who had been advised to spend the winter abroad. A short walk brought us to the hotel, a good-sized, comfortable building, commanding a fine view of the harbour and port of the town. On our way up, we passed a splendid specimen of the india-rubber tree, whose luxuriant growth almost hid the broad veranda'd cottage behind it. Speaking of this tree, Mark Twain says that, when he saw it, it was "out of season, possibly as there were no shoes on it, nor suspenders, nor anything a person would properly expect to find there." This tree was the first sign of tropical vegetation that we had seen, which fact had rather surprised us, as on the cover of a "bill of fare," which had been shown to us in New York, was a picture of the Hamilton Hotel, with an avenue of palms and bananas leading up to it. The fine palms—mountain cabbage—we afterwards discovered about half-a-mile off, and not even within sight of the hotel. But one cannot expect to find everything one sees, even on a bill of fare. We were informed by the clerk that we were the first visitors of the season. "But somebody else is here," said I, pointing to a solitary name in the visitor's register. "Oh," said he, "that's me;" and forthwith assigned us our rooms.

And now let me say a word about this hotel, which is notorious for having prevented many strangers from visiting Bermuda, and others who would have liked to return, from coming back. The rooms are simply but comfortably furnished, the situation is good, and the grounds might be very prettily laid out. The whole cause of discontent with the hotel has hitherto—that is, up to the winter of 1877-78—been with the management. The house had been leased to an American, a pleasant, agreeable person, but without the least idea of managing an hotel. People did not come to Bermuda for third-rate American hotel dinners, but there they got them, until they could stand it no longer. It was useless to speak to the manager; no redress was obtainable. Everything was served at once; an armada of little white dishes was placed before you, in one a dry cutlet, in another a few dried pellets of fried potatoes, peas like buckshot, boiled potatoes like cannon-balls; here an inch of tough chicken, there a slice of beef, baked until all its proper juices had been extracted; heavy pumpkin pies, tea and coffee quite undrinkable, butter that no one could touch; such, with but little variation, were the component parts of the three meals. Even the provisions of Nature were not made as available as they might have been. In the garden were two or three fine papaw trees, whose insipid green fruit was sometimes given to us as a delicious West-Indian preserve. It is said that the leaves of this tree, if rubbed on a bull's hide, would immediately convert it into tender beefsteak; now our meat was always of the toughest description.

Day after day I used to see my two friends, fresh from their home in Boston, rise from the table without having touched anything, and I felt quite ashamed of our English colony. Had the proprietor been English, I think I should have run away. As it was, we limited our visit to a fortnight instead of a month, the doctor accompanying me to the West Indies, whilst his mother returned home.

It seems a pity that quiet Bermuda should not attract more visitors—Americans especially—than it does. A well-kept hotel there would be very welcome to many who now winter in Florida or Nassau (Bahamas). The island is more interesting than either of those places, and equally picturesque; and I have no doubt that visitors, when they left, would carry away as pleasant recollections as they would probably leave behind.

CHAPTER II.

A WHITE TOWN—A CEDAR AVENUE—THE "DUCKING-STOOL"—SEA ENCROACHMENTS—FERN PITS—SPANISH POINT—FAIRY-LAND—THE ISLAND ROAD—AMUSEMENTS—A PAPER HUNT—REEFS—SEA CUCUMBERS—THE SOUTH WIND—SAND-HILLS—BOILERS—ARCHITECTURE—MUSEUM—A RARE SPIDER.

"Pleasant it was when the woods were green,

And the winds were soft and low,

To lie amid some sylvan scene,

Where the long drooping boughs between,

Shadows dark and sunlight sheen

Alternate come and go."

LONGFELLOW.

When you first look out of your window over the town, you imagine that there has been a slight snow-storm, so gleaming white are the roofs of all the houses. But you soon learn that, owing to the absence of springs and streams, the roofs are white-washed, and kept scrupulously clean, as the rain-water is thence conducted into cisterns, from which it is drawn for use.

The roads are white, the houses are whiter, and the roofs are whitest; but what would otherwise be an unpleasant glare is modified by the foliage, which half conceals the houses, and by the green Venetian blinds, which shade all the windows.

Nearly every house has a garden, and passion-flowers, morning glory, and other vines creep up the pillars and over the piazzas in great profusion and brilliancy. "Pride of India" trees border the sides of the streets, but these fail to give the delicious shade which is obtained under the cedar avenue which lies on one side of the small public gardens. Here you can stroll in the heat of the day, protected from the sun by a green roof, and surrounded by roses,[1] heliotropes, lilies, great beds of geraniums, pomegranates, gorgeous blossoms of hybiscus, gladioli, and all sorts of lovely creepers. Then when the sun's rays have lost some of their power, you can prolong your walk along the winding road, past the pretty country church of Pembroke, and leaving Mount Langton (Government House) on your right, behold at the bottom of a shady lane spreadeth a golden network, like a veil of gauze, stretching far and wide. That is the sea, and in a short half-hour you have crossed this part of the island.

Better still is it to come here in the morning, and after a plunge in the deep blue water, sit on the "ducking stool," and meditate on the feelings of the poor wretches who, in days gone by, suffered the water punishment for witchcraft, sorcery, and other imaginary offences. A notice prohibits bathing on Government grounds, but down below the steep rocks there are plenty of nooks and hollows, sand-carpeted and as private as your own chamber. For myself, I never could make out where the Government property began or where it ended.

On this north shore a delicious breeze tempers the heat of the sun, and it is enjoyment enough to look at and listen to the sea, to watch the men collecting the seaweed for their land, or to read, and consequently fall asleep. No one will disturb you; there are no tramps in Bermuda, and your watch will still be going, even should you sleep for hours. To return to town two different ways are open to you; both are along the same sea-shore road, but lie in opposite directions; the one leads to the north-east, until you branch off to the right past the barracks; the other—and the one we will take—runs south-west towards Admiralty House and Spanish Point. All along this road you cannot help noticing the encroachment of the sea, and you wonder how long it will be before the road on which you are walking becomes the edge of a craggy wall for the waves to beat against and undermine. Here truly does—

"The hungry ocean gain

Advantage on the kingdom of the shore."

The hollowness of Bermuda is very remarkable, and in many places the cavernous ground gives forth very musical sounds when struck.

As we proceed on our walk, we see but few signs of cultivation; here and there are strips of garden running up into the ubiquitous cedar bush, but most of the land is used for grazing, and very indifferent grazing, too. One peculiarity amongst the four-footed animals is that they are nearly all black and white; another is that they are all tethered; everything seems at anchor in Bermuda, cattle, goats, pigs, donkeys, even the hens are not at liberty. Occasionally one passes a deep well, originally dug out for the purpose of obtaining fresh water, but entirely lined with the lovely maiden-hair fern. This delicate species gives a special charm to the island, as it grows luxuriously on the walls and rocks, in caves and hollows, and drapes the numerous land-pits with its graceful fronds. Where the fern declines to grow, there the "life-plant" flourishes, and quickly covers up the bare places with its deep green, fleshy leaves. Of such vitality is this weed that a single leaf, if plucked and pinned to the wall, will live and send out shoots from its edges with perfect indifference as to its changed abode.

At Spanish Point the view across to Ireland Island is very picturesque, and one perfect horse-shoe bay, with white sandy shore, lingers a long time in the memory, not only on account of the peaceful scene of which it forms a part, but also for its own exquisite form. Near by is Fairy-land, well named, for it really is one of the most charming spots in Bermuda. The sea here runs far up into the island, forming a lake, with bays, islets, caves, isthmuses, and peninsulas. Just above one of the green bights stands a little nest called "Honeymoon Cottage," a gem of a place, where many a happy pair have passed the first week or two of their new life. The hall-door steps lead down to the bathing house, which, when I visited it, contained only one little shoe, but that worthy of Amphitrite herself.

Leaving beautiful Undercliff, our road now turns more inland, sometimes crossing a little hill, and sometimes running through a swamp with high reeds and flags, and with its edges planted with potatoes and tomatoes. Now it curves through a grove, anon it winds past home-like cottages, whose black occupants grin with delight at seeing a stranger, curtsey, and wish him a pleasant walk; then once more the sea is in view, pretty gardens line the road, life and activity betoken the neighbourhood of the wharf, and you are again in Hamilton. Have you enjoyed your walk? I must not ask whether you have a good appetite for dinner!

There is no doubt that the scenery of Bermuda improves on acquaintance. At first sight the visitor will probably be disappointed with the flat appearance of the island and the apparently few possibilities for the picturesque. But in a very short time he will discover that it is all hill and dale, on a minute scale, it is true, as the highest elevation hardly exceeds two hundred and fifty feet—but varied and even romantic. Take, for instance, the view from the Barrack Hill. Everywhere the coastland seems broken up in the most capricious manner. Deep bays, narrow promontories, and an infinite number of islands give to the sea the appearance of a series of silver lakes, which shine in the sun like the fragments of a broken mirror. The undulating country is clothed with cedar-bush, whose grey green is relieved here and there by the brilliant flush of the pink oleander and the white perpendicular walls of a stone quarry. Afar off a lighthouse is pictured against the sky, near at hand is a white fort, and a church spire shows itself above the trees. But it is the beauty of the sea rather than of the land that here takes the first place in one's affections; and in after-time it is the memory of the molten silver sea and its green islands that clings to one longest;

"Wherever you wander the sea is in sight,

With its changeable turquoise green and blue,

And its strange transparence of limpid light.

You can watch the work that the Nereids do

Down, down, where their purple fans unfurl,

Planting their coral and sowing their pearl."

Those who are familiar with the scenery of Puget Sound, or of Vancouver's Island, will recognise, I think, many points of similarity with that of Bermuda. The dense forests are wanting in the latter, but from a bird's-eye view the resemblance is striking. Above all there is the same air of absolute quiet and a subdued wildness characteristic of the two places. Certainly Bermuda is a quiet land; so still a place, it seemed to me, I had never been in before. You are perpetually wondering why the church bells are not ringing for service, and I have heard people ask, "Did you hear the dog barking yesterday?" But life here is by no means dull, a more friendly, hospitable, and fun-loving people you would not find, and what with military theatricals, croquet, cricket, lawn tennis, boating parties, and other amusements, time glides away very quickly.

There is little or no game on the island—one bevy of quails being the extent of my observations—but, as an Englishman must hunt or shoot something, a "paper-hunt" has been established. It may not be as exciting as fox-hunting, but, in a climate where you must take things easily, it affords capital exercise. The Bermudian foxes—or rather the Judases, as they carry the bag—are generally men from the garrison, and, with the thermometer 75 deg. in the shade, and 110 deg. or more in the sun, they have no easy task in giving a good run. Spectators are always invited to view "the finish" at some previously selected spot, and there refreshments of all kinds are served, making a very agreeable finale to an amusing day. A severe critic might remark that the hurdles and other obstacles placed near "the finish," were hardly worthy of the excessive ardour displayed in overcoming them, but he must remember that it perhaps makes up for a slight falling off where the jumps were more formidable. It is not only in Bermuda that the presence of a certain pair of bright eyes has driven many a Nimrod to deeds of heroism in the matter of hedges and ditches that otherwise would have been neglected.

For boating the Bermuda waters offer great facilities, and, if you want to see how near to the wind's eye it is possible to go, you cannot do better than hire one of the native sailing-boats—one masted and flush-decked—when there is a stiff breeze. You may get rather wet, but you will spin along at a glorious rate, and you certainly will admire the workmanlike way in which your crew—a man and a boy—manage the rakish craft.

Then, in calm weather it is delightful to pay a visit to the reefs and gather for yourself the brain corals and "sea-whips," specimens of which fishermen have brought to the hotel for sale. In these water-gardens may be seen all sorts of many-hued plants; crinoids like palm trees, gorgonias, mosses, sea-feathers, coral like creeping vines, sea-cucumbers,[2] and coloured weeds waving to and fro over the brilliant fish. On bright, sunny days, when the blue water sparkles, you may, perhaps, in fancy, hear snatches of low music and gay tones of laughter gurgling up from below, but, when it is dull and gloomy, the sounds will be of sorrow, telling secrets dire and tales of woe, wrung from restless spirits buried amid wreck and ruin beneath the flood that sweeps over those cruel, beautiful coral rocks.

We had heard so much of the disagreeable effects of the south wind, which generates so much moisture that everything is quickly covered with green mould, and a general clammy feeling prevails, that we were continually running round the corner of the hotel to note the direction of the wind by the flag at the signal station. As we were constantly expecting it—the south wind—the natural consequence was that it never came, and we were very grateful. I think it was a Frenchman who remarked that nothing happens except the unexpected, and I have found this true in many cases. For instance, when travelling in the tropics, if you are continually on the look-out for snakes, you will rarely meet them, and we all know that the best way to keep off the rain is to carry an umbrella. The climate of Bermuda is said to be capricious, but during our stay—a short one certainly—we found the temperature very pleasant, the thermometer seldom rising over 73 deg., and frequently a fire towards evening was very comfortable.

Small as Bermuda is—as the five principal islands connected by ferries and bridges only form a chain about twenty-four miles in length, and with a breadth varying from a few hundred yards to about two miles—it yet contains many points of interest. The splendid lighthouse on Gibb's Hill is worth a visit for itself, and for the fine view to be obtained from it; the fortifications, too, which, together with the natural barriers, are gradually making a second Gibraltar, must be inspected. The Paget Hills on the eastern shore show how the drifting sand is elevating the land, and probably increasing it as fast as the western waves are washing it away. Unfortunately, this overwhelming mass of sand is steadily advancing over the cultivated land, and has already buried one cottage, whose chimney alone is visible above the surrounding whiteness. It is merely a matter of taste which is preferable—to be washed away or to be buried alive.

Near the beach, at the foot of these hills, may be seen, at low water, great circular masses of rock, hollowed out like huge cauldrons. Similar ones occur at intervals round the islands, and are by no means the least interesting of the Bermudian curiosities.[3]

However entertaining the country and seaside may be, there is very little in the town of Hamilton worth noticing. With the exception of Trinity Church, the buildings are insignificant. The "Public Building" stands in an ill-tended garden and presents no inducement to the young Bermudian to prepare himself for the Legislature. But, perhaps, there will soon be no young white Bermudians, as the youths of these islands find the United States better adapted for their speedy advancement in life.

I had hoped to find in the museum a specimen of a certain spider, concerning which an ancient chronicler of Bermuda has said: "They are of a very large size, but withal beautifully coloured, and look as if they were adorned with pearl and gold. Their webs are in colour and substance a perfect raw silk, and so strongly woven that, running from tree to tree, like so many snares, small birds are sometimes caught in them." The Museum consisted of a few South-Sea Island shells, some coral, some moth-eaten skins, three bottles of alcohol containing marine specimens, two butterflies, and no spider. I had a better ungathered collection of insects in my own room at the hotel. I must return there and see if I can find a mother-of-pearl spider.

CHAPTER III.

BERMUDIAN ROADS—NIGHT BLOOMING CACTUS—A NATURAL CURIOSITY—EXPORTS AND IMPORTS—THE COLOURED NATIVE—HARRINGTON SOUND—DEVIL'S HEAD—NEPTUNE'S GROTTO—A SALT-WATER FOUNTAIN—A DIABOLICAL PLOT—THE CALABASH—MEMENTOES OF TOM MOORE—WALSINGHAM—THE CAUSEWAY—A NEW FEATURE IN CULTIVATION—ST. GEORGE'S.

We have not half exhausted the beauties of the neighbourhood, but, in case your patience should be at an end, please step into the carriage which is to take us to St. George's, at the other end of the island, whence we are to embark for the West Indies, and let us look about us on the way.

Three roads lead to our destination; we will take the middle one, which joins the ocean drive near Harrington Sound. Splendid roads these are, too! Bermuda may well be proud of them. Altogether there are more than a hundred miles of broad, white, smooth road. Sometimes the road-bed is so deeply hewn out of the white coral rock that Lilliputian canyons are formed with fern-hung walls, and capped with aloe or cactus. Several varieties of the latter plant grow in the islands, and a magnificent specimen of the night-blooming *cereus grandiflora* is to be seen in the small garden behind the Yacht Club in Hamilton. It runs in wild profusion over trees, walls, and bushes, and when in blossom is covered with hundreds of pale flowers, whose delicious perfume is quite overpowering. It may be inconvenient, perhaps, to visit it at the proper time—midnight—but it is necessary, as in the morning beauty and perfume have gone.

Dazzlingly white, but, fortunately, not dusty, is the road as we leave the snowy houses behind us, but soon we enter a stretch of cool forest. Here a deeper silence reigns than even on the sunny hill we have ascended, a melodious silence too, for the sweet note of the blue bird and the soft chirp of the "chick of the village" do not break the quiet, but rather adds to it. A crimson cardinal gives a rare flush to the grey cedar, and pretty little ground-doves sit perfectly unconcerned by the roadside as we drive past. Prospect is soon reached, and then we descend, again skirting a large morass, edged with cedars, mangrove, and palmetto. We see a new church, which makes a strong contrast with the old ruined one that stands farther on, near some really fine cedars.

Here we halt for a moment to inspect a natural curiosity, namely, a very ancient cedar, lofty and hollow, and in whose dead trunk is growing a young one, the green head of which appears high up, amid the dead branches of the old one. Patches of cultivated land with their great hedges of oleander were as common here as everywhere else, but, besides the usual tomato, onion, and potato, we saw for the first time that friend of our childhood—the farinaceous arrowroot. Could we do less than greet it with a friendly nod as we drove along? Alas! even the cultivation of this diminishes year by year; everything has to give way to onions and tomatoes—consequently, the supply of other vegetables, cereals, and fruits is extremely limited. With such a fertile soil the exports might almost equal the imports in value, but I am afraid to say how many times the latter exceed the former at present. No one would expect a black man to work more than he is absolutely obliged, and certainly in Bermuda he who can avoid doing anything makes the best of his opportunities. Possibly his nature is allied to that of the surrounding coral formations, and he becomes a sort of human coral-polyp, whose only labour of life is to get a little food and to eat it; the rest he leaves to nature. Well, who can blame him? he seems very happy and contented, he sends his children to school, he is very polite, and, if he is poor, poverty does not harm him, and he is content.

Look at that merry group in the doorway of that tumble-down old building! All smile at the strangers, and the mother who has been plaiting away at some palmetto work—which by the way is not half so fine and pretty here as in Florida—leaves it, to gather some magnificent roses we have stopped to admire. But surely an earthquake has shattered this little village; roofless cottages, mouldering walls, gardens in which papaws, prickly pears, and lantanas form a perfect jungle, everything has the appearance of some such catastrophe. No, these ruins are the land fragments of what was once an important harbour, and the splendid sheet of water before us is Harrington Sound. Very beautiful is this lake—as it may be called—which at its junction with the sea is crossed by a bridge a few yards in length, and only visible when approached quite close; for it lies at the foot of a circle of green hills, surrounded by cavernous shores, and with islands dotting its green transparent waters.

Taking the road to the right we pass some pretty cottages, one of which has such a tremendous portico, that we are reminded of the donkey that tried to convert itself into a deer by attaching antlers to its head. Then we arrive at the Devil's Hole. Across the water the Devil's Head rises up, its perpendicular cliff looking quite grand in miniature; there the tropic-bird builds its nest in perfect security in some inaccessible position. What the devil has to do with either place I cannot say; both names seem singularly inappropriate, and for the former "Neptune's Grotto" is more suitable, and just as easy to pronounce.

There is frequently, I believe, a good deal of difficulty in finding the proprietor of the pool in question, but at the time of our visit he was standing at the wooden door, and informed us we had come at a good time, as he was just going to feed the fish. Entering, we found ourselves in a pretty circular grotto, lined with shrubs, ferns, and creepers. Steps, cut out of the rock, led down to a deep pool of the clearest salt water, in which were a number of great fish called "groupers," gazing up with the most expectant look—if a fish-eye can be expressive—and evidently aware that feeding time was at hand. And how they did eat! there was no dainty nibbling, no coquettish trifling, a huge mouth opened and the morsel was gone. "What does that great fellow weigh?" "Oh, about two shillings," replied the proprietor, whose idea of weight was a marketable one, "and those angels will average one and sixpence apiece." Well, those angels were worth it, their exquisite azure hue vied with the wonderfully tinted water, and, what with gold streakings, waving plume-like fins, and really beautiful eyes, they well deserved their name. If some clever soul could discover a preparation for preserving the natural hues of fish, what a benefactor he would be! At present, the alcoholic collections of our Museums form a ghastly contrast with the brilliant birds and insects which surround them.

"While blazing breast of humming-bird and Io's stiffened wing,

Are just as bright as when they flew their earliest voyage in spring;

While speckled snake and spotted pard their markings still display—

Though he who once embalm'd them both himself be turned to clay—

The scaly tribe a different doom awaits—scarce reach'd the shore

Those rainbow hues are fading fast till all their beauty's o'er."

Right learnedly, and with the tongue of a gourmet, did our fisherman discuss the habits and qualities of the various fish that swim in Bermudian waters. Cow-fish, porgies, hamlets, hog, grunts, bream, and many others; a few he pointed out to us, amongst them a squirrel with large eyes, of a blood-red colour and peculiar shape; then he landed a "grunt," which gave vent to sounds that would shame a veritable porker. This natural aquarium is connected with the sea by an underground passage, consequently the water is always fresh; formerly, we were told, it was a cavern, but the roof had fallen in.

On emerging, we see eastward the pretty house and grounds belonging to the American Consul. In his garden is a salt-water fountain, in the basin of which we, during a former visit, had seen many strange fish, and also some good specimens of the sea-horse. On that occasion we had been told of the terrible plot concocted in these Islands by a Dr. Blackburn, for introducing the yellow fever into the Northern part of the United States, by sending thither boxes of infected clothing. Fortunately—and I believe chiefly through the instrumentality of our host—the plot was discovered in time to prevent the shipment, and a terrible calamity was probably averted. The worthy Consul does not confine his attention to fish alone, and his system of banana culture might be profitably adopted in many other parts of the Island.

Continuing our drive round the Sound, we are more and more impressed with its attractions; the apple-green water below us, the rocky inlets with white sandy edges, here and there a stretch of shingle or a wooden promontory, and, beyond, the blue sea with the foam on its distant reefs, form a lovely picture, and we are sorry when a turn in the road has shut us out from such a wealth of colour.

Our next halting-place is at a farm house, near which stands Moore's "calabash tree,"[4] beneath whose shade the poet composed his verses, and wove his amatory couplets addressed to "Nea, the Rose of the Isles." The tree lives still, in spite of the severe hacking it has received from tourists, whose carved names are continually blurred out by time and the hands of their successors. Even the seat under it is the object of much curiosity, and as each new one is placed in its proper position it is carried off piecemeal by enthusiastic admirers, who must have a bit of the chair the poet sat in. I never see the ravages made by relic hunters, or the desecration of historical places, without thinking of a certain tourist to whom an Italian monk was showing a consecrated lamp, which had never gone out during five centuries. Giving the flame a decisive puff, he remarked, with cool complacency, "Well, I guess it's out now." A few gourds are still left hanging from the topmost boughs of the tree, but the sable attendant will not allow any of these to be knocked down, so you must be satisfied with the one presented to you by the proprietor of the land at your departure. It may come from Moore's tree, but gourds are deceptive and much alike.

A short walk through tangled wild-wood leads to some limestone caves, which were also frequented by the poet. They differ little from other cavernous formations; there are vaulted arches, halls and aisles, gem-studded cornices, and upright columns; here there is a sheet of water so clear that the guide has to tell you that it is water; there, oozing stalactites embellish a Gothic temple, but the effect of brilliant crystallization is marred by the smoke of the rushes which light up the gloom of the interior. The visit is a scrambling one, but still worth accomplishing.

Shortly after leaving Walsingham we cross the causeway which connects the main island with St. George's; on our right, is the magnificent Castle Harbour, with numerous islands; on our left, a land-locked sound, with cranes and other birds fishing on the shallows and among the mangrove bushes, whilst in front, lying in the hollow of a curve under a hill, are the white houses of the town. Rapidly we drive along the fine causeway, the waves now and then almost dashing over us, so near is the sea; then, after crossing a drawbridge, we are soon among cottages and gardens. Here we see again potato fields and patches of cultivated ground, apparently planted with black bottles. These black bottles are quite a feature in Bermudian cultivation during the sowing season; they are not planted in the hope of their ever becoming quarts or magnums, or even of their being refilled by nature with their original contents, but, having held the seed, they merely indicate the amount sown.

A quaint old town is St. George's, with its high stone walls and winding alleys. So narrow are the streets that, if two carriages met in one of them, it is difficult to imagine what would happen, as they could not pass, and certainly could not turn back; but two carriages in St. George's on the same day would be an exceptional event. The whole place has the appearance of having been cut out of a single block of white limestone, rather than being built of bricks of that material. It is not in many places that a man can build his house from stone out of his own quarry, on his own premises, but he can in Bermuda. With a hand-saw he cuts out the soft stone, and the blocks then harden by exposure to the air.

The numerous square cuttings in the hill-sides and along the roads form a feature in the scenery, and by no means an unpleasing one, as the new are snowy white, and the old are generally draped with green bushes and creepers. Walls are built of the same material, and then receive, as the houses do, a coating of whitewash, which hides the seams and joinings, thus presenting a solid white mass. Over these walls, you see broad plantain leaves and flaming poinsettias; orange, lemon, and palm trees are more numerous here at St. George's than at Hamilton, and the tropical aspect of the town extends to its inhabitants. Of labour there is little or no sign, and what there is of life is hardly worth mentioning.

As St. George's is a garrison town—two regiments being considered necessary for the safety of Bermuda—it is probably gayer than when we saw it, which was in hot noonday, when all slept except one black man, who was shaving a white man under the shade of a tree in the square.

That evening the 'Beta,' from Halifax, left with us for the West Indies. Summer isles, in spite of that abused hotel, I would gladly revisit you; I carry away nought but a remembrance of white cottages and gardens, green islands, billowy masses of oleander, cedar hills, and coral rocks, and, above all, of a shining lake-like sea, as calm and restful as the happy homes which it surrounds.

CHAPTER IV.

ST. THOMAS—FORTS—BOATMEN—DIVERS—HOTEL DU COMMERCE—MAIN STREET—STABLE COMPANIONS—AMAZONS—A NEGRO POLITICIAN—DANISH RULE—A SORRY SIGHT—JUSTICE IN THE VIRGIN GROUP—A DAY'S DOINGS—KRUMM BAY—CHA-CHAS—AN OCEAN PAWNBROKER'S—LANDSLIP—ALOE—A CURE FOR LUNG DISEASES—UP THE MOUNTAIN.

Had the passengers on board the comfortable 'Beta' been as poetical as Childe Harold was when in his clumsy brig he sang:

"Four days are sped, but with the fifth anon

New shores descried make every bosom gay,"

they might have said something less prosy than "Thank goodness, there's land!" when, precisely on the fifth morning after leaving Bermuda, a vision as of misty clouds grew out of the sea! Then, as the yellow flush of dawn cleared the prospect, substance was given to the hazy outlines, and as the sun rose, touching the rugged peaks with gold and purple, the island of St. Thomas lay revealed before them.

As the vessel entered the spacious harbour and dropped anchor at some distance from shore, we thought we had seldom looked at a prettier scene. In front is a high, abrupt mountain range, from which three rounded spurs run down to the sea, and on these hills stands the town. On the right, a low, wooded savanna sweeps up to the hills which encircle the bay, whose mirror-like surface reflects the rocks and islands which close the entrance and almost join the promontory on our left. But it is the rich colouring that forms the striking part of the view. After demure Bermuda, with its white and grey-green, the bright red roofs and white, green, yellow, and blue houses are almost dazzling. There, clinging to the side of the hill, is a cluster of freshly painted cottages, looking very gaudy in the strong sunlight; nearer at hand are a few low houses, whose once brilliant roofs are now changed by time and weather to a golden russet-red highly picturesque.

The height of the dark mountains gives a diminutive appearance to the buildings, so that you imagine you are looking at a Dutch toy village—or rather three villages. This idea is enhanced by the toy fort which, with bastion, battlements, and barbican, is strongly suggestive of cake ornamentation. Commanding this Danish fortress are the two strongholds of those old pirates called Bluebeard and Blackbeard, which look feudal, and only want a few of Mr. James's horsemen slowly winding up the narrow causeway to be quite romantic. Over the trees of the toy public garden, which lies close to the landing, is seen a Moorish-looking structure, which proves to be the hotel, and gives promise of coolness and comfort, which I need hardly say is not realised. Behold, then, bright, cheerful little dwellings, with a prevailing hue of russet, perched on hills and nestling in the intervening valleys, amid tropical trees and flowering shrubs, forming the centre of a combination of mountain, sea, and island that is very pleasing, especially when seen in the soft golden light shining through the pearly grey mist of the rain storms which often sweep over the island—and such is St. Thomas.

The change of scenery from Bermuda is not greater than that of manners. There is no quaker-like simplicity in St. Thomas; noise and clamour prevail. Hardly has the anchor touched the bottom before the ship is surrounded with dozens of boats, manned by sturdy negroes, anxious to take passengers ashore. Here we find among the boatmen the same names as those borne by Egyptian donkeys at Cairo and Alexandria—Derby winners, heroes of popular songs, &c. "Champagne Charlie" urges his cognomen as a special reason for your patronage, whilst another, blacker than the blackest of imps, claims the stranger's old acquaintance with "Remember Snowball, massa, last time you here!"

Just as we stepped into our boat, a young Canadian on board, who had been assiduously fishing ever since we arrived, and without success, suddenly called out that he had a bite, and triumphantly pulled up his line, to which a bottle had been attached by one of the little urchins when diving for coppers. This little incident reminded one of our party of the tricks which Antony and Cleopatra used to play each other by the aid of divers. In the play Charmian says to Cleopatra:

"'Twas merry when

You wagered on your angling; when your diver

Did hang a salt fish on his hook, which he

With fervency drew up."

"And thus history repeats herself," said somebody else, as we landed on the wharf.

The inhabitants of St. Thomas are apt to boast of their Hôtel du Commerce, and to inform the stranger that it is the best in the West Indies; all I can say is that out of the few I saw, it was by far the worst. It was kept by a Spanish family, each member of which was master, and each cared less than the other for the comfort of the guests. The beds were bad, the mosquito nets were full of holes, there was not a comfortable chair or table in any bedroom, dirt and uncleanliness prevailed everywhere; clean linen was at a discount, and the cook evidently thought that wretched food was compensated for by the fine, broad verandah in which it was eaten. My friend, the doctor, was so overcome by the heat and discomfort that he determined to return to Boston by the first steamer, which was not due, however, for nearly a fortnight. As mine, also, was not expected until about the same time, we determined to make the best of it, and try to enjoy ourselves. On looking back, we afterwards found that our enjoyment principally consisted in going from the reading-room to the club, and from the club back to the reading-room. It was too hot to sit down, and we found it necessary to keep moving in order to get a little air.

Main Street, which runs along the sea, is the only level piece of ground in St. Thomas; beyond that all is up-hill; it is here, therefore, that you see life in its busiest and idlest aspect. The shops and stores are prepossessing neither in their exterior nor in their interior. Straw hats, ready-made clothes, tawdry trifles, and provisions predominate; there is nothing to tempt you, nothing strange to invite a purchaser. But in the street itself it is more amusing; look at that stately woman in flowing white, with the bright turban, on which is poised a tray of cakes—she is a Haytian; those children sitting on the doorstep, and dressed in the suit they were born in, are evidently natives; here comes a white horse, with a brilliant red saddle-cloth, followed closely by a sheep; is there a circus coming? No; the patriarchal rider is only Mr. So-and-So, and it is the fashion in many parts of the West Indies for sheep to accompany horses. They say it is healthy for sheep to live in the stables with horses, and they get so attached to one another that, out-of-doors, the former will not leave the latter as long as they can keep up with them.

Now groups of women pass; surely they are real Amazons! Jet black, and wearing only very short skirts, a twist of hemp round their heads, and with their woolly hair plaited in horns, or crowned with a half cocoa-nut by way of bonnet, they shout and sing like frantic Mœnads. They are coalers returning from their hard day's labour in the harbour. It is not in St. Thomas where "men must work and women must weep." That old negro who is declaiming with such vehemence in front of the hotel is a great admirer of Lord Beaconsfield, learns all his speeches by heart, and goes about reciting them. It is pleasant to observe this tribute of admiration to our great Minister, however odd the expression of it may be. English, French, German, Dutch, Creoles, all sorts of nationalities, are met with here, but of Danes, to whom the island belongs, there is a very limited supply. As for the Danish language, it is the only one not heard.

Of Danish rule the casual visitor can, of course, say very little. He sees clean, well-ordered streets, and evidences of continual improvements, sanitary and otherwise, although he cannot help thinking that the great open sewer, crossed by a bridge in Main Street, and down which, in the rainy season, come avalanches of dead cats, tin cans, and other despised articles, might be made less conspicuous, and answer its purpose equally well. He sees, also, a chain-gang on some public works, and the pitiful sight of women working with the male convicts; but the unfortunate creatures seem to care less about it than the spectator, and with a jaunty air shoulder their spade or pickaxe, and sing to a chain accompaniment.

The visitor to the island will probably hear—for at St. Thomas, as elsewhere:

"There is a lust in man no charm can tame,

Of loudly publishing his neighbour's shame—"

of the strange administration of justice (by the way, do we not, in our own neighbouring island of Tortola, present the strange spectacle of a president who himself combines the three functions of judge, prosecutor, and judge of appeal?), of harmless idlers being picked up by the police and exiled to the small island of St. John's, there to tend sheep and cattle; of theft being far more severely punished than murder, and of the general incapacity of the government. But the proverbial "grain of salt" must be taken with the tales, and I think the stranger will allow that things are carried on much the same as elsewhere; that harmony exists in spite of inharmonious elements, and that St. Thomas is not so bad as he had been led to expect.

The days here are monotonous, but variety cannot be expected in so circumscribed an area. In the early morning, just as you are about to drop off to sleep, after an intensely hot night, varied with earthquakes, and passed probably in opening and closing the shutters of your room—closing them against the driving rain, and opening them to get some air—the gun fires, and if that fails to waken you thoroughly, the negroes hold such a jubilee under your window that sleep is quite impossible.[5] A sudden screaming and wild vociferation makes you spring out of bed fearing an earthquake, but it is only the old black women having a "talk," or merely wishing each other "good morning." Then the men indulge in angry abuse, gesticulate madly, and just as you expect to see a knife plunged into somebody's bosom, the chief disputant walks off, singing the "Sweet by-and-by." There was no quarrel! You then go to bed again; but immediately bread and coffee are brought, and, as early rising is infectious, you go through the agony of dressing when, as Sydney Smith says, you would rather "take off your flesh and sit in your bones." St. Thomas is one of those places where, as the Irishman said, it is never cooler—it may be hotter, but it is never cooler. However, that is at last accomplished, and then comes a terrible gap of time until breakfast. There is little to explore, and ferns and shells are soon exhausted, so you ramble up Main Street, visit the much-enduring consul, or make one of the coterie in the grand réunions held in some store, where the affairs of the world are settled.

At last comes breakfast, which is dinner without soup, and where quantity tries to make up for quality.

"Such breakfast, such beginning of the day

Is more than half the whole;"

and very fortunate it is that such is the case, as until the heat of the sun has decreased there is not much inducement for exercise. By that time dinner is ready, and soon after—as early hours are the rule—you retire to your room, to turn out the centipedes, which are of enormous size in St. Thomas, from under your pillow, and the mosquitos from out of the netting. Then you perspire all night. And so passes hotel-life when there are no dinner-parties, nor theatricals, nor excursions to break its monotony.

One morning we took a boat to visit a very curious place called "Krumm Bay." It was intensely hot, but "Admiral Nelson" pulled away merrily across the harbour, past the western suburb of the town, and in among the islands and creeks, which in olden times afforded good retreats for pirates. Here Blackbeard was wont to retire after some filibustering expedition and take in fresh supplies of wines and provisions. A fishing boat sailed by, in which was an enormous Jew-fish, at which the "Admiral" pulled a very long face, and explained to us that, whenever a Jew-fish was caught, some one of high position in St. Thomas was sure to die, or perhaps was already dead. Strangely enough, next morning we noticed that all the flags were at half-mast, and heard that news had just arrived of the death in England of the head of one of the chief firms in the island.

The islets around were covered with thick under-bush, out of which tall flowering aloes shot up like telegraph poles, but on the mainland cacti predominated, with here and there masses of creamy blossoms of the fragrant Frangipani. I am at a loss to know how the latter plant gained its name, as its scent is by no means the same as that extracted from flowers by the great Roman alchemist Frangipani, and which as "a perfumed powder in a velvet bag," with

"———a cast of

Odours rare—of orris mixed with spice

Sandal and violet, with musk and rose

Combined in due proportion,"

was considered a wonderful cure for the plague. High up on the arid soil rose a giant cereus, with arms like candelabra; lower down were the round prickly forms of the echinocactus, looking like small hedge-hogs; then there were numbers of the melocactus, which they here call the Pope's head, and which finds a ready sale among the shipping. We had noticed dépôts for shells and cacti at the other extremity of the town, and probably these are the only exports from the island. Those large trees near the water are manchineel, whose fruit is deadly poison to all but crabs, who esteem it highly. These crabs are themselves considered a delicacy, but are generally kept for a week, and thoroughly purged before being eaten.

But who are those light-complexioned men in that crazy canoe? The Admiral smiles disdainfully as he informs us that they are only "Cha-Chas," who live on the outskirts of the town, and employ themselves in fishing. We afterwards visited one of their little colonies, and found an industrious people—natives of small adjacent islands—living in huts made of the tin plates cut from kerosene cans and biscuit cases, looking not unlike extra large sardine-boxes, and as closely packed. There they raised some fruit and vegetables, plaited straw, and made ornaments of tamarind seeds.

At the bottom of a deep bay, we found the object of our visit, viz., an establishment for wrecks. Here, lying on the beach and stowed away under long sheds, were fragments of all sorts of vessels and their fittings. Long masts lay near rusty boilers, paddle-wheels were mixed with broken screws; a deck cabin half concealed a ship's boat; anchors, helms, poops, sterns, funnels, beams, all the makings of a ship were there, and a large workshop showed where the useless was made good, and the broken repaired. It was not a working-day, and the only sign of life was a large and hungry dog, whose appearance did not render a landing very inviting. We had, therefore, to be satisfied with an exterior view of this marine pawn-shop, where Neptune had got rid of some of his worthless lumber, perhaps only to retake it when it had once more been made serviceable.

And now, before taking leave of St. Thomas, let us ascend to the top of the hill above the town, and risk a hot walk for the sake of the fresh air and view. After passing the theatre, where a black troupe had lately performed "Macbeth," the road winds up and up, past cottages hanging like bird-cages to the hill-sides, and only waiting for a landslip to precipitate them into the valley—in fact, one house that now stands close to the town originally stood far up on a hill, but in 1877 it was carried down entire to its present position, after an earthquake, followed by a landslip—and soon we were high above the red tiled roofs.

The vegetation is of the scrub order, and among the low bushes fly the repulsive "black witches," uttering rich but melancholy notes. The yellow flowers of the "cedar bush" sprinkle the mountain-side, and a species of bitter aloe is common; from the latter an old black woman of the town makes a decoction which is positively declared to be a certain cure for lung disease. The fleshy leaves contain a jelly-like pulp; this, after being extracted, is washed seven times in pure water, and beaten up with eggs and milk. To effect a cure, seven wine-glasses of it must be drunk. In Mexico I have frequently seen the same medicine used, and have heard wonderful stories of its power, but there the number seven is not included in the recipe.

Continuing up the path, we do not see much animal life; occasionally a lizard runs across, or we meet a few natives bringing down sugar-cane, and each carrying a "sour-sop"—a large green fruit, with pulp-like cotton-wool—or, perchance, a little donkey clatters down, so loaded with grass that nothing can be seen of it except the little hoofs.

The view from the summit is fine and contrasting. On one side, far below, lies the busy town, with its picturesque towers and harbour filled with shipping. On the other, a silent waste of water, broken up into fantastic bays and inlets, and with rocky islands scattered over its face.

On the town side, hardly any cultivation is visible, but on the other are long strips of cane-lands and patches of garden, groups of fruit-trees, and grazing pastures.

In the west, rises Porto Rico; in the south, the dim outlines of Santa Cruz are visible, and between the two, like a ship under press of canvas, appears Caraval, or Sail Rock, with its forked peak, white-shining in the sun.

To the east, lie the Virgin Islands in the midst of the "Grande Rue des Vierges," as the blue waters which surround them are called. But we have not much time to admire the scene, already the rose-pink in the west is changing to gold, a metallic lustre dances on the water, the Virgin group is fading in the purple distance, and we must descend to the steaming town.

As we approach, a sound of music floats up to us, and we hear children's voices singing a Christmas carol. Can this really be December? To-morrow we will go to Santa Cruz.

CHAPTER V.

TO SANTA CRUZ—BASSIN—A DOG-HOUSE—FRUIT STEALING—"THIBET" TREES—GREEN HERONS—PRETTY SCENERY—WEST END—SANTA CRUZ v. ST. THOMAS—CENTRAL ROAD—STEAM PLOUGH—A CENTRAL FACTORY—OPPOSITION—WAGES—CHILDREN—HOME AGAIN—RE-EMBARKATION—OFFICIAL DELAY.

Santa Cruz is situated about forty miles south of St. Thomas. To reach it, it is necessary to take the Government mail-schooner, which makes the passage generally in about six hours, though, with contrary winds, it has been known to take days, and even weeks. Nine o'clock in the evening was the hour for sailing, and precisely at that time we stepped on board. "Passports, gentlemen!" was the greeting we received. "What! passports to go from one Danish island to another!" We had none, so it was finally settled that we should pay the price of them—thirty-two cents. each—to the Commissioner of Police, who was expected on board to see his mother-in-law off. Ten o'clock came, and no sign of either Commissioner or his mother-in-law. The breeze was falling, and we began to doubt whether we should be able to get outside the harbour, but at half-past ten they appeared, and in a few minutes we were beating out.

When we gained the open sea, the north-east trade wind blew fresh and strong, so that by four a.m. next morning we had passed through the narrow reef-passage, and had anchored in a picturesque bay at the fort of Bassin (Christianstœd), the capital of the island. The scene differed widely from that of St. Thomas. From the white beach backwards, acres of sugar-cane extended over the level land and swept up over the undulating hills and across to the mountain background in a waving mass of green, broken here and there by long lines of cocoa-nut palms, windmills, the white buildings of the planters, and the cottages of their labourers.

The town looked antiquated, but clean, and with ample foliage. Originally, the island was covered with forest, but the French burnt it, and now it appears like one vast sugar plantation. But the loss of its forests may prove in time the ruin of the island. Formerly its rain-fall was abundant, and its productiveness enormous. Now years of drought follow in quick succession, and it is said that the barren belt beginning at the sea-beach in parts of the island is annually spreading inland. Ruin is following closely in the path of the forest destroyer.

In former years Bassin was a place of great resort, but now visitors are scarce, and the wretched building near the wharf, although it still bears the name of hotel, is closed and receives no guests. We had been recommended to take rooms at the Widow Brady's. This we did, and had no cause to regret it. The widow herself met us before we reached her house. It was only a short distance, but, before we had accomplished it, we knew all the gossip of the island, the sugar prospect, the history of the poor deceased, and had received a general sketch of past events, with a few prophetic remarks concerning the future. A refreshing bath made up for a sleepless night on the schooner, whose night accommodation—unless you preferred to stifle below— consisted of a few rabbit-hutches, or dog-houses, as they are called, with a mattress spread on the floor. After our bath we started on a tour of inspection.

It did not require many minutes to find out that the sleepy old town was not a success as regards its buildings, and that Santa Cruz rum was its chief article of commerce, but its gardens and trees were delightful. There were sapodillas, fine, lofty trees, with clusters of leaves and brown fruit, avocados, trees of the mess-apple, sour-sop, and other insipid fruits; then there were mangoes, tamarinds, and guava bushes, overrun with bright convolvuluses, and still more brilliant ipomæas; roses, jessamine, and honeysuckle grew most luxuriantly, but they were overmatched in profusion, if not in fragrance, by the Mexican wreath plant, with pretty pink flowers like clusters of coral, and by the quiscualis, whose sweet jessamine-like flowers—white, pink, and red on the same stalk—peeped out in hundreds from their glossy green hiding places.

A pleasing feature in this island is the number of good roads which run in all directions. On one of these we drove over to Friderichstœd, or West End, as it is called. I do not know why the latter name should be used, but I suppose for the same reason that Christianstœd is called Bassin, and Charlotte Amalia, St. Thomas. During the drive, we saw to perfection that system of cultivation which commencing in this island continues all through the West Indies, with the exception now of Trinidad,—namely, the systematic neglect of all other products for one, and that one—sugar. There comes a drought, a deluge, or a blight, and great is the outcry of planters, who have nothing else to fall back upon. Here, outside the town, even the fruit trees had been cut down, because, as long as fruit is on a tree, the labourers instead of working will lie down and pick and eat. The same complaint exists everywhere against the fruit-loving workmen, whether native or imported, and it is said that the only way of stopping the evil is the ruthless cutting down of the trees.

Our road ran through a sea of cane, or an occasional acre of Guinea grass in different stages of ripeness, crossed at intervals by long rows of cocoa-nut palms, whose beauty was diminished by a blight which seems to have prevailed in all the West Indian Islands. Fortunately, it had not touched the mountain-cabbage palms, which rose straight and majestic, and with the greenest of plums, beside their faded brethren. These trees, although beautiful to look at, did not afford much shade, and as the sun was intensely hot, it was a relief occasionally to rest under the "Thibet," whose long brown pods made a strange rustling sound as they were shaken by the breeze. The branches and mimosa-like leaves of this tree make nutritious food for cattle, and it is therefore especially valuable in dry seasons. Now the planters were especially jubilant, as there had been an abundant fall of rain, and the prospect of good crops was cheering, after six or seven bad years. Rivulets trickled past us, and in the marshy ground small green herons peered at us inquiringly or plunged their bills into the soft earth.

As we approached the western side the scenery improved; high hills rose up on either side, and below us ran a mountain stream in a dell rich with mango and bread-fruit[6] trees, and gaily decked with heliconias, yellow cedar bush, and the crimson flowers of the "Pride of Barbadoes." On the high points of land, windmills stretch out their long arms, or, armless, resembled Martello towers guarding the cane valleys beneath. In the valleys, the smoke issuing from the tall chimneys showed that sugar-making was in progress, and at one of the plantations the owner kindly asked us in. Here they were ploughing, or placing the cane slips on the ridges ready for planting, there they were hoeing, and in another place, cutting the ripe cane or carrying it to the mill. The various processes were shown and explained to us, and then our host refreshed us with cane juice in different stages, from "sling," which was served in large jugs, to the material beverage—rum—which, as real old Santa Cruz, was drunk as a liqueur. We both agreed afterwards, that "sling" was the most unpleasant beverage we had ever tasted. The dwelling house was well situated for business and pleasure, as from one window the owner could overlook his workpeople on the plantation, and from the other he often shot the little Santa Cruz deer, which abound in the low underbrush of the uncultivated parts.

After a short visit we took our leave, and continued our drive. At length, the hills were left behind, and before us lay a flat rich country—cane-laden of course—stretching to the sea. In the fine roadstead, only two or three vessels lay at anchor, and we at once exclaimed that surely this ought to be the converging point for trade with the West Indies; that instead of the small town of Friderichstœd there were capabilities for a city. We were ignorant perhaps, but we could not understand what advantages St. Thomas possessed over this pretty island. True, its geographical position is not equal to that of St. Thomas, but the very few extra hours taken to reach it would be compensated for by its superior land facilities and its healthiness. Possibly, shipowners and merchants at home may say, what is health in comparison with three hours' extra fuel? but those who live out here, and those who travel in ships, may reverse the saying. Would hurricanes in the commodious roadstead be more dangerous than in the harbour of St. Thomas? Well! in 1867, a tidal wave at the latter place destroyed an immense amount of property and lives, and swamped the shipping, and to the present time particular prayers are offered in the churches at the beginning and end of the hurricane season. It is said that, in a sanitary point of view, St. Thomas is very different from what it was years ago, but of the two islands we certainly preferred Santa Cruz.

Towards evening, after we had paid a very pleasant visit to Major M—, one of the principal planters in the Island—we drove back to Bassin by the central road, which was straight and flat in comparison with that of the morning. As before, cane and palms surrounded us, but many of the cocoa-nut trees had been robbed of their beauty and were headless; and, as the fresh breeze swept over the land, their bent shafts resembled the bare poles of a stricken ship scudding along through a waving green sea. At the corners of the different plantations by the roadside, were small white-domed buildings like Eastern sepulchres; these were watch houses, necessary to prevent stray passers-by from cutting the juicy cane. A steam plough next claimed our attention, and after that a Moravian[7] Church; then darkness closed in, and before long we were home again.

Another of our drives was to the new "Central Factory," about which Santa Cruz was then very much disturbed and divided into two factions. By a "Central Factory," the functions of the cane producer and the sugar-maker are divided, just as those of the wheat farmer and the miller. All the planter has to do is to grow the cane and take it when cut to the nearest dépôt belonging to the "Central Factory," and then his duty is finished.

The complaints against the one being erected in this island were many; among them, it was said that the Government—it was a Government project—had forced the planters into joining the Company, most of the estates being in debt to the Government, owing to a series of bad years; that the planters had their own machinery and could make larger profits by manufacturing sugar themselves; that there was not enough sugar on the island to make so large a factory pay; that small farms and sub-lettings would spring up among the black population (which was already fast superseding the white), which would withdraw labour from the large estates and deteriorate agriculture. The "piping" was also objected to; miles of this had been laid down to convey the juice from the five dépôts to the Central House; up hill and down hill ran this piping, and its opponents declared that the means (pressure) adopted for its utility could never succeed. Nor was the price to be paid by the Company, viz., the value of five and a half pounds of sugar for one hundred pounds of cane, considered sufficient, and altogether so disheartened were the opponents that some of them who had one hundred shares in the Factory, and had paid up a half, were ready to give away the remaining fifty to anyone who would take them up. Whether the project has proved successful or not, I have never heard. To our eyes, the chief drawback seemed to be in the great cost of the buildings and machinery, which were on a far too magnificent a scale for the small island.

A cause of failure in the West India Islands has been the superabundance of central factories; where one would have been sufficient for the neighbourhood, three and four have been erected, to the detriment of all.[8] In Martinique, for example, there are no less than thirteen, and out of these only six are profitable. Wages in Santa Cruz could not be considered excessive, the average for the negro labourers being ten cents per diem, with bread, sugar, and rum thrown in. But poverty was not noticeable, as it was at St. Thomas, and the number of plump, healthy-looking children was remarkable; when we wanted some memento to take away with us, and asked if they made nothing peculiar to the island, the answer might have been that given by an old lady at Martinique to a similar question:—"Rien que les enfants, Monsieur, en voulez-vous?"

The vast preponderance of the black population over the white ought to be a subject of deep consideration to the island planters, and to us it appeared, from the rumours of discontent and negro outbreaks, that the very existence of the white property-owners was in danger.[9] Home we went by the beach, where the fresh-smelling seaweed lay in great banks, and near us was a wonderfully bright colouring of green, blue, and yellow, as the still water lay over deep or shallow shoals, enclosed within circling coral reef, white with the foaming waves of the blue-black sea beyond.

When we re-embarked on the schooner for St. Thomas, we were delayed for more than three hours, which we knew would seriously imperil our chances of getting anything to eat on our arrival at the hotel. This time the delay was caused by the mail, and when it did arrive it consisted of one skinny bag, apparently containing one letter. Fresh passports to take us back! truly there must be "something rotten in the state of Denmark." We lost our dinner by just half-an-hour, but were compensated in some degree by the arrival of our respective steamers, which were to sail on the following day. We had therefore to forego the pleasures of a shark hunt,[10] which had been arranged for us, and in a few hours the doctor was on his way to America, and I was bound South.

CHAPTER VI.

SABA—CRATER COLONIES—ST. EUSTATIUS—ST. KITTS—
BRIMSTONE HILL—MOUNT MISERY—AN ATMOSPHERE—
BASSETERRE—CROWN COLONY SYSTEM—THE NARROWS—
NEVIS—REDONDO—MONTSERRAT—ANTIGUA—ITS
HARBOUR BY MOONLIGHT—GUADELOUPE—
MARIEGALANTE—DOMINICA—CARIBS—ISLAND SCENERY—
ROSEAU—FROGS.

The meeting of the steamers at St. Thomas brings together a varied company, and those on board the 'Tiber' formed no exception to the rule, clergymen, colonial officials, military officers, planters, engineers, commercial travellers, tourists, only a few of each denomination certainly, but those few all the more prepared to enjoy sea-life by having superior cabin accommodation.

Passengers just from England were of course well-acquainted with one another after a two weeks' voyage, and of the others even the most frigid had thawed out before we passed Saba. Strange little island! only a volcanic cone rising directly from the water. We glided by so close that we seemed to hear the lap of the waves as they gently kissed its rocky base, but no harbour, no habitation was visible. It must be an active volcano, for near the summit a faint blue smoke curled upwards and joined the floating clouds. No; that smoke is raised by human hands, for the crater out of which it ascends is the home of a small colony. A mixed population of Dutch and negroes live there, raise fruit and vegetables, and build boats it is said, though timber must be getting scarce in spite of the trees that we see edging the crater's rim.

Some years previously I had visited a crater colony in beautiful Apolima—one of the South Sea Islands; there the whole of the interior had sunk, and we paddled through a narrow opening into a lovely bay, on whose bank stood the village. But here there was no ingress, save by a rocky staircase leading to the interior. I should much like to have gained an insight into the life of the inhabitants, who may, indeed, be said to "live with a volcano under their feet," but time and opportunity were wanting, and in a very short time we had lost sight of the green nest in rough and rugged Saba.

Then another volcanic island, St. Eustatius, appeared. The northern end is broken and rocky, with here and there a ravine filled with trees, then a stretch of land leading up to the crater. Unlike its sister isle, it is the outside which is green and cultivated, and houses dot the scene. It is picturesque, and, before we are tired of looking at it, it fades like a dissolving view, and, ere the accompanying music has had time to change from a Dutch to an English tune, we are coasting along St. Kitts.

Now we begin to realize the fact that we are in the West Indies. The long promontory, which slopes up to the chain of hills intersecting the island, is fresh and green with sugar-cane; tall factory-chimneys and planters' houses are scattered about, and the soft beauty of the cultivated land contrasts with the bold mountain heights which shoot up in culminating masses towards the centre.

Near the shore stands a lonely rock, huge and precipitous as if flung from the summit of Mount Misery, which, in the distant background, towers above it to a height of nearly 4,000 feet. Brimstone Hill, as this imposing pile of igneous rock is called, is accessible only from one side; formerly it was the seat of the garrison and was fortified, the fortifications being still visible.

Further on, a shapely mount, flat-tipped and wooded, raises itself above a black ravine cut deep into the lower hills, which are cultivated in many parts to their tops. A white cloud floats across the volcanic chasm over which Mount Misery frowns, leaving the summit crag bare and distinct, and, for the first time since we entered the West Indies, atmosphere lends its charm to perspective.

Hitherto the clearness of the atmosphere had brought the island views strangely close, without a distance, and with a monotone of tint most unpaintable, but here there was cloud and mist enough to have satisfied Corot himself. It was pleasant to feel that there was a beyond that we could clothe with our own fanciful colours, and that our gaze did not enfold the entire landscape.

Basseterre, the capital, where we stopped for an hour, looked very bright and sunny. Red roofs, peering out of thick green foliage, a gleam of white among the palm trees, and a picturesque church-tower, formed the foreground to a valley of rustling cane, extending the circle of hills, whose links are here of a less elevation than in the other parts of the chain. To us, it looked a quiet, fertile little place, and, no doubt, uncommonly dull. Of its native products we only saw some very good white grapes, and some very indifferent cigars which were brought for sale. St. Kitts is the only one of the Leeward[11] Islands that can be said to pay its way; the others seem to retrograde year by year. Now, however, that the constitution of the islands has been changed to the Crown Colony system, an improvement may be expected, and the same progress looked forward to as in the Windward group.

From Basseterre, the hill chain runs in a south-easterly direction in a series of low ridges covered with scrub mimosa, dwindling away until they reach the "Narrows," as the two-mile stretch of sea is called which separates Nevis from St. Kitts. A shallow dangerous passage is this, full of shoals and hidden reefs, and almost in its midst rises a sharp triangular rock.

Across the "Narrows," a long low plain slopes up to a single cone, whose summit for ever sleeps in mist and clouds. Much bush covers the lower lands, but windmills here and there show that some cultivation is carried on, and light-green patches of cane are seen divided by rows of cocoa-nut palms, which, in their blighted state, alas! have more the appearance of feather dusters. A dreamy-looking little island is this Nevis, whose chief interest to a stranger lies in the fact that here Nelson lived after his marriage with Mrs. Nisbet for a few quiet years.

We sped along swiftly past the graceful southern slope of old "Ben"—as the volcanic cone might be called—but he would not deign to lift his fleecy cap to us, the shifty clouds merely paling or growing blacker, until they were lost to view. The steep and picturesque "Redondo" next claimed our attention. It is only a cavernous rock rising out of the waves, and sea-birds are its sole inhabitants. From it the eye wanders off to the more distant island of Montserrat, whose bold headland stands out in relief against the thickly wooded gorges which traverse the broken uplands. In the centre, a three-headed mountain range, like a crouching Cerberus, guards the fruitful lemon groves and plantations that lie far below. How pleasant it would be to spend a few days on each of these West Indian islands! to visit their *souffrières*, their mountain forests, their wild hills, and their cultivated estates! but, at present, to set one's foot on land necessitates a two weeks' sojourn. Such being the case, and with Roraima ever beckoning me on, I had determined to halt only at Martinique and Trinidad before reaching British Guiana, and therefore glimpses—sometimes near and sometimes far—were all I could expect of the Antilles.

It was night before we reached Antigua, but a full moon rendered the coast scene as clear as day, and added romantic effect to the lovely harbour. A bay within a bay, a semi-circle of wooded hills and ravines, a few white houses, lava cliffs which almost meet at the narrow entrance, and a rampart-crowned rock were the principal points in the picture. The basin in which the vessel lay moored by hawsers seemed but another sky, the stars scarcely quivering in the still deep water; and, as the moon's rays silvered the sharp-leaved aloes, or touched with a bright gleam the angled fort, here softening the rough-edged tufa, and there defining more clearly the outlines of the palm groups, the whole scene wore a delightful aspect of unreality, which was heightened by the extreme quiet, broken only by an occasional plash of oars.

From Antigua we crossed over to Guadeloupe, whose broad and irregular heights were hidden by clouds; as it was night when we coasted along, we saw little except cliffs, green pasture land, and ravines leading up into the heart of the mountains. Next morning we sighted Mariegalante, far away on our port side, and then, in broad daylight, for several hours, beautiful Dominica sat to us for her picture. Up to this time the various island scenes had been pretty, but could not have been called grand, but now the first glance raised our expectations to a high pitch. Nor were we disappointed, for a more lovely island, a finer combination of grandeur and quiet beauty, could hardly be found in the West Indies.

Towards the north, the waves beat against a rock-bound shore, above which rise wooded hills, increasing in size until they join the seamed and contorted mountains. Here, in a retired village, dwell the Carib Indians, once the owners of the island. Reduced to a few score in numbers, these relics of a great tribe live peacefully under their own king, intermarry, hold but little intercourse with strangers, and seldom appear in the capital, Roseau, except now and then to sell their beautifully woven basket-work. On the western side, along which we coast, the sea-board extends further back; there is not much cultivation, but in the bush clearings are a few cane-fields, and beyond, out of the green sloping lawns, spring many hills, some bare and craggy, others cultivated to the summit. Behind, rise the great mountains in a thousand fantastic shapes, here buried in forest, there frowning black and barren over some tree-filled gorge. Everywhere there is a romantic mingling of hill and valley, mountain and gorge. Lifting clouds reveal wooded eminences crowning steep precipices, from whose feet the green sward stretches down in waves to the white beach, and, as the silver veil floats higher and higher, still loftier ridges are unbared, where the pale green of the sugar-cane is plainly distinguished against the dark setting of the forest background. So high and steep are the hills on which many of these cane-fields are perched that the crop, when cut, has to be let down in bundles by ropes.

At Roseau, where we stopped for an hour, we were gladdened by the sight of a river in which many washerwomen were at work. The scene was very pleasing; in the midst of palms and verdure, stood a pretty church and old grey and white houses with deep verandahs; on the right was Government House, with diminutive fortifications, on the left, the land rolled up in cultivated terraces, and a magnificent ravine behind the town ran deep into the cloud-capped mountains.

If Dominica is celebrated for anything, it is for its frogs, some of which are of enormous size. A curry of frogs' legs is a very delicate dish, and we were in great hopes that some *grenouilles* would have been brought on board alive, but they only brought the large *crapauds*, stuffed and varnished. A basketful of them, together with some huge beetles, was quickly disposed of, but a promised cargo of live ones never arrived. Roseau appeared to be an interesting place to pass a few days in, but we were assured by those who knew, that the accommodation was bad in the extreme, that there were no roads in the island, that it was difficult to obtain riding animals, and that, if we wanted to carry away a pleasant memory of our English isle, we had better be contented with its view from the sea.

So we sail on. Still the same fair scenery; mountains gathered up "like a woven garment, and shaken into deep falling folds," here a velvet slope, there a gigantic rib, sharp but forest-covered, or a bare perpendicular cliff with its feet bathed by the sea. Now a farm nestling in some winding glen, overshadowed by brown-red rocks tipped with cane, and again a narrow fissure feathered with evergreen foliage, and opening into a deep bowl full of close and thick vegetation. Clouds rest on the mountain sides, or hanging above cast fitful shadows on upland and valley; a hundred varying shades give colour to the landscape, and, over all, the blue sky, in perfect harmony with the green tints of earth, blends with the sparkling sea into one bright frame for the beautiful island.

The land ends abruptly in a mass of grey rock, sparsely clad, which juts out into the sea. On its summit stands a cross. Passing this corner, we see palm-covered slopes and gentle depressions, then a high needle-like cone with perpendicular sides rising from the ocean, and, beyond, the southern extremity of the central mountain range. Soon after, Dominica fades from us in mist and rain.

CHAPTER VII.

MARTINIQUE—ST. PIERRE—MUSCULAR FEMALES—FEVER—
GRANDE RUE—TAMARIND AVENUE—SAVANNA—
SKETCHING FROM NATURE—BOTANICAL GARDENS—
MOUNTAIN CABBAGE PALM—THE GREAT TROPICAL
FALLACY—WATERFALL—THE LAKE—MUSEUM—A
FORSAKEN GARDEN—TO MORNE ROUGE—COUNTRY LIFE—
THE CALVARY.

"Here the pilgrim may behold

How the bended cocoa waves

When at eve and morn a breeze

Blows to and from the Carib seas,

How the lush banana leaves

From their braided trunk unfold;

How the mango wears its gold,

And the sceptred aloe's bloom

Glorifies it for the tomb."

The above lines, appropriate enough for any West India isle, yet for me associate themselves with Martinique more than with any other. It may be because I lingered long enough to know that island better than the rest, or it may be because the remembrance of a certain ride across the rich country—a ride ever memorable as the most beautiful I had ever enjoyed, and which must be described later on—abides with me as a practical lesson in botany by nature herself.

It was late in the afternoon when we anchored off St. Pierre—the chief town in Martinique. The character of the island had not seemed quite so broken and romantic as Dominica, there was more low table-land and more cultivation, but the mountain range, with its grand pitons looking out over the clouds, gave promise to the expectant imagination of many beautiful scenes.

From the roadstead, we saw in front of us houses thickly massed together and extending round the bay. Close behind the town, on the eastern side, rose a precipitous hill, crowned with waving sugar-cane, and its deep-wooded side dotted with white villas. Towards the north, a broad ravine, through which a river ran, divided the town into two parts, and beyond rose the soft uplands, green with cane, and stretching to the delicately coloured hills which reached the high mountains in the background. On our right, the coast line was varied with rock, hill, and valley, and on one summit a large white statue stood out conspicuously against the green foliage; on our left, the palm-fringed shore, with here a solitary house, and there a little white village, ran northwards in a gently undulating line.

On landing at St. Pierre the traveller finds himself the object of a popular demonstration; he is assailed by a swarm of stalwart women, some of whom dispossess him of his book, umbrella, or whatever he may be carrying, whilst others, after a short fight among themselves, seize on the luggage, toss great portmanteaus and boxes on to their heads with the greatest of ease, and amid shouts of laughter rush off with loud cries, "A la douane! à la douane!" It is useless to protest that you want to carry such and such a thing yourself, you may recapture it for a second, but it is lost again; everything goes aloft on female heads and shoulders, and to avoid a similar fate yourself you follow in the wake of the flying Amazons and arrive at the Custom House. Then a strict inspection ensues, after which the luggage is remounted and a procession is formed to the hotel.

We—one other passenger and myself—had been advised to go to the Hôtel des Bains, so when our porters said of course "les Messieurs" were going to the "Hôtel Micas," we answered of course not. Eventually we made out from the extraordinary Creole patois, that the former hotel was closed, and that its proprietor had opened the latter. We soon arrived there, and it looked clean and comfortable, but the landlord was "désolé," there was not a single vacant room; "would the gentlemen be satisfied with a billiard table for to-night, then to-morrow——?" This offer was declined, and finally we found rooms in the Hôtel du Commerce, a place of very second-rate pretensions, but with a very obliging proprietor.

The first few days of my sojourn in this "Faubourg St. Germain of the tropics"—as the French love to call it—were certainly depressing. The heat was great, the food very indifferent, and the rain almost incessant. Much stress has been laid on the streams of clear, crystal water which here run through the streets. I should call them gutters, and, after one has seen the use to which they are put—the houses being entirely free from what we consider the most necessary requirements—the crystal romance is dissipated. Fortunately, owing to the slope of the streets and the ample supply of water which is brought down through fine aqueducts from the mountains, the flow is swift, and thus the gutters are kept pretty clean. Otherwise, the town of St. Pierre would be unbearable, as even now it rivals Cologne in the number of its smells. Under such conditions, it is not surprising that the stranger feels the effects of an "acclimatizing fever," as they here designate it.

Morning after morning I awoke dull, listless, and tired, and with all sorts of pains and aches in my limbs, but as the day advanced health returned and fever was forgotten.

St. Pierre is not a cheerful town even on its sunniest days; the streets are narrow, with side-walks of infinitesimal dimensions, the old stone houses, with heavy outside shutters, are gloomy and comfortless, no bright verandahs attract the eye, and the roofs are dingy with moss-covered tiles. But the outskirts are more attractive, and the road to the Botanical Gardens particularly so. Passing up the Grande Rue towards the north, we see shops and stores filled with gay-coloured foulards, straw hats, finery of all sorts, and an excess of gold ornaments. On the left is the Batterie d'Esnoty, with a few seats under the shady trees, and affording a fine view over the sea. Farther on, some fine mangoes overshadow a heavy fountain, and soon our road turns off eastward before reaching the bridges which cross the intersecting river. We follow its left bank under a beautiful avenue of tamarinds, whilst on our right is the Savanna or public park. And here commences picturesque Martinique. Down below in the wide rocky ravine flows the brawling stream, alive with dusky "blanchisseuses," whose methodical beat on the smooth stones with the clothes they are washing, keeps time with their patois songs. White houses rise in tiers over the opposite bank, their gardens filled with many bright flowers, and crowning all are clusters of palms and ceiba groves. Across the Savanna rises the mountain screen that shades the town; its steep side a perfect network of hanging vines. Here and there a mango has gained a precarious footing, its dark green dome contrasting well with the crimson blaze of a neighbouring Bois Immortelle;[12] and these lofty trees look like out-stretched arms on which is hung a close-textured mantle of flowering creepers. Far up, at the head of the cultivated river-valley, rise the mountains, whose dark gorges, veiled by almost constant mist, are arched by the most brilliant rainbows.

In a few steps after leaving the Savanna, the Botanic Gardens are gained. At the time of my first visit the road outside was lined with cadets from the French training ship "Flore," who were sketching a handsome Traveller's Tree—*Ravenala speciosa*—which grew near the entrance. A crowd of little urchins hovered about them, and it was very amusing to hear their outspoken opinions on the efforts of the different artists, who worked away with perfect composure. Several times afterwards I met the young scholars eagerly acquiring, under able tuition, that most desirable accomplishment— sketching from nature.

The Botanical Gardens are delightfully situated in a wide ravine through which a stream flows. Terraces have been cut out of the sides, and winding walks and avenues lead to pretty scenes and charming outlooks. Art here has done much in laying out the grounds and forming the various rills, fountains, and waterfalls, but nature has supplied a very beautiful site. Particularly beautiful is one avenue of "Palmistes Royals,"[13] whose perfectly straight grey stems, ending in a light green shaft and crowned with a leafy diadem of dark green spreading leaves, form an aisle of living Corinthian pillars, seventy or eighty feet in height. This magnificent species of palm reminds me of an article which appeared in the June number of "Belgravia," 1878, entitled "The Great Tropical Fallacy." In it the writer declares that "waving sugar-cane, graceful bamboos, spreading tree ferns, magnificent palms, &c., may be found at Kew, but not in the tropics." He also says "a true fern can scarcely be seen through the foul mouldering fronds that cling around its musty stem."

The amusing article certainly would dispel "The Great Tropical Fallacy," if it was true, but it can only have been written as a joke, as the writer adds that he has "lived for years in the tropics, but never yet beheld an alligator, an iguana, a toucan, or an antelope in their wild state. Scorpions do not occur." It is an undoubted fact that these creatures—with the exception of scorpions—do not frequent the streets of towns or villages, nor are they much addicted to highway travelling, but had the writer ever visited "the bush," or walked in the "country," I think he would have hesitated before making such a statement, that is, supposing he has the full use of his eyesight and has lived where these animals exist.

As regards the palm, it is true that cocoa-nut trees, especially when blighted, are not very imposing; but there are many other splendid species, and to depreciate the mountain cabbage-palms is to be guilty of high treason against the princes of the forest. They are simply wonderful. To admire them it is not necessary to be a pantheist, or one of those to whom a forest is a cathedral, each tree a missionary, and every flying creature a sacred spirit; one who bows down at the sight of a daisy or buttercup, and kneels before an oak as the wild Indian does before his ceiba. For these palms are so matchless in grace, so simple and yet so stately, that they lend an indescribable air of dignity to any spot where they may chance to grow.

To return to the garden. Leaving the palm avenue one comes suddenly upon a beautiful waterfall rushing down a steep rock amidst a mass of hanging grasses, ferns, and waving cannas. A little way below it runs into the heart of a garden-wilderness rich with bamboos, plantains, thickets of tangled vines, and fragrant coffee trees. Here shrubs and trees are more cultivated than flowers, but the former with their brilliant blossoms save the place from the monotonous effect of a too prevailing green. Gloxinias and primulas are scattered over the sloping banks, and overhead are interlaced the branches of various trees. The bright flowers of the "Flamboyant,"[14] form a red canopy which vies in richness with the large crimson blossoms of the mountain rose.[15] Here may be seen South Sea Island bread-fruit, cinnamon from Ceylon, and sandal-wood from the Marquesas. That tree with bunches of wax-like and pear-shaped fruit is a Eugenia;[16] its trunk is a perfect fernery, and its branches are hung with parasites. Next to a stilted pandanus rises a tall "poui" with saffron flowers, and beyond are the long white trumpets of a datura. Close at hand is the much prized persimmon of Japan, having a wood like ebony, and a reddish-yellow fruit. The ground is everywhere strewn with the red beads of an erythrina, and occasionally the large uneatable fruit of a species of inga comes down with a thump, that a passer by, if hit, would not soon forget.

Perhaps the prettiest spot in the garden is a small lake fed by a slender fall, whose water trickles down a moss-covered rock through ferns and drooping grasses. The three tiny islets are fringed with arums, heliconias, and bamboos, amongst which are scattered dark glossy green and gold-marbled crotons, purple dracœnas, and crimson hybiscus blossoms. In the centre of each stands a "Traveller's Tree," like a gigantic fan, surrounded with a few flowering shrubs and graceful plantains. But here as elsewhere, there is an air of neglect, the shady walks are full of weeds, the stone seats under the trees are damp and green, a broken canoe half full of water lies on the yielding bank, the few remaining tree labels are illegible, and, in a word, the gardens are not tended as they deserve. Their charm seems to have vanished with their novelty, as they are seldom visited by the inhabitants, and the funds granted for their maintenance are insufficient.

Within the grounds there is a building which contains a small natural history museum, and the native products form a very interesting collection. There is also an interior nursery-garden, where some delicate orchids and rare exotics are reared.

A primitive people these French Creoles must be, as a printed notice strictly prohibits bathing in the small fountains in this inside garden. Unhappily the people appear disinclined even to walk in the pleasant grounds, and the casual visitor feels that a time may come when the few labourers will be withdrawn and a "Forsaken Garden" realised:

"Not a flower to be prest of the foot that falls not;

As the heart of a dead man the seed plots are dry;

From the thicket of thorns when the nightingale calls not,

Could she call, there were never a rose to reply.

Over the meadows that blossom and wither

Rings but the note of a sea-bird's song,

Only the sun and the rain come hither

All year long."[17]

One of the pleasantest drives from St. Pierre is to Morne Rouge. The village is situated high up in the hills, and near it and cut out of a rocky wall is a celebrated grotto dedicated to "Our Lady of Lourdes." Morne Rouge is one of the localities which the negroes say is at certain seasons visited by the celebrated Dominican Friar, Père Labat, who arrived in Martinique in 1693. He is said to appear in the guise of a lambent flame.

The road thither passes the Botanical Gardens, and for some distance is lined with country houses standing in pretty grounds. It was in one of these villas that the Empress Joséphine was born. The hedges and banks are covered with blue flowers of the "ipomæa" and the buff-coloured "thumbergia," whose dark brown eye attracts the attention of numerous humming birds.

The houses for the most part look cool, but comfortless and devoid of privacy. The foliage of the tall trees shades them, but the bare trunks leave an uninterrupted view into the interior. Here, one sees Madame in a very airy costume enjoying her early coffee; there, Monsieur in his dressing-gown lounges on a long cane chair.

Grass is conspicuous by its absence, but rich and gaudy flowers are in abundance. Tall yuccas guard the entrance, and the lavender spikes of the "petrœa" cluster over the verandahs. Many varieties of "dracœna" are scattered about, their slender stems and bending blades contrasting well with the showy hybiscus and the bright green bananas. In each garden one sees a tall clavija, like a giant papau, and with panicles of the fragrant white flowers beloved by Creoles. Thick stone walls surround some of the villas, but tropical nature heeds no such barriers. Creepers of every hue fling themselves over, then catching the hanging air-roots scramble up to the tree-tops and mingle their blossoms with those of their more lofty brethren. Among the numerous trees with hanging pods, the "rosary bean"[18] is very prominent, as the curled and split pod displays the bright red seeds within. Gradually the houses are left behind, and the road becomes more steep and winding. The high banks are thickly carpeted with begonias, both pink and white. From a neighbouring hill a high waterfall—caused by a deflected stream—descends and turns the wheel of a sugar-mill situated at its foot.

At last we reach the village of Morne Rouge. A long straggling street with pretty cottages and gardens. From trellis-work hang great granadillas, fruit which is only palatable when cunningly compounded with sugar, ice, and wine. The life around is simple, but full of colour, and picturesque. Old women spin in the doorways. Mothers, with bright kerchiefs round their heads, watch their children playing in the road. The children themselves, often only dressed in a plain suit of gold earrings, have fresh, happy faces, brighter and ruddier by far than those in the hot town below. Round the fountain are groups of girls with water-jars poised on their heads, and in the bright sunshine each touch of red and blue in their dress shines out clearly and effectively. From this fountain a beautiful view is obtained seaward, but from the higher Calvary there is a more extended landscape. The prayer-stations leading to the chapel stand between hybiscus hedges, and are surrounded with roses, lilies, azaleas, and palms. The little shrines contained terra cotta representations of the Passion, but the protecting glass was broken and the figures were defaced. Within them green lizards played at hide and seek, and humming birds searched the flower-offerings that had been thrust through the torn grating.

The view from the top is worth the climb. On one side a mass of undulating hills sweeps off to the sea; through the intervening pasture land a winding stream threads its way, and here and there a cottage is seen half buried in clumps of palms and bamboos, and with its cane patch or banana grove. The lofty "pitons" form the background. Below us lies the village, and extending westward towards St. Pierre are cane-covered hills, fertile valleys, and a broad cultivated plain, squared like a chess-board by the dividing palm rows. Beyond rises the glittering blue sea far into the sky, white sails catch the sunbeams, and nearer is the dark line of anchored ships. On rare occasions— one of which favoured me—rounded masses of fleecy clouds of intense brilliancy float over land and sea, and pour down such a flood of light that the panorama is illuminated. The white glare is almost painful, but the strong sea-breeze soon drives the wandering rain-heralds back to the mountains, where they wreathe themselves round the higher peaks and lie like snow-drifts in the hollows between the summits. And thus the scene changes from sunshine to shade, from rest to storm, and from light to darkness, each a life-phase typical in itself, but not more significant than the solemn Calvary above us in its bright frame of green trees and flowers.

CHAPTER VIII.

A GALA DAY—COSTUMES—CINQ-CLOUS—BATTERIE
D'ESNOTY—A CASSAVA FARM—PANDEMONIUM—
PREPARATION OF CASSAVA—A "CATCH"—COUNTRY
SCENES—FRESH ATMOSPHERE—A STORM—RAINBOWS—
FOREST SCENES—TROPICAL VEGETATION—NOON-DAY
HALT.

On Sundays and gala days St. Pierre brightens up. The band plays in the Savanna, and thither the inhabitants flock. In the matter of carriages and horses, Rotten Row would certainly outvie this favourite drive, but in brilliancy of colour the latter would carry the day. On ordinary occasions the Creole woman is content with a simple long-flowing dress of light material, but on state occasions her costume is bright and picturesque. Then you see a bewildering display of silk or satin skirts, short enough not to hide a daintily shod foot; embroidered bodices and gauzy scarfs, a profusion of necklaces and bracelets, all of plain gold—for precious stones are never worn—and jaunty turbans ornamented with gold pins and brooches. But the most striking as well as the commonest feature in the national costume of Martinique is the quaint earrings—cinq-clous. These consist of five gold tubes welded together at the sides into a circular form, not unlike the barrels of a revolver, and vary in size from the dimensions of a toy pistol to those of a full grown Colt's. Many girls carry their entire future in their ears.

Those splendid beds of tulips were not in the Savanna when we last passed through! As we approach, we see they are not composed of flowers, but are merely gorgeous head-dresses. Another trait, and a charming one too, of Martinique costume. Here you see no dyed feathers, or artificial flowers and fruits, decorating the flashy hats and bonnets so dear to the negro soul. Bright coloured foulards, twisted into various pyramidal, circular, and oval shapes, crown every head with rainbow hues. There are ten different ways of tying these kerchiefs, and the initiated can tell by the twist whence the wearer comes.

Near the band is a motley group. Two or three old negresses dressed in flowered chintz, and with trimly turned head-dresses gossip over the last scandal; slowly sweeping along comes a majestic creature, her long white dress hitched up on one side and displaying a foot neatly blacked by nature; in that family coach are some white Creole ladies with charming faces, and tastefully dressed in the latest Parisian fashion, while the youngsters who force their bouquets on them are habited in little else than "native" worth. The excitement is of the mildest kind, but enjoyment is universal. Here and there some little maidens dance to the music, boys run races, the elders give the prizes, handsome carriages and wretched *fiacres* continue their monotonous round, and meeting is so perpetual that everybody smiles at everybody else, till at length the sun goes down. Then the vehicles are turned towards home, dandies prance off on their rocking horses, old ladies put up their umbrellas against the dew, peasants take off their shoes preparatory to their homeward tramp, and very soon the Savanna is deserted.

Wonderfully clear are the nights in Martinique. You see distinct shadows, and on looking up for the moon you find they are cast by a star (Venus probably) shining with a radiance of most remarkable power.

From the Batterie d'Esnoty you look down on a sparkling sea in which every vessel stands out distinctly. You can almost count the piles of merchandise and barrels on the wharf. It is so quiet that you can catch the words of the song that the black crew are singing as they pull to shore from some outlying ship, and their strange rising and falling to each stroke is plainly visible. Suddenly a hideous bray rings out close beside you. It comes from one of three buglers who make this their starting point, and in turn repeat the discordant sounds until they reach their distant barracks. This is the Martinique tattoo. The stranger in St. Pierre will notice the quantity of thin white cakes about the size of a cart wheel. These are made from cassava[19] which here, as in many of the islands, and in parts of South America, affords the chief sustenance of the poorer classes.

We drove out one day to a farm to witness its manufacture. We soon came to fields covered with the plant, which grows to a height of about four feet. In appearance it is a slender-knotted grey stem, with branches at the top from which spring red stalks of broad digitated leaves. The root, which is cylindrical and about a foot long, is a deadly poison in its natural state, but by a simple process it is converted into nutritious food. As we approached the wattled shed in which it was being prepared, we heard sounds of a veritable pandemonium. On looking in, we saw thirty or forty jet black Africans stripped to the skin and furiously grating the white roots against a rough board, the meal falling into great tubs.

The exertion was apparently immense, as they steamed with perspiration, and, as if the fumes of the poison got into their heads, they would every now and then utter yells or bound into the air. To this wild scene there was a musical accompaniment. The instruments consisted of tom-toms, pipes, chac-chacs, and long bamboos, struck by pieces of wood, and a strange concern made of cane-work, from which issued a grating sound by drawing a stick quickly up and down. Music from such sources was not likely to be of a high order, but it was conscientiously gone through at all events. All that lungs could blow was blown; all that fists could do to break a drum skin was done. White, eyes rolled, black lips blew, and black fists struck. The "grater" sounded worse than the grating, and the monotonous chant of one of the performers was more horrible than the howls of the workers. Never had I heard a like "charivari." "Ils ont de la couleur," said the pleased proprietor, as he rubbed his hand and glanced at the rapidly filling tubs. The next operation is to get rid of the poisonous juices. Here, as the factory was on a large scale, the meal was put into a great sort of oven and the poison extracted by heat or pressure. But the usual mode, and the one invariably applied by the Indians of Guiana, where in after-days I many a time witnessed the operation, is as follows: A long plaited tube—matapi—made of a certain reed is filled with the grated meal; its upper end is fastened to a beam so that its lower end, which possesses a loop-hole, hangs a few feet from the ground. A pole is then passed through the loop and the shorter end firmly fixed so that the longer, when pressed down, serves as a lever; the elastic tube presses the meal together, and the poisonous juice escapes through the interstices. The flour is then dried and sifted. When required for use, a handful is baked over a fire on a flat plate, and in a few minutes "cassava bread," resembling an enormous oatmeal cake, is ready. If required for a journey, it is thoroughly dried in the sun until it is as hard as a nail, and will then last for months; if not properly dried, it quickly gets mouldy and uneatable. Cassiripe, which is the extracted poison-juice of cassava, is the foundation of the well-known "pepper pot," which is an "olla podrida" of meat and peppers cooked in an earthen pot, and always on hand in the West Indies. Fortunately, the deleterious principle of the juice is so volatile that it is entirely dissipated by heat, and it then becomes a wholesome seasoning; and thus the good is extracted from the evil in this strange blending of life and death, as exhibited in the cassava root.

That evening, before we reached home, we witnessed a scene of excitement. As we drove along the sea-shore there was a sudden rush of people to the beach, boats were pushed hurriedly out, men jumped into the water and swam out, women waded up to their knees and ran back again, and children did their best to get drowned. Presently, a series of long nets formed a semi-circle and enclosed a large shoal of sardines which had been the cause of the uproar. Gradually the nets were drawn in, and so large was the haul that in a few minutes five boats were filled with the little silvery fish. Buckets, barrels, baskets, and cans were then put into requisition, and, even after every article from the neighbouring cottages that could hold a fish had done its duty, there were still sardines enough left on the beach to have stocked a market.

Next morning I started for a ride across the island to Trinité, a distance of about thirty miles. The scenery on the road had been so extolled that I attributed enthusiastic descriptions of it to patriotism, and was prepared for a disappointment. When I returned, I acknowledged it was the most beautiful ride I had ever taken, and one whose like I should probably never see again.

It was dawn when my mule drew up at the hotel door, and we were soon clattering over the rough cobble stones which pave the narrow streets. We passed the Promenade, which was deserted by all save a solitary sentry, who slept in his box under the Palace of the Archbishop, and then the road commenced to wind up the hill under whose shadow the town lay, dark and quiet. Before we reached the top it was broad daylight, the great crimson blossoms of the hybiscus and the fragile bells of the abutilon, which we had left sleeping below, were now unfolded, and the white flowers of the night cereus and of the ipomæa, had already drooped and faded. For some distance beyond the summit the road is walled in with sugar-cane, then bends inwards towards the mountains by a gentle acclivity. Here and there, one passes a little *cabaret de ferme*, where the market people are drinking coffee, or, more probably, rum.

Down in the valley lie cottages and farms, and the hill-sides are flecked with groups of trees, whose light and dark green foliage is very conspicuous. Fine mango trees are dotted about here and there, and fringing rocky heights, or clustered in hollows, are aloes in various stages of their growth; some fully flowered and rapidly collapsing, others whose tall stalks are covered with fresh blooms, and more still whose rich green expanding heart is suggestive of a thyrsus—"thro' the blooms of a garland the point of a spear."

On approaching a small and picturesque village, cane culture is superseded by cassava, and the country becomes more rugged and grander. Cottages are perched upon jutting cliffs, and immediately above the road is situated a delightfully quaint old church, which is reached by a flight of rough stone steps. Near this, a large wooden cross overlooks the valley. The view looking west is lovely. Afar off is the bright blue sea, to which extend the mountain arms and the undulating hill spurs. The valleys between are partly tilled and partly bush-covered, and the few houses stand in garden patches high up on the hill slopes. Through the central valley a twisting thread of green, darker than the surrounding foliage, marks the course of a stream, and clumps of trees of a similar contrasting hue, above and around us, show where orange groves and mangoes lie amid the paler green of cane fields and bananas. Behind rise the forest-clad peaks of the mountains, through which runs the road to Trinité.

Up to this point we had enjoyed a very beautiful morning. Here spring was in the air, and we had left hot summer below. There was such fulness of life in the cool air that all nature seemed affected by it. The flowers looked brighter, the birds sang sweeter, and even the running water seemed to tinkle with a more silvery sound than in the valleys.

A simple circumstance, but one that impressed me very vividly, occurred as I was looking over the blue shadowed valley. An old peasant woman, very brown and wrinkled, laid a bunch of flowers on the cross, and as she knelt at its foot an oriole flew on to one of its arms and poured forth such a trill that it seemed as if the bird-voice was carrying aloft her mumbled prayers. When she entered the church a few minutes later, tears were in her eyes, but she looked so happy that I am sure the bird had not sung in vain. The romance of the little episode was injured by an unsentimental goat who completely demolished the flower-offering, and then tried to butt some children who had done nothing to offend it. They, however, did not seem to mind it, and laughed merrily at the antics of the creature. These children's voices were just what was wanted to give a charming finish to the bright picture. What the flowers were to the garden, the stream to the valley, the birds to the air, and the sun's rays to all, were the happy child-tones to the surrounding scene, gladdening everything in accord with each, and freshening with rippling music the fragrant uplands:

"Ah, what would the world be to us

If the children came no more?

We should dread the desert behind us

More than the dark before."

I had hardly whispered these lines to my mule before the last two words sounded ominous. The animal showed signs of uneasiness which could not be attributed to the verse; for among his many faults a mule cannot be accused of sentimentality, and he cares as little for poetry as he does for a stick. He is so stubborn and self-willed, and yet carries it off with such a nonchalant air, that there is no way of knowing what may be passing in his mind, except by watching his restless ears. Fortunately, these appendages are so expressive—more so in fact than some human faces—that they explain his feelings and foretell his movements. On this occasion they were suddenly pointed straight forward, and as suddenly laid limp on his neck, then pricked again.

The air grew hot and still, a black mist was descending on us from the now hidden mountains, and it was plain that a heavy storm was about to break. On looking round, I saw a hand beckoning to me from a door, and in a few minutes my mule was under cover, and I found myself in a clean room drinking coffee with the kind hostess. Then the rain came down in torrents, and held me prisoner for some time. Here I saw one of those terrible snakes known as the "Fer-de-lance," which had been killed not long before on the road to Trinité by the old lady's husband, who had preserved it in a jar of spirits.

At the first lull we started again, and soon reached a stream spanned by a stone bridge of a single arch. This we crossed, and in a few minutes entered the forest ravine. Turning in the saddle, I was dazzled by a brilliant rainbow, which in a broad band struck the bridge at a right angle. It was so close that I could not resist the novelty of riding back into the middle of it. Then it danced off up the deep bed of the river, and before I re-entered the forest it had formed a bow, stretching across the mountain sides like a grand triumphal arch. A last look from the wooded portals revealed a bright blue sky and the sun shining over the lowlands, whilst around us the rain still fell, and through the dripping branches of the trees that met overhead only dull grey clouds were visible. Here commenced a series of mountain pictures in bewildering variety. For almost all the rest of the journey the path runs up and down hill, with a deep ravine sometimes on one hand and sometimes on the other. Through the ravine runs a stream, on the other side of which the mountain rises in a grand and almost perpendicular wall. On the near side the path is edged with banks which slope away to the higher hills, and diversified with glens and hollows, and an occasional overhanging rock.

The vegetation is of the most luxuriant description, as numerous waterfalls descend from both the mountain sides, here crossing the path in a broad stream, and there trickling down in a slender thread, which loses itself in thick ferns and grasses. Each turn in the road presents some new combination of rock, tree, and falling water. You emerge from an avenue of bamboos, to enter another arched over by the fronds of magnificent tree-ferns. The latter grow everywhere; you look up at their rough fibrous stems, and you look down into their very hearts. The banks are covered with begonias and primulas; above these rise the dark green blades of plantains, or dark green heliconias, with their red and yellow flowers. Then come the great forest trees, such as the locust, the angelim, the bois violon (fiddle wood), the bois immortelle, &c. Of begonias I counted four varieties, one of which was sweet-scented. For some time I searched, wondering whence the delicious fragrance—very like that of the lily of the valley—came.

I had never heard of a sweet-scented begonia, but at last I discovered one, and gathered a large bunch of the delicious blossoms. The flowers of this variety were very small and of a pink colour, but the elephant-eared leaves were as large as those of much finer flowering species. I regret much that I did not endeavour to transplant some specimens, as I have since heard that a scented begonia is unknown. The extraordinary wealth of tropical vegetation was such that, in spite of heavy rain, I constantly stood for many minutes lost in astonishment. And there was no questioning the down-pour; sometimes a perfect stream would enter the sensitive ears of the mule, and the poor animal would actually squeal and kick, and then droop, until he presented a spectacle of abject misery. Thoughts of fever hovered about me, but I had a change of clothes in my saddle-bags, and even without it I doubt whether I could have hastened my steps, so fascinating was the scenery.

Our progress had been so slow that it was noon before little more than half the distance had been accomplished. Then a certain spot offered such irresistible attractions for a halt that I picketed old Solomon—as the mule had been named—under a hanging rock, and lunched. There could not have been a prettier place, with its rich banks of flowers, feathery bamboos, and silvery fall, trickling down through a fernery of frail, shivering beauty. Across the wild ravine rose a perpendicular mass of black rock, hung with long waving grasses and tufts of green. Large trees clung to its side where there was, apparently, no root-hold, and their branches were loaded with orchids and red-spiked bromelias. The only sounds were the pattering of the raindrops and the murmur of the rapids below, which foamed over the rough stones that were hidden by the fringing arums, bamboos, and branching ferns.

Suddenly a whirring sound broke the silence, and I immediately saw a "Purple Carib"[20] humming-bird, hovering over a flowering vine. It was the first time I had ever seen one of this beautiful species alive, and he seemed determined I should not forget him. After every plunge into a flower, he retired to a favourite branch and preened his velvet black feathers and shook his wings, until their metallic green and the deep purple of the throat flashed again and again. His resting-place was a magnolia tree—numbers of which line this woodland path—and the dark, shining wet leaves formed a lovely frame for the dainty *oiseau-mouche*. He looked like a living gem, set in green enamel, and diamond sprays. I saw no other birds, and the silent woods raised in me a fancy to pull the long bell-ropes hanging from the trees, and thus set the forest chiming. I did so, and got nothing but a shower bath; and the falling leaves and sticks stilled for a moment the melancholy croak of the frogs, in their perpetual lament for the departed Indian race, "Ca-rib, Ca-rib." Then I saddled Solomon, and we resumed our journey.

There is little more to describe. Everywhere beautiful scenes, and blending of loveliness and grandeur. Sometimes from the overhanging cliffs a landslip, caused by the heavy rains, rendered the path—which, with a very little trouble, might be made good enough for a carriage—almost impassable; otherwise, the road is remarkably easy and free from obstructions.

The finest view remains for the last. When the highest point to which the road ascends is reached, a narrow ridge, with a deep ravine on each side, commands a magnificent prospect over Trinité to the sea. Near by are rocky gorges, mountain peaks, and half-hidden glades. The rank vegetation forms green vistas above the descending terraces, and through them shines the deep blue water, out of which rise the bold outlines of Dominica on one side, and St. Lucia on the other. That these islands are visible, I only know from hearsay, as mist and clouds enshrouded so much of the landscape that I could only form an idea of what its beauty would be on a clear day. In rain I went to Trinité and in rain I returned. No feeling of ill-will towards the weather was felt by me, but rather one of gratitude, as, had it not been for the rain, I might never have torn myself from those enchanted grounds. It was my last and pleasantest excursion in Martinique.

CHAPTER IX.

A CURIO HUNTER—FORT DE FRANCE—BATHS OF DIDIER—
DIAMOND ROCK—FLYING-FISH TRADE—BARBADOES—
CARLISLE BAY—HOAD'S—TRAFALGAR SQUARE—THE ICE-
HOUSE—ST. ANN'S—SCOTLAND—CONFEDERATION—COAST
OF TOBAGO—BIRDS OF TOBAGO—FAUNA OF THE WEST
INDIES.

"Yeo-ho, boys, ho, yeo-ho," rang out merrily from the crew, and before the last notes of "Nancy Lee" had died away, the 'Eider' was slowly steaming from Martinique on her way to Barbadoes. A slight delay had been occasioned by the prolonged absence of one of the passengers who was an enthusiastic curiosity hunter, and who, having rifled the other islands and bought up all the frogs and beetles at Dominica, had gone on shore to buy Eau de Cologne, dolls in native costume, and the various liqueurs for which Martinique is celebrated.

Soon we pass Fort de France—the Fort Royal of Imperial days—which is nominally the capital of Martinique, though far inferior in size and population to St. Pierre. A small steamer runs daily between the two places, and Fort de France is well worth a visit. The fine harbour and the pretty town, backed by the great Piton, are more thoroughly tropical in their surroundings than is St. Pierre. In the neighbourhood are some picturesque walks, and the "Baths of Didier," where there are some mineral springs, is a very favourite resort. In the outskirts dwell a few of the Carib Indians, who occupy themselves with their peculiar basket work. It is a quiet little town, but gains an air of industry and life from the freighted wharfs and the busy dockyard with its spacious floating dock.

From the deck of the 'Eider' all eyes are centered on a steep island pyramid, which rises out of the water to a height of about five hundred and fifty feet. This is the celebrated "Diamond Rock," whose history forms a memorable page in the annals of the West Indies, where nearly every link in the chain of the Antilles has been the scene of England's naval warfare.

The well-known story may be briefly related as follows. In 1804, the English admiral determined to prevent the escape of French ships, which hitherto had baffled him by running between this rock and the opposite Diamond Point into Fort Royal harbour. The deep water that surrounded the almost perpendicular rock permitted an anchorage within a few feet of its side. The admiral therefore laid his ship, the 'Centaur,' close alongside, and performed the surprising feat of hoisting heavy guns from the top-sail yard-arm, and mounting them on the summit of this improvised fortress. Here Captain Morris was established, with men, ammunition, water, and provisions, and the rock was recognised at the Admiralty, as His Majesty's ship 'Diamond Rock.' For months the gallant captain and his crew defied the exertions of the French to dislodge them, destroying their merchant vessels and gunboats, and harassing them to desperation. Finally, want of water and ammunition necessitated a surrender, and the rock-ship was once more untenanted.

On approaching Barbadoes, it is surprising to see the vast shoals of flying-fish. Like flights of silver arrows they shoot over the water on all sides, and just as you are beginning to think they must be birds, down they drop into the waves. No wonder that the catching of them is a trade in that island, and that flying-fish in Barbadoes is the staff of life—and a very delicious one. No time is lost in their pursuit, nets surround them by day, and at night, by means of an attractive lantern, they fly against the outspread sail and fall victims by the hundred.

After Martinique and Dominica, the appearance of Barbadoes is flat, and tame. One misses the central hill range, which is so marked a feature in the other islands. The wide-stretching fields of bright green cane, and the windmills, recall Santa Cruz. Like that island, Barbadoes, when discovered by the Portuguese in the early part of the sixteenth century, was covered with thick forest. From many of the trees hung the beard-like Tillandsia, whence arose the island's name. In the present day there is no forest, and the one little wood, with its boiling spring, is reckoned among the "lions" of Barbadoes.

But if the island is devoid of great physical beauty, it is interesting, as being the most ancient colony in the British Empire, one also that has never changed hands, and the only one which thrives—or shall I say has thriven—without foreign labour.

From Carlisle Bay, the harbour of Bridgetown, which is the capital of the island, the view is one of bright colour. One sees gleaming sands broken on by blue water, and edged with deep green avicennias, with here and there a bending cocoa-nut palm. From the busy wharfs white houses extend back into the country to a limestone ridge, and to the undulating hills which are covered with sugar-cane and dotted with lines of palms, leading to the planters' houses. White roads wind through the green fields, and a church tower peeps over the shady trees; a windmill rises above a cluster of cottages, and near by is the tall smoking chimney of a sugar factory. There are no clouds in the intensely blue sky to cast their shadows, and the breeze rushes across the cane slopes in white green waves. On all, the sun pours down with a pitiless glare, and its strong light brings to full view the finished cultivation and well-to-do aspect of the island.

"Passengers for Bimshire all aboard," was the cry, as the ship's cutter pulled for the shore, thus disappointing the clamorous native crews of several expected fees. Presently we landed in Bimshire—as Barbadoes is sometimes called—and were at once surrounded by an agitated crowd of "Bims," both black and white. As there are no hotels—properly so-called—our luggage was carried to "Hoad's," the best boarding house; and after escaping numerous blind beggars who pursued us from the wharf, we were soon ensconced in clean lodgings. Here we found small but comfortable rooms, good food—flying-fish served in two or three different forms being particularly tempting—and indifferent bathing accommodation.

After Martinique, where there are no mosquitoes, one looks disconsolately at the stuffy nettings, and cannot help wondering why the detestable insects should patronize the English islands and not the French. The Barbadian mosquito is of an exceptionally dissipated disposition, as it keeps up its revels far into the morning, and with the heat increases the misery of the late as well as of the early riser.

As may be expected in an island whose population averages a thousand to the square mile, Bridgetown swarms with negroes, whose high-pitched voices and incessant "talk" effectually relieve the streets of any air of dulness. The town is not imposing. Its architectural features are collected in Trafalgar Square, where are situated the Government Buildings. Their style, though striking, is a marvellous blending of Gothic and Venetian architecture, mixed with bow windows and Moorish arches, and as much out of keeping with the adjacent Cathedral as the National Gallery in London is with its neighbouring Church of St. Martin. The statue of Nelson, which stands in the centre of the square, cannot be considered as complimentary to the great admiral, and in its present condition fairly represents "the triumph of Nature over Art." Shops, stores, and warehouses are good and thriving, and, last but not least, there is an excellent tea-house, which is an institution peculiar to the West Indies. It vies with the club as a place of resort, contains a restaurant, and a well-kept bar, provides the latest papers, and disseminates the freshest news.

In the matter of ice, which is of no small importance in hot climates, the English are ahead of the French. Here it is admitted free, I believe, of duty, whilst in Martinique it is heavily taxed and monopolized.

Most of the white inhabitants live in the suburbs of the town, and in a drive one passes many pretty villas and pleasant gardens. The roads leading to them are lined with negro huts and cabins, shaded by flowering trees, and now and then surrounded by an ill-tended garden plot. On some of these abodes we noticed hanging-boards, on which quaint greetings had been written; one of these bore the words, "A mery Krismas and a hapy New ear to everybody;" on another was printed, "Welcum home 1 and all."

Towards evening carriages wend their way past the seaside villages of Hastings and Worthing, or, when the band plays at St. Ann's, stop there to listen to it. The latter appeared to me to be the most agreeable place in or around Bridgetown. The barracks are situated there, and fronting them is a fine savanna, surrounded by shady avenues. Here there is the race course, the cricket ground, a ball court, theatre, and opportunity for the various amusements which relieve the monotony of life in the tropics, and which, fortunately, are always to be found where England has established her garrisons. I should have liked to have visited "Scotland," as the northern part of the island is called, for it is said to be picturesque and interesting, but time would not permit. Mount Hillaby, which has the highest elevation, is not quite 1200 feet in height, but the scenery is bold and mountainous, though of course on a small scale.

About twelve miles from Bridgetown is Codrington College, and above it, near the edge of a cliff, stands the old St. John's Church, celebrated for containing in its churchyard the tomb of a Palæologus, supposed to be the last descendant of the Christian Emperors of Greece.

At the time of my visit, the island was somewhat excited over impending Government changes, and the "storm in a tea cup," raised by the late Governor, Mr. Pope Hennessy, had not subsided. The scheme of confederating it with Tobago, St. Lucia, St. Vincent, and Grenada met with strong opposition. The Leeward Confederation had not proved a success, and the Barbadians objected to having the Windward group joined to them in the same way. Very conservative in their manners and customs, the white inhabitants look with no friendly eye on change and innovation; but I have heard it said, by some whose opinion was valuable, that the Crown Colony system would eventually prove the saving of the island. There were rumours too of fresh negro disturbances; provision grounds were pillaged daily, and the already incredibly conceited blacks were growing more and more pretentious. No other negro can come up to a Barbadian in impudence. If in any of the other islands you meet or hear of a case of peculiar insolence, the offender is sure to be a Barbadian. "You do not like me," says the deservedly-rebuked servant, "find one more bettar," and then walks off.

In Barbadoes, you hear that only the worst negroes leave the island, as their love for it is so great that few can be induced to emigrate, in spite of small wages. In time, however, even the most home-loving may find himself compelled to agree with the African philosopher, who, when asked what he thought of freedom, replied, "Well, sir, freedom is a mighty fine thing, but I can't eat freedom, and I can't wear freedom, and now I'se got to export myself." Two days were all that were allowed us in Barbadoes, and then the steamer arrived to carry us to Tobago and Trinidad.

On approaching Tobago from the north, the island presents a mass of high hills, terminating in abrupt precipices. Heavy forests clothe the central ridge and the hill spurs which spring from it. There is hardly a break in the luxuriant vegetation, and except here and there, where a patch in the valleys or on the hill sides has been cleared for cultivation, not a single bare spot is to be seen. We skirt the small island of Little Tobago, the haunt of boobies and tropic birds, and then come in sight of a pretty estate on the mainland, which greatly brightens the wild and gloomy scenery. Soon we round a point, and anchor in Scarborough Bay.

On the right rises a hill, crowned by the dismantled fort of St. George. Below it, and forming the central feature, lies a cluster of grey, steep-roofed houses, grouped on a low conical hill which slopes towards the water, and ends in a steep bank fringed with bamboos.

On the left, cane-fields extend from the shore far back over the undulating land to the hill-range, which curves round in a southerly direction towards a long, low promontory, called Sandy Point. Government House is prettily situated on the rising ground at some distance behind the town, but there is nothing of the slightest interest to induce a passenger to land for the short time during the exchange of mails. For a longer stay, that is if you have a friend's house to go to, Tobago is very interesting, both to the geologist and naturalist.

Up to the present, over one hundred and thirty different species of birds have been discovered there, among which a "Penlope" is peculiar to the island, and is known as the Tobago pheasant. A bird-seller, who came on board, had some fine skins of trogons, jacamars, humming-birds, manakins, and others. It is to be hoped that the bird laws which have been wisely established in Trinidad will be adopted in Tobago, as at present the bird-killers from the former island gain their supplies from the latter.

A curious circumstance in connection with the fauna of the West Indies is the number of species of birds, animals, and reptiles peculiar to certain islands, and those islands actually within sight of others. For instance, the Santa Cruz deer is distinct from the deer of St. Vincent or Tobago. The frogs of Dominica and the snakes of Martinique differ from those found elsewhere. The "Imperial Parrot"[21] from Dominica, is unknown in the other islands. Regarding humming-birds, Wallace says that "the West Indian islands possess fifteen distinct species, belonging to eight different genera, and these are so unlike any found on the continent that five of these genera are peculiar to the Antilles."

The cave-haunting Guacharos are found in Trinidad, as well as on the mainland of South America, but they have not reached the more northerly islands. It may be that the isolation of species is not so in reality, but owes its apparent existence to a want of knowledge, as the recesses of many of the densely wooded islands have still to be explored.

It was with no regret that we left Tobago, as the heat was intense, and we could sympathize with a certain officer, who, when quartered here, was once found sitting in his tub, uttering the most vehement denunciations, with the invariable refrain, "D— Columbus, confound the fellow! why did he discover this rascally island?"

CHAPTER X.

TO TRINIDAD—BOCA DE MONOS—GULF OF PARIA—PORT
OF SPAIN—SAVANNA—BOTANIC GARDENS—A HINDOO
VILLAGE—STAPLES—A CACAO PLANTATION—THE BLUE
BASIN—FALLS OF MARACAS—THE PITCH LAKE—START FOR
THE ORINOCO.

AS Tobago and Trinidad are little more than eighteen miles apart where
nearest, we were soon coasting down the latter island. The scenery was bold
and picturesque, and the richly clad mountains were of a deep green, flushed
in spots, with the crimson canopies of the "bois immortelle." Fertile valleys
gently opened to the sea, which here dashed angrily against the caverned
limestone walls, and there rippled to the feet of the cocoa-nut palms which
encircled the bays.

On reaching the "Boca de Monos"—monkey's mouth—the mountains of
Cumaná on the mainland of South America loomed up before us. Stretching
far out into the sea, these mountains resemble islands similar to those which
form the different entrances to the Gulf of Paria, and so near do they appear
that it is hard to believe that they are really part of the mainland. As so often
happens, whether travelling by sea, lake, or river, the finest scenery is sure to
present itself at dinner time. I regret to say that, in our case, enthusiasm was
damped by the thought that the soup was getting cold, and that probably the
"pepper-pot" would be finished before we got through the "mouth." The
scene was striking, as must be the case where wild woodland, reaching to the
water, and bold mountain cliffs combine with steeply rising islands, fringed
with palms and mangroves, and covered with a thick vegetation wherever a
plant can cling. As if the passage was not narrow enough, a rocky islet, tufted
with cactus and draped with euphorbias and cistus, stood in the way; but we
slipped past it, and soon sailed into the broad gulf. On we went, past wooded
islets crowned with white houses, to which the Trinidadians retire in hot
weather, and at last anchored off Port of Spain at a long distance from shore.

The view from the water can hardly be called picturesque, the flat shores
stretching on either side of the town in a long line hardly above the level of
the sea. But the town itself is prettily situated in a profusion of foliage trees
and feathery palms, which half conceal the white houses and graceful church
towers. Higher up lies a green savanna, with the handsome "Queen's House"
on its outskirts, and close behind rise the forest hills of Montserrat.

At a short distance from the wharf, the main street is entered. A broad shady
avenue runs up its centre, terminating with the mosque-like Roman Catholic
Cathedral. Half way up, a break in the avenue is caused by Marine Square,
with a fountain in the middle, and two of its angles occupied by boarding-

houses. The nearest of these is known as Emma Clark's, and is supposed to have the best accommodation in the town. Here, we accordingly entered, and were received by the hostess, a Creole lady, of ultra Junoesque proportions, and of renowned verbosity. Good-tempered beyond measure when not annoyed, but terrible in her wrath when aroused. I shall never forget her sublime indignation and torrent of words once, when one of her guests had the temerity to ask for an extra pillow. He did not get it, nor did he even repeat the request. Altogether, Miss Emma did not treat us so badly. Certainly, some people did say that her food, though good, was very limited as to quantity, that the wine and beer she supplied were execrable, that the solitary bath-room might have been kept cleaner, and that the apartments might have contained a little more furniture. But then somebody is always sure to grumble about something, and those who were not satisfied had the option of leaving—only there was nowhere else to go. What a benefit it would be to travellers, and probably to the entire West Indies, if the Government—Home or Colonial—were to erect suitable hotels in the different islands, and lease them to competent persons who would render a sojourn among them more attractive than at present!

The town of Port of Spain is not very interesting. Stores and shops are good, and Brunswick Square is adorned with a handsome cathedral and a curious old Government building. Beyond the latter are the new Court Houses, of massive and striking design, and large and expensive enough to satisfy the requirements of the entire West Indies. It is a handsome town, and with that all has been said. Its chief features, irrespective of Emma Clark, are buzzards[22] and smells. Of the birds there are an immense number; they line the roofs of the houses, perch on the fountains and wade in the basins, blink at you from the trees, and refuse to get out of your way in the streets. Alive, the noisome creatures sweep close to your face when you look from a verandah; and dead, they greet your nostrils in your walk, as they generally choose the centre of a road as a suitable place to expire, and where they fall, there they lie.

In smells, Port of Spain vies with St. Pierre. Our rooms were sometimes unbearable from the odour of salt fish, raw onions, potatoes, and coffee, which ascended from the provision stores underneath, and equalled in intensity the fumes from the small courtyard in which a cow, goats, pigs, a sheep, puppies, naked black children, and parrots wandered at liberty. Often did we exclaim with Mrs. Partington, "How flagrant it is!" Perhaps these odours account for the number of chemists' and druggists' shops that exist in Port of Spain. But the outskirts of the town are fresh and bright. Pretty houses and lovely gardens line the approaches to the park-like savanna. The only blot on the fair scene, is an unsightly building—originally erected for the Duke of Edinburgh—which stands in a conspicuous position, unrelieved by a tree or flower.

On approaching Queen's House, which is situated in the Botanical Gardens, the eye rests on, what to me, was the most charming sight in or around Port of Spain. Grand clumps of the most magnificent bamboos here line the roadside. Splendid ceibas, tamarinds, and samans are dotted about close by, but to my mind, could not compare with the bamboos, whose feathery arches and drooping boughs seemed like a "forest fit to fringe fairy land." The gardens disappointed me, perhaps from over-expectation. Unlike those of Martinique, nature has not here granted a picturesque situation. Art has only partially succeeded in rendering the grounds attractive. There are many beautiful varieties of palms, deep-green nutmeg groves, towering erythrinas, ceibas, and various rare shrubs and trees, but there is something wanting to make up an effective whole. The gardens are of small extent and are deficient in any leading feature of special interest. There are no fountains, no pieces of water, no falls, no rockeries, and the only flower-garden proper is a small one under the windows of Queen's House. Great care and attention are bestowed on the gardens, and in the nurseries I saw some rare orchids, luxuriant ferns, and many species of begonias, caladiums, and morantas. I was also shown some Liberian coffee trees, whose berries were far larger than the common. Formerly, there was a small Zoological collection here, but that is of the past.

The drive round the savanna in the cool evening is a very pleasant one. Here a black game of cricket is going on, amid much laughter and noise; there a white one is being conducted, in a very sedate and orderly fashion. Near the ugly Prince's building is a croquet lawn, and close to the opposite Grand Stand an impromptu race has been organized. Moon-eyed Chinese trot along, with a basket of vegetables slung at one end of a long bamboo and a bundle of clean clothes at the other. Delicate-looking cattle are being led to water by still more delicate-looking Indian coolies, and scattered over the grass are brilliant patches of colour, caused by the gay robes of Hindoo women, whose arms and ancles, heavily hung with bangles, glitter brightly as they milk soft-eyed cows, to the music of laughing babies riding astride their hips.

Coolie immigration from India has been very successful in Trinidad and Demerara, and speaks well for the system of labour which has been adopted in those places. And, certainly, the coolies have no cause for complaint. From the time they leave India until they return there—that is if they choose to return—every suitable provision is made for their comfort. Unlike the Chinese, whose only object is to make money and get back to the Celestial Empire as soon as possible, the Indian coolies become attached to their new home, and in Trinidad a great number—nearly three thousand—have obtained grants of land instead of "return" passages, and have settled down as colonists. Many of them possess sugar estates, and one owns several good race-horses.

Hindoo villages are seen in many parts of the island, and near Port of Spain, on the road to St. James's Barracks, is a coolie village, so oriental in its character, even to its native priests, charmers, and prayer-house, that, if an aeronaut suddenly descended there, he might readily imagine himself near Calcutta.

From the moment a stranger sets foot in Trinidad, he recognises that he is in a flourishing island; and the more he sees and hears of it, the more convinced does he become of its prosperous future. In the large and busy town, he can form some estimate of its resources, but, when he visits the interior and more distant regions, the fertility of the soil speaks for itself. To use one of Jerrold's witticisms, the land is so fertile "that, if you tickle it with a hoe, it smiles with a flower." Though sugar is the chief produce, there are other staples to which Trinidad directs her attention in a greater degree every year. The chief of these is cacao, which is a product continually increasing in value, and which is admirably adapted to the soil. Apart from the ease with which it is cultivated and prepared, a cacao plantation is a very desirable one, on account of its beauty. It has none of the monotonous stretches of a sugar plantation, as cacao has to be protected from the sun.

In some picturesque valley, or on undulating slopes, with a forest background, and probably with a glorious sea view from a neighbouring hill, you see a dwarf forest whose trees are about the size of apple-trees, and on whose stems and red-brown branches grow hundreds of pods like great golden lemons. Through this forest, run rows of "bois immortelles"— Madres del cacao—tall, elm-like trees, with bright flame-coloured canopies which afford a complete shade. On an eminence stands the white house of the planter, and near it a few rustic cottages and provision grounds; there is no tall smoking chimney, no din of machinery, no mingling of negro and molasses, all is cool and quiet, and you feel that, out of the few agricultural pursuits in the tropics, that of cacao-growing, must be the pleasantest.

Around Port of Spain the absence of bird life makes a sad void in nature; one misses the humming-birds, which in Martinique dart from every shrub, and even visit the balcony-flowers in the town. Even at a distance inland, it is only occasionally that the yellow "sucriers" are met with, or that the amusing, glossy brown "trembleurs" are seen bowing and scraping to one another in their usual polite fashion, but in some other islands these birds are very common. The "Wild Birds' Protection Ordinance," which was passed in 1875, has hardly had time to bear fruit as yet, but before long the feathered tribe may once again abound. Especially rare is that most beautiful of all humming-birds, the "Tufted Coquette,"—Lophornis ornatus—and once the species was as numerous as the "Ruby-crested,"[23] the "Savanna Sapphire,"[24] and the "Snowy-throated Emeralds,"[25] which are still abundant in Trinidad. Some lovely specimens of the above-named were offered me for sale, and I doubt whether I could have refused them, even without the assurance that they all came from the "Main." I must have made a mistake in thinking that the "Snowy-throated Emerald" was peculiar to Trinidad!

From Port of Spain there are many delightful excursions to be made. There is the Blue Basin, at the head of the Diegomartin Valley, and above it is the Signal Station, from whence the land and coast views are very beautiful. Then there is the celebrated Maracas waterfall, the road to which affords an opportunity of seeing the most picturesque plain, forest, and river scenery in the island. Besides the mud volcanoes, there is also that natural phenomenon, the Pitch Lake of La Brea. A weird, uncanny, intensely hot locality is that in which this strange lagoon is situated. The lake itself, which is nearly three miles in circumference, is surrounded by wood and jungle, growing luxuriantly from the pitchy soil. Out of the black sea rise little green oases covered with flowering shrubs, and occasionally lines of grass streak the surface. In the asphalte, which is hard in some places and soft and sticky in others, are numerous cracks and channels, often filled with clear brown water. Here and there a massive tree trunk or tapering pole protrudes through the pitch, like the hull and masts of some wrecked vessel sinking gradually out of sight.

Charles Kingsley has already fully described the sights and wonders of Trinidad, and since "At Last" was written the face of the country has little altered. Civilization of late has progressed, a railroad and coast steamers now connect different parts of the island, plantations have increased in number, and trade is augmenting annually. But Trinidad is still in its infancy, as by far the greater part of the island is still unreclaimed and unopened forest.

When Trinidad is traversed by proper roads, it is hardly too much to say that her prosperity will out-rival that of Jamaica in her palmiest days. On this subject a good authority has recently said:

"Unfortunately, the same conditions of soil, &c., which render Trinidad a very productive country, make the construction of roads, which are essential to the prosperity and advancement of a country, very difficult and expensive, and the peculiar conditions of the colonial community allow of little interest being manifested in the well-being of the island, beyond the immediate concerns of the moment. Thus it is that our highways, such as they are, are mostly very narrow, devoid of footwalks, and for many weary miles without a single tree which might afford shelter to man or beast, who are thus exposed to the fierce rays of a blazing tropical sun, the direct effects of which are heightened by the scarcely less pernicious ones of reflection and radiation from all the surfaces around. The correction of these and other evils can hardly be expected, unless there should arise a spirit of enlightened public feeling which at the present time does not exhibit itself."

Let us hope that the writer is too severe on the community of Trinidad, and that the road-making difficulty will soon be overcome. I ought to add that in the neighbourhood of the capital the roads are remarkably good, but glaring.

From Trinidad I proceeded to Demerara, and there found, as I stated in the preface, that the Government was about to send an expedition to Roraima, and with great kindness allowed me to accompany it. As it was not to start until the end of February, I determined to return to Trinidad, and from thence ascend the Orinoco. In the next chapter I must describe that trip.

CHAPTER XI.

THE "HEROE DE ABRIL"—APPROACHING THE ORINOCO—
MOUTHS OF THE ORINOCO—THE MACAREO CHANNEL—
MACAWS—WATER LABYRINTHS—GUARANOS—INDIAN
CAMP—TROUPIALS—BARRANCAS—LITTLE VENICE—LAS
TABLAS—CARATAL GOLD MINES—VENEZUELA—THE
CARONI—ROCKS OF PORPHYRY—CIUDAD BOLIVAR—PIEDRA
MEDIO—ANGOSTURA BITTERS—UPPER ORINOCO—FEATHER
HAMMOCKS.

Before a traveller can ascend the Orinoco, it is necessary—or said to be necessary by the steam-ship company—to obtain a passport. It is, I believe, quite unnecessary, but as the salary of Venezuelan officials depends in a great measure on perquisites, it is an act of charity to purchase your passport from the consul at Trinidad. This is the first of the many blows which go far to destroy the romance of the great river. At least we—my companion being a master from the college at Barbadoes—had an idea that the Orinoco must be a romantic river, for had not Raleigh cruised about it in search of golden palaces and of El Dorado!

We obtained our passports and tickets, and at the hour of sailing were informed that our vessel—the "Heroe de Abril"—was in the hands of the sheriff and could not leave. The following day, however, we received notice to be on board at a certain hour, as the steamer was to be allowed to depart on this occasion only. The owners chuckled over this, as, owing to defective boilers, neither she nor any of the passengers were expected to return at all. The "Heroe" proved to be an old Hudson River tug-boat, with sufficiently comfortable cabins on its upper deck, whilst its lower deck was open and crowded with second-class passengers who slung their hammocks wherever they could find space. Nearly all on board were bound for the gold mines of Caratal, and a very motley crowd it was.

Regarding the food and service, I will merely say that both were of the worst possible description. Those who had made the trip before had brought their own provisions, and were kind enough to share them with the novices. Without this aid, it is doubtful whether some of the passengers would have arrived at their journey's end.

It was late at night when we left Trinidad, so that early the following morning we found that we had crossed the Gulf of Paria, passed through the "Serpent's Mouth," and were approaching the gruel-like water of the Orinoco. On either side, but many miles apart, stretched two long, low lines of trees, which extended from the equally low coast line in front. To all appearance it was a deep ocean bay, but the colour of the water and the fact that there was no longer any heaving of the lead, told us that we had crossed the bar and had entered the Macareo channel of the Orinoco. Of the numerous other mouths which form the enormous delta of this river, but two are used by vessels, and of these two the "Boca de Navios" has fifteen or sixteen feet of water on the bar, while the "Pedernales" has barely six feet.

On nearing the mainland, we saw numerous islands covered with bush and shrubs, and on one, which looked like a floating mass of weeds that might be swept away by the waves caused by our paddle-wheels, an Indian fisherman had established himself. Two sloping sticks covered with leaves formed his shelter, which was half concealed from the prying eyes of fish and birds by a wide-meshed net. A little bark canoe showed that, in case of inundation, means of escape were at hand. Gradually the channel mouth narrowed, and the dense mangrove thickets which line the banks became more and more conspicuous. It is chiefly to these ever-extending mangroves that the great delta of the Orinoco owes its development. The twisted and matted roots stem the tide, retain the soil, and gradually raise the surface. Year by year the mangrove increases its dominions, and, judging from its present wide extent, it seems that ere long the smaller delta mouths will be choked.

All we saw was a low but vast expanse of bright green foliage. At one spot the mangroves appeared to be mingled with large bushes of hybiscus, covered with enormous crimson blossoms. Suddenly the blossoms took wing, and we recognized a flock of scarlet ibises. At length, we were fairly in the river channel, with a width across of less than a quarter of a mile. Various shrubs were now mixed with the mangroves, and at some distance from the banks tall clumps of trees, with masses of creepers, fringed the outlying lakes and open swamps. From these arose clouds of wild-fowl, which, after a look at the steamer, returned to their feeding-grounds, or in endless strings took long flights to more distant solitudes. There was no scarcity of birds here; there were geese, ducks of various sorts, bitterns, spoonbills, crested pheasants, herons, egrets, water-turkeys, and many specimens of the huge tantalus.

After a time the vegetation assumed a forest aspect, and we entered a palm region. Here we were greeted by the harsh cries of the blue and yellow macaws, which in numberless pairs flew overhead, and in flocks rose screaming from lofty trees. The scenery was very tropical, and we began to think that perhaps a trip up the Orinoco was not the mistake that it was said to be by a gentleman on board, who had made the voyage before. Palms predominated, but there were also splendid trees, from whose branches the hanging creepers formed a perfect wall. Here and there these green curtains lifted, and disclosed an aquatic maze threading its way deep into the wild forest. The monotonous green was varied with white-plumed ingas, crimson poivreas, and yellow bauhinias, which overhung the arums, the thick-veined caladiums, and the bamboo-like grasses growing on the banks. White egrets stalked along, tortoises flopped into the water from the branches, water-turkeys dived and always came up just ahead of us, and solemn cranes with one eye on the stream and the other on a fish, did not stir from their one-legged position as we puffed past them.

Only on the beautiful little Ocklawaha River in Florida, have I seen such lovely vistas as here penetrate the recesses of the border forests; each one, in fact, was a tropical Ocklawaha. Once, on turning a bend in the channel, we came suddenly upon a canoe whose occupants had not time to disappear in the side labyrinths, as they had done previously. It was evidently a family party of Guaraños or Kirishana Indians. The poor creatures looked terribly frightened, and the trembling women turned their faces towards the forest. Such modesty was hardly to be wondered at, seeing that the only clothing of any description that one of them had on was a baby, which she hastily caught up and wore as an impromptu apron.

It was with no small interest that we gazed at these few members of an almost extinct tribe, whose home is—or used to be—for the greater part of the year in the tree tops. For this Delta, which is always wet, is for several months inundated. The swampy soil is then many feet under water, and, therefore, high up in the trees, the Indians build their houses. If it was on account of its freedom that they selected such an unpropitious spot for habitation, they chose well and were certainly safe from intrusion, as none but an Indian could thread in his canoe the water-paths of the dismal forest. But probably their choice was determined by the extraordinary abundance of a certain palm called the "Mauritia" or "Ite."[26] This has been well named *arbol de la vida*, for it supplies the Indians with food, drink, clothing, habitation, canoes, and hunting and fishing implements. Food is made from the scaly fruit, which resembles pine cones hanging in clusters, and also from the soft pithy substance contained in the trunk; the two are treated like cassava and mixed into a cake of the consistency of sago and called "yaruma." From the juice of the flower-spathes toddy is made, and from the sheaths at their base sandals and girdles are manufactured. Hammocks, nets, and lines are woven from the fibres, canoes are fashioned out of the trunks, and bows and arrows from the leaf-stems.

Besides these necessaries of life, some luxuries are also supplied, as from the pith of the large arm of the leaf, split longitudinally, a sail is made for canoes, and by raising the fibres of the arm and placing a bridge under them, a rude kind of musical instrument is formed. To make their domiciles, four suitable palm trees are selected, notches are cut, and beams, stretched from trunk to trunk, are lashed together with fibre. A layer of mud, which hardens and is capable of bearing a fire, is then spread over the flooring, a roof of trees is added, and the dwelling is complete.

Whether these Indians still take to the trees in the wet season, or whether they find more comfortable lodgings on the ground, I know not. Higher up the river we passed one or two small Indian settlements, where the huts, pitched on elevated ground, consisted merely of a thatched roof supported by poles, but whether the inhabitants were Guaraños or not we could not say. They were better dressed than our old friends, as each individual was provided with fully six inches of cotton girdle. But their attire did not prove that they were not Guaraños, as it may be that they only put on their Sunday best on the approach of the steamer. Nature has admirably assisted these beings in their hiding propensities, as the reddish brown colour of their skins assimilates with that of the bush stems and tree trunks, among which they conceal themselves. In one place where we had seen a canoe enter, we saw a camp with hammocks slung and fire burning, but not a trace of the occupants, although they were probably looking at us from out of the bushes a very short distance away. They must have been close, as the canoe was there and empty.

It is not surprising that these timid savages consider everyone who does not belong to their own tribe as their natural enemy. At a "wooding" station where we had stopped, a canoe hovered about for some time but would not approach. At last, just as we were starting, it came alongside, and we found that it contained several cages of black and yellow troupials. The owners would not come on board, and could not be induced to hand up their birds for inspection until they had received payment, and then they paddled hurriedly away. On inquiry, I heard that the ship's company (Venezuelans) made a good deal of money by the sale of these beautiful birds in Trinidad and other places, and it had been the practice to obtain them from the Indians and delay payment until it was too late. Thus the unfortunate natives lost their birds and their money.

Besides the sight of an occasional Indian, we had no other excitement. Once in the night the steamer came to a halt owing to a thick fog, and at another time a loud crash preceded the stoppage of the engine; loud cries of "Has the boiler burst?" came from different parts, in various languages, but we had only run ashore, and soon steamed off again.

On the morning of the third day after leaving Trinidad, we arrived at Barrancas, where the mouths of the Orinoco separate. We did not anchor, but sent off the mails in a small boat to the little town which stands on the left bank of the main river, and then proceeded on our way. Here the scenery changed completely. The forest had disappeared, there were no more palms, no bright creepers, even the mangroves were absent. Macaws, parrots, troupials, all were left behind, and we looked over a river some miles in width, with sandy banks and low, dry, unprepossessing hills in the distance. It was a barren, desolate scene, and even a great, lean heron sitting on a withered branch, with his long neck sunk between his shoulders, seemed to think that life with such surroundings was not worth fishing for. We were certainly in Venezuela, but "Little Venice," with its water lanes and streets, lay behind us.

After several hours of slow steaming we arrived at Las Tablas, which is the nearest port to the mines of Caratal. It was a dreary-looking place, consisting of a few houses and one large tree. No one was allowed to disembark as there is no Custom House, consequently passengers for the mines have to proceed on to Ciudad Bolivar and wait there some days, until the steamer returns to Las Tablas. Thus, for want of a Custom House, passengers, as well as goods, have to travel nearly two hundred miles out of their way. The mines of Caratal are taking a very conspicuous position among the gold mines of the world, and already there are over 4,000 British subjects—mostly natives of the West Indies—at work there.

Strange to say, we have no representative at Bolivar. Some years ago our Consul was dismissed by the President in the most arbitrary manner, and no notice was taken of the insult, neither was the office refilled. The need of a representative is very great in a country where the authorities are in the habit of raising troops to suppress perpetual insurrections, and where they seize on anyone without regard to nationality. I have heard it hinted that, were the boundaries of Venezuela and British Guiana properly assigned, it would be found that the valuable mines of Caratal belong to the latter. This, however, is by no means the opinion of Venezuelans, and as these boundaries have been of late under much discussion, I have appended the translation of some official reports which have lately been published on the subject in Carácas. The Venezuelan idea of the correct boundary line—that of the Essequibo—is so different from our own, that a perusal of the papers may be interesting.

Close to Las Tablas the Caroni joins the Orinoco, and a curious effect is produced by the differently coloured waters running together for a long distance without mingling. This was the farthest point reached by Raleigh in his search for El Dorado in 1595, when, finding that his men were discouraged and nothing was to be gained by remaining, he returned to England. From Las Tablas upwards, the scenery was almost identical with that from Barrancas. Here and there on the banks stood a cottage and plantation, beyond stretched wide plains edged by green slopes and woods, which imparted a brighter aspect. Soundings were continually taken, and in many places there was barely sufficient depth of water to carry us over. From the waste of waters rose numerous islets of porphyry as smooth as glass, and which, being covered with a crust of oxide of manganese, sparkled in the sun and formed remarkable objects in the scene. Sand-banks were frequent, and on one a brig bound for New York lay stranded, and had been there two weeks, owing to the captain's refusal to pay a steam-tug from Ciudad Bolivar the enormous sum demanded for towing her off. As she was in the same position when we returned, it is probable she remained there until the rising of the river in the wet season.

Animal life was reduced to a few cranes and some enormous alligators, which basked on the sand in utter indifference to the noisy anathemas heaped on them by the black crew, who yelled again whenever they caught sight of the scaly bodies.

On the day after leaving Las Tablas, we anchored off Ciudad Bolivar, the capital of Guayana, which is the largest state in the Republic of Venezuela. The town was built in 1764, by Mendoza, who named it Santo Tomas de la Nueva Guayana, which was afterwards changed to "Angostura," and then to its present one, Ciudad Bolivar. Angostura—the Narrows—was a very appropriate name, as here the Orinoco, whose breadth above and below averages about two miles and a half, contracts to less than half a mile. In the middle of the river stands a famous rock, called "La Piedra del Medio," which serves as a metre to gauge the rise and fall of the flood, which at its highest rises no less than sixty feet above its summer level. As our visit was during the dry season we had to land in a boat, struggle over a sandy beach, and then clamber up a high bank, whereas in the wet season you step from the vessel on to the Alameda.

From the river the town looks picturesque, as it is situated on a conical hill, with the houses rising in tiers and crowned by the cathedral. The streets are narrow and steep, with the exception of the principal one, which skirts the river, and which is partly shaded by a double row of fine spreading trees called "mamon." The most prominent building is the market-place, which stands on a rocky eminence overhanging the river.

After a strict inspection of our luggage at the Custom House, we went to the only hotel in the town which the two Germans who keep it call "the Club." Here we found clean rooms without furniture of any kind, but the proprietor promised to give us canvas cots, and, if possible, two chairs. We were glad to sit down to breakfast after our long fast on board the "Heroe," but alas! the food was almost as bad as that on the steamer, and, as we were informed that it was impossible to cook any dish without garlic, we had to live chiefly on bread during our stay. Some claret that we ordered was so bad that we sent for another and much more expensive brand; finding it equally bad we complained to the servant, who laughingly informed us that it all came out of the same cask.

A more uninteresting town than Ciudad Bolivar it is impossible to imagine. In half-an-hour you can see the whole of it, including the cathedral, a bronze statue of "the Liberator"—Bolivar—and a very tall pillar with a small bust of Guzman Blanco—the late President—on the top of it. The cemetery contains the monument of the first Dr. Siegert, of "Angostura Bitters" celebrity, and, when you have seen that and the two above-mentioned statues, you have seen the "lions" of Ciudad Bolivar. Apropos of "Angostura Bitters," the manufactory is no longer carried on here owing to its exorbitant taxation by the Government, but has been removed to Trinidad.

Near the cemetery are the barracks, and these are buildings worthy of their occupants. We were told that the soldiers collected here were not good specimens of the Venezuelan Army, and we hoped not. In Carácas I afterwards saw some troops that were well equipped and presented a soldier-like appearance. But here half-starved, ill-clad, of a wretched physique, in height averaging about five feet, and with miserable arms and accoutrements, the troops that we beheld presented a sorry spectacle. Their pay is hardly worth mentioning, but they are fortunate when they receive it. This circumstance reminded me of a distribution of pay that once occurred in a certain town in the United States.

A number of Pinte Indians had been brought in to take part in a 4th of July procession, and after the parade each man received a dollar. It had been customary to hand over the entire amount to their chief—Captain Bob—for distribution, but the fact had become known that coin did not readily leave his grasp. The captain observed this new method of paying with more complacency than was anticipated. He was out-generaled, but not beaten. Being a great poker player he took his men to one of his favourite haunts, and before sunset had cleared his entire army out of the last cent.

From the pitiful condition of the troops when we saw them, it was difficult to imagine what the state of the private soldiers must have been in 1822, when hundreds of officers were seen begging from house to house in the streets of Carácas. Even as late as 1862, the army was in want of the necessaries of life.

It is not from a lack of generals that the troops are uncared for and ill-disciplined, for the supply is unlimited. Two boatmen, who once rowed us over from Ciudad Bolivar to the opposite shore to visit a cattle ranch, were both generals. The butcher who supplied the hotel was a general, and, if his military tactics were as good as those he exhibited in his steady resolve not to furnish good meat, he ought to have been a success. But in Venezuela it is not necessary either to be, or to have been a soldier, to become a general. The title is distributed indiscriminately, and sent about like a bouquet of flowers or a box of cigars, with the compliments of so and so. A late aspirant for the Presidency intimated that he would abolish this distinction, by making everybody a general. Needless to say he lost his election. In more recent times, did not the son of Prince Bismarck lose his nomination to the Reichstag by a premature declaration of his policy?

At Carácas, one day, I was looking over a book called *Cervantes y la Crítica*, by Urdaneta. In it was a list of subscribers to the volume, and out of four hundred names I counted two hundred and seventy-eight generals, and all the rest were doctors. Well might the Irishman exclaim in Venezuela, as he did upon his arrival in the United States, "What a divil of a battle has been fought near here, where all the privates were kilt!"

Finding so little to see or do in Ciudad Bolivar, we were anxious to ascend the Upper Orinoco, but heard to our dismay that the small steamer "Nutrias" no longer went up the river. We therefore had to pass a week in the town until the "Heroe" returned to Trinidad. Formerly, the trade with the Upper Orinoco was very considerable, and four steamers used to ply on the river, bringing down coffee, indigo, hides, cotton, &c. Revolutions have destroyed that, and now almost the only trade is with the mines of Caratal. Now and then large Indian canoes from the Rio Negro descend the river, bringing birds, hammocks, and curiosities, which they exchange for necessaries, and then return. Some of their feather and grass hammocks that we saw were marvels of skill, and must have been highly remunerative to the merchants, who demanded from one hundred to one hundred and fifty dollars apiece, having probably obtained them for ten or twelve dollars worth of goods.

It was excessively hot during our stay, but fortunately a dry heat, and there were no mosquitoes, although a lagoon on one side of the town gave promise of an abundant supply. In the wet season the heat is almost unbearable. As our hotel was close to the river—in fact, just outside the door was the hull of a vessel which had been left there high and dry when the water fell—we generally had a good breeze, and the verandah was the coolest place in the town. Few of the other houses possessed verandahs, as in Ciudad Bolivar the roof is the favourite family resort in the evening. Some of the roofs are prettily laid out with flowers and shrubs, and there the ladies sit and talk, receive visitors, promenade, and enjoy any breath of air that may relieve the stifling heat.

Ciudad Bolivar used to be a very hospitable town, but that was in the good old days when Señor Dalle Costa was President of Guayana, and there seemed a fair chance of good government. Then there was a good deal of amusement; travellers, English officers from Trinidad, and others were gladly welcomed and entertained, puma and jaguar hunts were organized, and a trip up the Orinoco was a great pleasure. Now trade is depressed, the town is woefully dull, and I doubt whether any traveller would visit Ciudad Bolivar for pleasure a second time. Whether the community—which numbers 7,000 or 8,000 souls—is an intellectual one I do not know, but I do know that I was unable to obtain a book in any language or of any description—except grammars—at any store or shop in the town. After a long search in stores that contained a little of everything, from pomatum to ship's cables, I was told that I might find some books at the chemist's. His stock consisted of a few grammars, very useful in their way, but hardly entertaining enough to wile away the hot hours. It must be remembered that this was in the capital of the largest State in Venezuela, a republic whose area is larger than that of France, Spain, and Portugal taken together.

Trinidad is very little better off for books than Ciudad Bolivar, as the only bookseller there has very few works except an old collection of volumes of Tauchnitz—an edition, by the way, which I think is "particularly requested not to be introduced into English colonies." A collector of coins might visit Ciudad Bolivar with advantage, as a more miscellaneous currency could not be found. Not only do you receive in change coins from every country in the world, but also chips of silver and blocks of copper that would be utterly valueless anywhere else. The scenery around the town was flat and tame, but it acquired a charm from the great river and the wonderful transparency of the atmosphere.

From the Calvary behind the town, easy of access, but fruitful in rattlesnakes, the eye embraced a vast extent of country. For the most part it is covered with thick *chaparro*, with here and there an undulating line which marks the course of a rivulet. Dotted about are what look like specks of pasture, but which, when approached, prove to be wide savannas, which afford grazing for countless cattle. Dark masses of trees show where virgin forests lie, and on the verge of the horizon the hills rise, looking pink and purple in the brilliant sunlight. The environs are dry and uncultivated. A few Indian huts and cottages with plantain patches are all that are to be seen.

Every evening we used to go to the old fort near the market and watch the sunset, and the last we saw surpassed in colouring any that I have ever witnessed. We looked up the river towards the west, and were fairly dazzled by the rich lights in sky and water. An arch of dead gold spanned a dip in the distant purple hills; below it was a crimson disc, and above a clear blue expanse. Radiating from this arc were bars of distinct shades, which shone for a few seconds and melted into a sheet of yellow and rose. The light was continuous from the sky far down the river, where it touched with pink the great cross on the black rock "del Medio." Turning from the rainbow-tinted water to the north-east we looked down the river, and, though a rose flush still tinged the horizon, the broad flood flashed like burnished steel as the rays of a full moon fell directly upon it. After the glare of the sunset, the change was as sudden as from noon to midnight. But gradually the eye became accustomed to the chastened silvery light as it touched the dark green foliage and brought into clear relief the houses and cottages on the bank, and, when once more we turned towards the west, it was there where the seeming darkness rested. Only for a moment though, and then we discerned a beautiful olive-green horizon, which gradually faded in the clear silver moonlight. For sharp, decided colouring, we had seen nothing like it, and in spite of our anxiety to leave Ciudad Bolivar we regretted that we should not witness one more sunset there.

Before we left our rocky standpoint, a loud exclamation from some bathers below us drew our attention to a black object floating down the stream. It proved to be an alligator, who would, doubtless, have made short work of anyone who ventured beyond the shallow pools that bordered the river. When the river is high, it is not an unfrequent occurrence to see one of these monsters in the very street. Waterton says: "One Sunday evening some years ago, as I was walking with Don Felipe de Yriarte, Governor of Angostura, on the banks of the Orinoco: 'Stop here a moment or two, Don Carlos,' said he to me, 'while I recount a sad accident. One fine evening last year the people of Angostura were sauntering up and down in the Alameda. I was within twenty yards of this place, when I saw a large cayman rush out of the river, seize a man and carry him down before anybody had it in his power to assist him. The screams of the poor fellow were terrible as the cayman was running off with him. He plunged into the river with his prey; we instantly lost sight of him, and never saw or heard of him more.'"

Humboldt also saw an alligator seize an Indian by the leg, while pushing his boat ashore, in the lagoon behind the town. He was dragged into deep water, and his cries collected a crowd, who saw him search for his knife. Not finding it, he seized the reptile by the head and pressed his fingers into his eyes. But the creature held on and disappeared with the unfortunate Indian.

Our descent of the Orinoco was as uneventful as our ascent. The only change was a substitution of cattle for our former second-class passengers. Freight, human and mercantile, was discharged at Las Tablas; we were stopped by frogs and impeded by shallows, but the boiler did not burst, thanks to the untiring watchfulness of the Scotch engineer, and we arrived safely at Trinidad. Soon afterwards I proceeded to Demerara.

CHAPTER XII.

TO GEORGETOWN—FIRST IMPRESSIONS—BATHS—A
DROUGHT—STREET SCENES—AN OIL PAINTING—VICTORIA
REGIA—THE CANNON-BALL TREE—SWIZZLES—A
PROVISION OF NATURE—DIGNITY BALLS—CALLING
CRABS—FOUR EYES—KISKIDIS—FEATHER TRADE—
COLOURED SUGAR—A VERSATILE AMERICAN—DEMERARA
CRYSTALS—PHYSALIA—OFF TO RORAIMA.

A dark thread stretching across the horizon, only a faint streak, which
thickened into a fringed skein as the tops of cocoa-nut trees came in view,
told us that we were in sight of British Guiana.[27] Soon the blue water
assumed the hue and consistency of pea-soup, as we approached the mouth
of the Demerara river. A pilot came on board, but for six hours we had to
await the pleasure of the tide before crossing the shallow bar that guards the
entrance to the river.

The first impression on beholding Demerara is that a wave of moderate
proportions would submerge the country. You see no background, no hill or
rising land, nothing but a thin coast line of avicennia and mangrove bushes,
above which rise cocoa-nut palms and high chimneys. Presently you discover
that there is land behind the coast line, as beyond a fine sea-wall on the left
you can see the barracks, fine spacious buildings with deep verandahs, and
several white houses. A fort is passed, and a goodly array of shipping at
anchor in the river, and lying alongside the wharfs, betokens a busy town.
Groups of royal palms, spires, and steeples rise up in the rear of large
warehouses and go-downs that line the bank, and before the vessel anchors
you recognize the fact that Georgetown is the first and most promising town
in or near the West Indies.

We anchored in the river, but now the steamers run alongside a wharf, which
is a comfort that cannot be too highly estimated. A hundred voices greeted
us on landing, with offers to convey our luggage to the hotel, and "Kerridge,
sir, kerridge," resounded on all sides. Not only were there "kerridges" of
different descriptions, but there was actually a "hansom" in waiting. Had it
not been for the numerous black faces, we might have landed on the coast
of England, but, then again, the numerous bangled women and turbaned
men suggested India.

We were quickly driven to the new "Tower" Hotel, which looked clean and
comfortable, but not a room was vacant. In Georgetown, house-rent is so
exorbitant that many resident bachelors, and occasionally families, live
together at the hotels; consequently, strangers often find accommodation
unobtainable or indifferent.

Across the road was the "Kaieteur Hotel," a large, rambling, wooden structure, but with the prestige of antiquity, and kept by Captain Holly, the American consul at Barbadoes. Here we found rooms, and the worthy proprietor did his best to make us comfortable, but it must be allowed that, with all his kindness and attention, he had not then attained the art of keeping a good hotel. But as the two I have mentioned are by far the best hotels in the West Indies, allowances must be made for a few short-comings. There is one item though for which no allowance ought to be made, and in the tropics it is a most important one. In the matter of baths and bath rooms the hotels and boarding houses in the West Indies are disgracefully negligent.

At St. Thomas, to reach the cobwebby and tarantula-occupied bath room, it is necessary to descend a flight of dirty stone steps and to pick your way across a courtyard which is never swept, and which is a repository for old boots, rags, banana skins, and fowls. At Martinique there were no bath rooms in my hotel, and I had to hire a tub; I was told that even in the best hotels— the Hôtel Micas—there were no baths. At Barbadoes, one very small shower-bath taken on the bare bricks did duty for the whole establishment at Hoad's. At Trinidad, a green, slimy tank into which fresh water ran, but which was never emptied or cleaned, was the sole bathing accommodation for Miss Emma Clark, her boarders, and servants. And here at the "Kaieteur," the two bath rooms—one on each floor—were not fit for sculleries, a use by the way to which they were frequently put. Their size was such that they barely held a small tub, and it was difficult to stand upright in them; as for a chair, there was not room for one, and, what with the intense heat and the want of space, I have frequently seen people come out of the wretched hole streaming with perspiration after their bath. The supply of water, too, was very limited, as in Demerara rain water alone is used, and when we arrived there the long continued drought had nearly emptied the tanks.

The average rain-fall in Demerara is estimated by feet instead of inches; but last year (1877) had been very dry, and now the absence of rain in the usual short wet season—December, January, and February—had already created more loss to the planters, and as it was too late to expect rain before May, a water famine was anticipated. It used to be positively asserted that the year was divided into two wet and two dry seasons in British Guiana, but it is gradually dawning on the public mind that no uniformity in weather ever did, or can exist, and that, though the climate remains, the weather changes.

Georgetown is a handsome, well-built town, with broad streets, avenues, excellent stores, and shops of all descriptions, and with a lively, well to-do air that is as invigorating as the heat is depressing. In the streets, besides the white race, you meet sharp-featured Madrassees, Hindoos of various castes, Parsees, Nubians, and half-breeds. Stepping timidly along may also be seen two or three "bucks," as the natives from the interior are called, dressed—if dressed at all—in a motley suit of old clothes, and only anxious to sell or exchange their parrots and hammocks, and then return to their wilds. From a merchant's store filled with European goods, you step into a little shop redolent of the East, and stocked with bangles and silver ornaments worked by their Cingalese proprietor. There stands a Portuguese Jew, ready to fleece the first "buck" whom he can entice into his cheap general-store, and here sits stolid John Chinaman, with his pigtail wreathed round his head, keeping guard over his home-made cigars.

The Government Building is a large, fine-looking structure, the numerous churches are graceful and picturesque, and everywhere there is a home look about the town, without pretension, that is very attractive. The reading-room is cool and very comfortable, the library well managed, and the museum in the same building is likely, under the care of Mr. Im Thurm, the new curator, to become a very valuable acquisition to the colony. Under his superintendence, a very interesting exhibition of native produce and industry had been held previous to my arrival, and I was sorry to have missed it.

It has been said that hospitality is on the wane in the West Indies; well, if that of Demerara may be taken as an example, may it always be on the wane! A kinder, more hospitable community I never met. It seems to be the object of the residents to make a stranger's sojourn among them as home-like and agreeable as they can. Some one once remarked, and it has been the fashion to repeat, that the French alone in the West Indies make the land of their adoption their home, and that the English make it merely a place of business, from which they hasten at the earliest opportunity. This may be so, for the English of all others are a home-loving race, and "the old country" is more, I think, to them than "fatherland" to the Germans, or "notre pays" to the French. But, whilst they are in exile, they, at any rate in Demerara, surround themselves as far as possible with home comforts and home reminiscences, and infuse something of the far off country sweetness into the inner circle of their lives. No heart—no, not even a Savoyard's—feels expatriation so deeply as an Englishman's, and none, save those whose lot has been to sojourn far from home, can imagine the intense longing to see again the native shores. Do you remember that old poem called "The Home Fever: A reminiscence of the West Indies?"—the first verse is—

"We sat alone in a trellised bower,

And gazed o'er the darkening deep,

And the holy calm of that twilight hour

Came over our hearts like sleep,

And we dreamed of the banks and the bonny braes

That have gladdened our hearts in childhood's days."

and the last,

"Oh! talk of spring to the trampled flower,

Of light to the fallen star;

Of glory, to those who, in danger's hour,

Lie cold in the field of war;

But ye mock the exile's heart when ye tell

Of aught save the home where it pines to dwell."

It will be asked, where do these good people of Georgetown dwell?

Opposite the "Kaieteur" hotel is the Club, which is the pleasantest resort in the town, as it receives the full benefit of the trade wind, which on certain occasions by-the-bye wafts other zephyrs than those fresh from the beautiful hybiscus hedge in front, and is much frequented by its members. Stretching far away from this club towards the sea-wall is Main Street, and there and in the neighbouring parallel one the principal houses of Georgetown are situated. Main Street is broad and picturesque; a series of wide trenches[28] with green sloping banks divides it, and on each side runs a fine road. The residences which line it are all detached, and of various styles of architecture, from a three-storied edifice with towers and cupola to a low wide-spreading structure with but one floor above the basement. But all are built for coolness as well as comfort, and their wide shady verandahs are the favourite resorts of the family. Many of the gardens are brilliant masses of colour, resembling a rich oil-painting, rather than a delicate water-colour of those of European lands. The tints are so gorgeous and heavy; there are bushes of the crimson hybiscus, scarlet cordias, flaming poinsettias, trailing corallitas, the bright flowers of the bois immortelle, the drooping clusters of the red quiscualis, the vermilion blossoms of the flamboyant, all vying in splendour with saffron petrœas, deep blue convolvuluses, abutilons, and the white trumpets of the datura. In one garden I remember seeing a resplendent mass of Bougainvilleas, and on a neighbouring tree some equally showy blossoms of a magnificent crimson orchid—*Cattleya superba*; between them crept pale clusters of English honeysuckle, not a bit abashed by their grand neighbours, but rather exulting in the fragrance denied to their bright-coloured companions.

Marbled crotons and purple dracœnas are tipped by strange-looking papaws, whose wax-like blossoms grow direct from the trunks and branches, and above these tower shade-trees and tall palms. Very conspicuous are the royal palms, standing either singly or in groups, and near them bend the cocoa-nut trees, as if in acknowledgment of the superior majesty of their kings. Besides the houses, some pretty churches, half-hidden in trees, give a finish to this the most picturesque street in Georgetown.

In the adjacent street are also some neat houses, and on one side of it are the Public Gardens with the small but ever hospitable Government House opposite. In the gardens are some specimens of the Victoria Regia—the lily which was discovered by Sir Robert Schomburg on the Berbice river—but in size they are not to be compared with some in other parts of Demerara; for instance on one of the plantations, Leonora, is a plant whose leaves are over six feet in diameter, and strong enough to bear the weight of an average-sized man when a board has been placed across to distribute the weight properly. There is also a fine cannon-ball tree,[29] under whose shade the weary traveller may experience sensations similar to those of Damocles, as the huge fruit, which is as big as a twenty-pound shot and nearly as heavy, seems always ready to fall from its slender hanging stem. The gardens are not very interesting, but afford a pleasant playground for children, and a delicious gossiping ground for their attendant nurses.

Let me now recall the usual daily routine in Georgetown. A little before six o'clock tea and toast; after that I never knew for certain what anyone did up to breakfast at half-past nine, probably because my time till then was entirely taken up in getting a bath, dressing, and trying to keep cool. I believe though that business was the occupation. As for riding or early walking exercise, I saw none of it, but then again that may have been through my own dilatoriness, although I doubt it. Breakfast was a very substantial meal, too substantial in fact at the "Kaieteur," and not tempting enough for a hot climate.

Long before the traveller reaches Demerara, he will have discovered that no meal in the West Indies is without salt-fish from Newfoundland; that and pepper-pot are standard works. Good fresh fish in Georgetown is something of a rarity—at least it was with us at the hotel—and when Jew fish is in the market a bell-man goes round proclaiming the fact and the price per pound. The flesh is coarse, but appreciated by the poorer class when it is cheap. Housekeepers also complain of the scarcity of good meat, and certainly the beefsteaks and mutton chops furnished to us were poor.

After breakfast, business is attended to with decreasing energy up to luncheon, and then dies a natural death in the course of the afternoon. About five p.m. all the world—with the exception of the steady whist and euchre players at the club—takes an airing. Those who have carriages drive out to the sea-wall, which is the promenade, and those who have not walk there.

Nursery maids take their charges to the public gardens, coolies lead out cows and oxen to graze, black boys exercise their masters' dogs, horsemen ride out to the race-course, and unfortunate cripples—chiefly Chinese—in all stages of terrible disease, come forth and beg. A late dinner, followed probably by some delightful music—as Georgetown boasts of a very excellent Philharmonic Society—winds up the day.

I must not forget to add that it is just possible that its interludes have been filled up by a certain institution of Demerara known as "swizzles." Most cities and towns have some small peculiarity, for which they are as well remembered as for their greater. Demerara and swizzles are inseparably connected in my mind. The exact recipe for a swizzle I cannot give, although I have seen it concocted not unfrequently; but it is a deliciously cold drink, of a delicate pink colour, and when lashed into a foam by the revolutions of a peculiar instrument called the swizzle-stick, and imbibed out of a thin glass, it makes a very pretty drink. By a wonderful provision of Nature the tree which furnishes the pronged stick, without which the beverage would lose much of its charm, grows abundantly in Guiana. The exact time for indulging in a swizzle has not been clearly defined, but as a general rule in Demerara it is accepted whenever offered. It is taken in the morning to ward off the effect of chill, before breakfast to give a tone to the system, in the middle of the day to fortify against the heat, in the afternoon as a suitable finale to luncheon, and again as a stimulant to euchre, and a solace for your losses. Before dinner it acts as an appetizer, and it is said that when taken before going to bed it assists slumber. And very frequently in Georgetown anything to induce sleep would be welcome, as the incessant "dignity" balls of the negroes are fatal to slumber. The noisier they are, the better they are enjoyed, and a lull of a few minutes only gives fresh energy to subsequent demonstrations. Verily the coloured folk give a literal interpretation of their own proverb, that "what you lose in de jig, you gain in de reel."

Even the guttural notes of the frogs, of which there are an extraordinary number in the trenches, are preferable to the negro discord. When Bacchus was rowed along the Styx he could not have been greeted with a more varied frog's chorus than that which day and night salutes the inhabitants of Georgetown. "Awnk, awnk, awnk," roars the bass, "week, week, week," pipes the tenor, "cru, cru, cru," screams the soprano, and then the full choir joins in a refrain which swells and falls with the breeze. One quaint little fellow has a peculiarly sweet note, so exactly like a whistle that I have frequently stopped in my walk and turned to see who it was that wanted to attract my attention. Just as plentiful and more amusing are the crabs which frequent the dykes and mud flats around the town. The "calling crabs"[30] are especially entertaining, as they wave and beckon with their great claw, and then scurry away at the least attempt to approach them. Often in their fright they miss their holes, then in despair place themselves in fighting attitude, and dare you to the attack. Another common and very hideous creature is the little fish known as "Four Eyes,"[31] which takes amusement in shooting along the water and stranding itself at every opportunity.

The feathered tribe are not strongly represented around Georgetown, but, as a "Birds' Protection Ordinance" has lately been passed in Guiana as well as in Trinidad, they may have a chance of multiplying. The commonest bird is a species of flycatcher called "Qu'est-ce qu'il dit," which are the exact words it utters; it is pretty and sociable, and its querulous notes are heard from many a tree and house top. It will be interesting to learn after a lapse of time whether the bird-law has tended to the increase of birds in towns and settlements. Of bright-plumaged birds the humming-birds alone frequent habitations, and it will be chiefly their increasing numbers that will tell the tale. The brilliant family of chatterers, the troupials, the cocks-of-the-rock, the trogons, toucans, the tanagers, fire-birds,[32] macaws, manakins, and other gay denizens of Guiana live so far from the haunts of white men that any increase in their numbers can only be assumed.

It is singular to note the constant development of the feather trade; the day is long past when every fine gentleman, king and commoner, decked himself with plumes, but now, when fashion requires them for ladies alone, the demand is far greater. Forests, mountains, and swamps in all parts of the world are ransacked to supply the dealers, and probably, not before the last bird becomes as extinct as the dodo, will the mania for feathers have died out. And it cannot be denied that the plumage of birds makes a most beautiful adornment, and, though in dress, a head here, a wing there, and a bit of the breast somewhere else, is not the most advantageous mode of showing off the glistening beauties, yet even the dismembered parts shine with matchless and inimitable tints. In the present day there is little that cannot be imitated; artificial flowers, stones, plants, fruit, fish, and human limbs are so skilfully fashioned as sometimes to deceive the sharpest eye. It has been said, too, that glass eyes have been made so perfectly that even the wearers themselves cannot see through the deception. But birds and their nests defy imitation.

A short time before my arrival in Georgetown, the community had been much amused by the advent of a series of commissioners who had come from the United States to inquire into the manufacture of "coloured" sugar. Some cargoes of this sugar had been detained at the custom-house in one of the American ports, under the impression that the sugar had been "artificially" coloured, thereby avoiding the high duties on light sugars.

Duly furnished with Government credentials, they came, saw, and departed, fully convinced, I believe, that the "coloured" sugar outcry was what is vulgarly called a mare's nest. One of the commissioners—a very pleasant young fellow—on finding, when he arrived, that he had been forestalled by others, wisely relinquished his sugar researches, and instead established the first telephone in British Guiana between Georgetown and Berbice. The last I heard of him was that he was about to be appointed consul either in British, French, or Dutch Guiana. The versatility of the true American is indeed wonderful.

Sugar-making has been so often described that I must refrain from giving an account of a visit to a Demerara plantation, much as I should have liked it. It must suffice to say that there you see the latest improvements in machinery, the latest scientific appliances for vacuum pans, centrifugals,[33] &c., and in fact sugar manufacture on a grand scale.

You also see a veritable "little Holland," as water forms the boundaries of estates, and by water the produce is transported to the mills. Dams and canals intersect the estates, and the navigation system is complete. You see, too, how the welfare of the coolie is attended to, his hospital, his home, his provision grounds, and how much better off in every way he is than in his native land. I once saw a coolie vessel arrive in Georgetown, and though her passengers wept and embraced the captain and officers in their sorrow at having to leave, yet they looked very lean and emaciated in comparison with those I afterwards saw working on the estates. The ships which bring them over are well regulated, and as comfortable as circumstances will admit, but the voyage is trying for a non-sea-going race. One of the mates, in answer to a question, told me they were "a docile, uncomplaining lot, but dirty, as they were always using water."

The visitor to a Demerara plantation is sure of a hearty welcome, that is always fresh and invigorating, however hot the day or tame the scenery may be. And even in the scenery there is always something interesting besides sugar, some strange fruit-bearing tree, some flower or bird, and the cane-laden boats, with a brightly clad figure among the green blades, are always picturesque. The country is flat certainly—the only hill I ever found about Georgetown was on the cricket ground—but it is not monotonous if one chooses to look about and enjoy it. Even the muddy river has its attractions, as the last time I crossed it after a visit to a plantation it was covered with hundreds of Portuguese men-of-war[34] whose large air sacks and vertical crests shone resplendently in every shade of purple and blue.

I must not conclude this sketch of social Demerara without alluding to a certain distribution of the government of the colony which, I believe, is peculiar to British Guiana. Besides the Governor, there is what is called a Court of Policy, and also the Combined Court, which consists of the members of the Court of Policy together with six financial representatives chosen by the people for two years. The Court of Policy is composed of ten members, five of them being Government officers, and five elected from the college of Keizers or Electors. This college is a body of seven members chosen for life by the inhabitants who possess the suffrage, for which an annual income of six hundred dollars qualifies. The Court of Policy carries on the general legislative business, whilst taxation and expenditure are in the power of the Combined Court. Every member of the Combined Court has an equal vote, and also the power of rejecting, if he thinks proper, a bill passed by the majority. Thus Kings, Lords, and Commons rule in Demerara, and to their enterprise and liberality I owe my visit to Roraima.

Mr. McTurk a Government official, who was experienced in bush life, and possessed of qualifications well suited to the purpose, had been commissioned by the Governor to superintend the expedition, and towards the end of February I received intimation to join him at the settlement near the junction of the Cuyuni and Mazaruni rivers, where he awaited me with his boats.

CHAPTER XIII.

TO THE ESSEQUIBO—BARTICA GROVE—THE PENAL SETTLEMENT—CUYUNI RIVER—EL DORADO—RALEIGH'S CREDULITY—TENT BOATS—CAMP IN SHED—CARIA ISLAND— AN ARCHIPELAGO—KOSTERBROKE FALLS—ASCENT OF CATARACTS—WARIMAMBO RAPIDS—MORA—A NEW YEAST.

Early on the morning of the 23rd of February the steamer, which was to take me part of the way to the settlement, started from Georgetown. The wharf— or stelling, as the wooden pier is called—presented an animated scene as the fruit-boats were being unloaded, and the vast quantities of pine-apples and mangoes, especially of the latter, were surprising; some of the canoes were actually overflowing with the golden fruit, and were weighed down to the water's edge. Mangoes form no inconsiderable item in the food of the blacks of Demerara.

We were soon clear of the native and foreign craft, quitted the Demerara river and proceeded in a north-westerly direction towards the Essequibo. To the mouth of that river from Georgetown is only about five and twenty miles, and so in spite of one or two delays at different landing-places on the west coast, it was not long before we found ourselves in a vast island-dotted expanse that suggested a lake rather than a river. From one side of the mainland to the other, the embouchure of the Essequibo is seventeen or eighteen miles in width, and is divided into four separate channels by islets and sandy shoals.

At Wahenaam, one of the largest of these islands, we changed steamers, as from that point a smaller one alone runs up to the settlement, fifty miles further on. Then we were fairly in the Essequibo River, whose breadth here is about eight miles. Of the mainland, we could only see now and then the fringing line of courida[35] bushes and the chimneys belonging to the plantations, but the island scenery was pretty and varying. In places the luxuriant vegetation had been cleared and plantain farms were seen extending far back into the surrounding bush, with a few tumble-down but picturesque huts in the foreground. These farms are chiefly owned by Portuguese, who make considerable profit out of them. Here and there in the open spaces were ovens for burning charcoal, and their proprietors—Chinese—were busily employed cutting down trees or planting rice and other vegetable products.

Mingled with the bamboos and larger trees were several varieties of palms, of which the most prominent were the Mauritias—Ite—easily recognised by the bunches of red fruit, and the dead drooping fronds which give an untidy aspect to the useful tree. There were also specimens of the jagua and numberless fan palms,[36] whose leaves furnish a sort of wax, but the most graceful of all were the manicoles, very straight and slim, and rising to a height of about forty feet.

At last, after some hours, the monotonous green of the land scenery was broken by a narrow promontory, on which stands the small village of Bartica Grove, which is situated at the junction of the Essequibo and the Mazaruni. This little settlement is a favourite resort of the Indians from the interior, who come down to trade with the few Portuguese who live there. Besides the latter there are but few whites, the greater number of inhabitants being river-men, who, as their name implies, pass their lives in navigating the waters, their principal occupation being in carrying timber from the various wood-cutting locations. They are a strange race, a mixture of Dutch, Indian, and negro descent, and though skilful and hard-working in their own vocation, yet possess in a marked degree, it is said, the attributes of the half-breed, *i.e.*, all the vices of civilization and none of the virtues of the savage.

Leaving the Grove on our left, we proceeded up the Mazaruni, and in half-an-hour arrived at the settlement. The view here is fresh and charming. On land the rising ground is planted with mango, palms, and shade trees, behind which are seen the neat prison buildings—for it is a Penal Settlement—and the houses of the Superintendent and other officers. Across the river some houses are situated on the bank, and also on the cleared sloping forest land, which is diversified with pasture and huge granite boulders. Below, at Bartica Grove, the mighty stream of the Essequibo is joined by that of the Mazaruni, and higher up there is another meeting of the waters, as there the Mazaruni is joined by the magnificent Cuyuni, whose mouth is nearly a mile in width.

About thirty miles up the Cuyuni is an abandoned gold mine, the sole spot in Sir Walter Raleigh's "El Dorado" where gold has up to the present been discovered, and even here in such small quantities that the working of it did not pay. Since the days of Raleigh, Guiana has earned a fictitious fame, chiefly through the extraordinary stories set abroad by that adventurer. Historians differ regarding Sir Walter's own belief in the existence of "El Dorado," but it seems probable from his writings that he was capable of believing anything. For instance, he says, "A similar people were said to live in Guiana, on the banks of the Caora; this may be thought a fable, yet for my own part I am resolved it is true, because every child in the province of Arromaia affirms all the same; they are called Ewaipanomi, and are reported to have their eyes in their shoulders and their mouths in the middle of their breasts, and that a long train of hair groweth backwards between the shoulders." Again, in speaking of the supposed city of El Dorado, he says that, "for greatness, riches, and the excellent seat, it far exceeded any city in the world, and founded on an inland sea two hundred leagues long, like unto the Mare Caspium."

The historian Hume says: "So ridiculous are the tales which he tells of the Inca's chimerical empire in the midst of Guiana; the rich city of El Dorado or Manoa, two days journey in length, and shining with gold and silver; the old Peruvian prophecies in favour of the English, who, he says, were expressly named as the deliverers of that country long before any European had even touched there; the Amazons, or republic of women; and in general, the vast and incredible riches which he saw on that continent, where nobody has yet found any treasures!"

As regards the Amazons and the Ewaipanomi, there are plenty of civilized Indians who still assert the existence of a wonderful race of beings who inhabit certain portions of Upper Guiana, which as yet have been untrodden by white men. Concerning the golden city on the inland sea, it is not improbable that the origin of the romance arose from the fact that the low alluvial lands around Lake Parima were inundated every year to such an extent that the natives navigated the forests in their canoes. The chief of a certain tribe who inhabited this locality, is said to have indulged in the luxury of a golden shower-bath every morning, that is, he powdered himself with a glittering but valueless substance called golden sand, which is merely iron ore in minute particles. Hence his cognomen, El Dorado, or the Golden Man. His palace was found to be a natural grotto, the walls of which were formed of micaceous rock that shone with a yellow metallic glitter. It may be that the glittering mica, derived from the granite which is prevalent in Guiana, deluded Raleigh into the belief that it was gold, for he says, when speaking of a ledge of "white sparre or flint," that he endeavoured to break it by all the means that he could, "because there appeared on the outside some small grains of gold ... of which kind of white stone (wherein gold is engendered), we saw divers hills in every part of Guiana wherein we travelled."

To return to the settlement. Immediately on landing I was met by McTurk, who, in spite of the day being far advanced, wisely determined to start at once; and so, throwing aside those trammels of civilization, coat, collar, and waistcoat, we stepped into our boats and were ready for our trip of two or three months into the interior. Two ordinary-sized boats—or bateaus, as they are called—and a strong well-built canoe composed the fleet. In colour they had been respectively painted red, white, and blue, and each was named after a certain species of frog; the largest was the "Bura-buraloo," the next was the "Adaba," and the canoe was the "Akoora." The crew consisted of fifteen civilized Indians—Arawaak and Acawais—good and tried men, most of whom had been on short expeditions with McTurk, and who therefore understood his ways and were aware that when he said a thing he meant it, that faithfulness and good conduct would be rewarded, and laziness and bad behaviour as surely punished. They nearly all understood a little English, but they preferred a sort of "pigeon" English peculiar to McTurk, and which always reminded me of a stage Dutchman's language. The strongest and most intelligent Indian in each boat is the captain, who, seated in the stern, uses his paddle to direct the course. Next to him in rank is the bowman, who has to keep a sharp look out for rocks and shoals.

Each boat was laden with provisions,[37] which were limited as far as possible to absolute necessaries, as after leaving the boats we knew that the difficulties of transportation would be very great. In addition, there was our own clothing—a very slender supply—guns, ammunition, trading articles, pots and pans, &c., everything, certainly, reduced to a minimum, but nevertheless, forming sufficiently heavy loads.

Before starting, I cast longing eyes at two or three luxurious tent-boats, provided with awnings, lockers, and curtains, all of which were denied us; but before many days I recognised the superiority of our own, as the long drought had shallowed the river, and it would have been impossible for the deep tent-boats to have ascended some of the cataracts. Taking our seats in the centre of our respective boats, McTurk gave the word, and in an hour the strong paddles of our crews had placed a considerable distance between us and the settlement, and we were really on the way to Roraima. At one time we feared that our start would prove inauspicious, as the strong wind blowing up the river raised such waves that once or twice we were almost swamped, but gradually we gained the opposite coast, and under the lee of the land entered comparatively smooth water.

Owing to the lateness of our departure we soon had to camp, and spying an old shed near the water's edge, we landed, slung up our hammocks, and there passed the night. To a traveller, I know of no cheaper luxury than a hammock. On a former long journey through the tropics I had burdened myself with a folding bed, thinking from very slight experience that to sleep in a hammock would be impossible. But now I discovered that a well-slung hammock, in which you have placed yourself diagonally, not parallel, so that your head and feet are too elevated, is a very delightful place of rest. By day a pleasant lounge, by night a clean bed even in dirty hovels, unscalable by insects, light and compact, easily put up and easily taken down, a hammock becomes an indispensable companion, especially dear when travelling in countries where even the most necessary articles have to be limited. We could hardly have selected a more likely spot for those pests of Guiana, namely, vampires and jiggers. The former frequent the clearings around sheds and houses, and in the dead of night when all are asleep—they never pay their visits as long as even one person in a party is awake—they fasten on an exposed toe or some part of the foot and cup the sleeper, who awakes faint and exhausted. Horses and cattle suffer equally from their attacks, and fowls frequently drop dead from their perches, their life blood drained to the very last drop. As a provision against these unpleasant visitors I had provided myself with a long double blanket, so that under no circumstances could a forgetful toe exhibit itself outside its covering.

A jigger (*Pulex penetrans*), as everyone knows, is a toe-loving creature, and makes its nest under the nails, and, if allowed, lays its eggs. As they swarm in every deserted hut and in every old Indian shed, and in sand, it is impossible to avoid them; morning and evening a strict examination of the feet by a competent Indian is absolutely necessary when travelling in the interior. In spite of great care and watchfulness on our part a search was seldom unrewarded, but we never approached the number once collected by Sir Robert Schomburgh, of whom it is related that a negress once extracted eighty-three from his feet at one sitting.

But, notwithstanding jiggers and vampires, the nights on the Mazaruni are always enjoyable because there are no mosquitoes; in many parts of Guiana, especially on the Pomeroon River, these plagues are so bad that cattle have been driven wild by them, and are always obliged to be shut up at night in mosquito-proof sheds; there, also, a mosquito net is invariably included in the agreement between master and labourer. Here we were free from them, and a patent hammock mosquito netting that had been given me by a kind friend in Georgetown was devoted to other uses.

Next morning we made an early start, and soon passed Coria island, on which a Dutch fort once stood, and the last that we saw of civilization was the little mission-house of St. Edward's, picturesquely situated on the opposite bank of the mainland. Above this point we entered that labyrinth of islands which, together with the innumerable rapids and cataracts, form the chief features of the Mazaruni River for nearly one hundred miles. Only one of our crew had ever ascended the river before, and, as he did not appear to remember much about it, we determined to keep to the main channel, as being the safest, out of the numerous ones into which it was divided. This was no easy matter, as, on account of the lowness of the water, and the great breadth— between three and four miles—of the river, it was often very difficult to decide which was the main channel, and sometimes we found our passage barred by shallows and had to return and seek another.

We ascended two rapids, and then came to the rather steep falls of Kosterbroke. A sad interest is attached to this place, as it was here that in 1863 seven young men lost their lives. A pleasure party, consisting of visitors from Trinidad and others who had been engaged in a cricket match at Georgetown, visited the settlement and ascended the Mazaruni as far as these rapids; whilst descending them, the tent-boat capsized and seven of its occupants were drowned. Report says that a midshipman, who formed one of the party, was swept away and given up for lost, but was discovered later on sitting on a rock in mid channel, drying a five-pound note in the sun.

The ascent of these cataracts affords a very lively and exciting scene. All hands, except the steersman, leave the boat, a long stout hawser is fastened to her bow, and by sheer strength she is hauled up through the rushing waters. Some of the crew wade by the side of the boat, to keep her from the rocks, others swim or dive across from adjacent points to where the best purchase can be secured, and the rest, holding the rope, pull with might and main straight up the current. A charming variety exists in these rapids; sometimes they may be ascended by taking advantage of the different currents and paddling with great power diagonally across the channel; others have short but steep falls, and others again extend for a long distance in a series of steep inclines, whilst the volume of pouring water in a few is so great that boats have to be carried round them overland. At the Warimambo Rapids, which we reached soon after passing Kosterbroke, we had to unload the boats and make a portage of about two hundred yards. A lot of negro woodcutters, who sat grinning at us on the rocky banks, informed us that it would be impossible for us to haul the boat up those rapids, but our men worked splendidly, and in about two hours we had loaded the boats and were off again.

The river here presented an extraordinary appearance from its great breadth and the innumerable rocks which cropped up in every direction. Many of these rocks were covered with the pretty pink flower of some water-plant. The islands and the low mainland were covered with virgin forest, whose intense green was relieved at intervals by the blazing crimson spikes of the kara-kara[38] or the various tinted canopies of the giant moras. The mora[39] may be termed the oak of the tropical forests of Guiana, as it far exceeds other trees in dimensions; its lofty wide-spreading branches, with glossy foliage changing from purple to red, add a distinctive charm to the scenery, but a deceptive one, as frequently we would exclaim. "At last there is some rising ground," which on approach proved to be only two or three moras towering above the rest of the forest trees. Besides the moras, we were continually passing many varieties of the valuable timber with which Guiana is so plentifully supplied. Now a green-heart[40] or a splendid purple-heart, occasionally a "letter-wood" tree and numerous "ballis," such as mora balli—balli meaning wood, and when attached to a word signifies akin to: itaballi, hubaballi, silverballi, &c.[41]

McTurk from practical experience in superintending Government wood-cutting was quite an authority on timber, and cast many longing eyes on grand trunks that would have squared from twenty to twenty-eight inches, with a length of from seventy to eighty feet. Overhanging the river, were also many shrubs of the "mahoe,"[42] whose bright yellow flowers contrasted with climbing purple petrœas and crimson passion-flowers. But the bright colours were mere islets in the surrounding sea of green, and it was necessary to observe closely in order to note the varying forms of vegetable life.

After the Warimambo, we came almost immediately on some very steep rapids, but which fortunately had sufficient depth of water to allow of the boats being hauled up without unloading. Here one of the crew nearly lost his life, as he was swept off his feet by the strong current, and only just caught the rope in time to save himself from being carried over a dangerous eddy, in which, as he was a weak swimmer, he would probably have been sucked under and drowned. He attributed his safety to the strictness with which the Indians had observed the proper respect due to a trogon that had flown over our heads in the morning; they have a superstition that, if on setting out on a journey they should turn their backs to this species of birds, ill luck will surely follow.

That evening we camped under some fine green-hearts that grew on the banks, which were here higher than we had hitherto seen. At this period camping was a very short business with us, as owing to the prevailing fine weather no shelter was necessary. On landing, some of the crew collected fire-wood and the cook prepared his provisions; two or three cut away the underbrush and slung up our hammocks on suitable trees apart from the others, and after they had hung their own the camp was finished. As McTurk had been unable to obtain at Georgetown a cook who was willing to work and carry loads like the other men, we were entirely at the mercy of the Indians, whose ideas of cookery were of the most primitive description. To them their rations of salt fish, rice, and fat bacon were luxuries, and a small alligator they considered a prize, but McTurk and I often agreed that our very plain fare would have been improved by even moderate cooking. Of canned meats and relishes, we had to be very sparing, but of flour we had an unlimited supply. But here again we failed in having any means of rendering the flour palatable, although it perforce formed the chief item of our meals. It was prepared in two ways; in the first, the flour was kneaded into a cake of dough, roasted on the embers and called a "bake;" in the second it was kneaded into a ball of dough, boiled in a pot and called a "dumpling;" under either name it was equally leathery and indigestible, and only with butter, of which we had a very small supply, and brown sugar, was it possible to eat it. Later on in our journey we made a slight improvement in the bakes and dumplings by adding some of "Eno's Fruit Salt," which had been recommended to us as containing valuable properties for a cooling drink in case of fever, thereby causing the flour to rise and the cakes to become lighter. It was certainly a novel baking-powder, but it succeeded. In future years should a traveller discover one of these "bakes" on the banks of the river, he will be puzzled about its origin, and will probably conclude that it is the fossil remains of some extinct species of shell-fish.

The crew took it in turns to cook for themselves, whilst the smartest of them became our own particular "chef," and a strong active young fellow, called "Charlie," acted as our trenchman. Charlie could turn his hand to anything, from building a house to making a basket, and was always ready and willing; he and his duplicate, Sammy, were the ones who worked hardest in and out of the water; they carried the heaviest loads, they shot the most game, were most skilful in raising shelters, and were the two who were never ill. Sometimes in the night a rain storm would come on, and Charlie was always ready with tarpaulins to stretch over our hammocks.

The nights were usually warm, but the mornings were chilly, and an early plunge into the river was like a warm bath, so great was the difference between the temperature of the air and water. And those morning and evening swims in the clear brown water—brown from the colouring matter of the wallaba[43] trees—of the broad Mazaruni were delightful, especially when contrasted with the tiny bucketful and the narrow bath-room of the hotel at Georgetown!

CHAPTER XIV.

A NEW HOUR—MARABUNTAS—SINKING OF THE BURA—
ROCK FORMATIONS—ARA HUMMING-BIRD—FALLS OF
YANINZAEC—JABIRU—CABUNI RIVER—SHOOTING FISH
WITH ARROWS—PACU—AN INDIAN CAMP—GREEN-HEART
BREAD—INDIAN LIFE—A PAIWORIE FEAST—DUCKLARS—
CURRI-CURRIS—SUN BITTERNS.

"Thirteen o'clock," was the extraordinary and invariable announcement with
which McTurk roused the slumbering Indians at daybreak. The origin of such
an unwonted hour has always been wrapped in mystery to me, but it sufficed
that the men understood it, and, a few minutes after the cry had resounded
through the camp, coffee was ready, hammocks taken down, boats loaded,
and we commenced another day of river travel. Our nights under the purple-
hearts had been cool and pleasant, and had prepared us for a day which
turned out to be one of incessant falls and rapids. The crews were hardly ever
out of the water, and the sun poured down with such power that even the
well-tanned backs of the Indians were scorched and blistered.

Between the wooded islands acres of rock rose two or three feet above the
water, revealing the most curious formations and indentations, varying in size
and shape from perfectly rounded bullet moulds to smooth oval cauldrons.
About half-past ten we stopped for breakfast, and whilst it was being
prepared I wandered around the island with my gun in search of game, but
found nothing. I was not quite unrewarded however, as on passing under a
low-hanging bough I received a sharp and painful nip, as if a pair of red hot
pincers had taken a piece of flesh out of my back. At first I thought a snake
must have stung me, but to my relief on looking back I saw it must have been
done by a "marabunta," whose nest was hanging near.

The sting of these Guiana wasps is extremely painful, and it was predicted
that fever would probably set in; although it caused a good deal of
inflammation, however, I was none the worse, but avoided marabunta nests
in future. When paddling, the Indians were continually annoyed by large
bumble-bees, which buzzed about their heads, and sometimes followed the
boats for more than a mile; I do not know what attracted them, but as they
did not trouble me I could afford to laugh at the frantic efforts of the men
to drive them off.

That evening we camped on the left bank of the mainland near a creek,
whose cold stream was very refreshing after the warm river water we had
been drinking. Here McTurk and some of the crew suffered from slight
feverish attacks, but a good dose of quinine set them up again, and next
morning they were ready to proceed. On this day we met with an accident

which might have occasioned a very serious loss. Two of the boats had been hauled safely up a long rapid, down which the water was rushing with great velocity, but the large one—the Bura-buraloo—was struck by a wave and commenced to sink; the crew, instead of slackening the rope, held on, and only loosened it when it was too late, as the boat drifted a short way down and sank. Fortunately it was not deep, and in less time than it takes to relate we had reached her, and rapidly unloading conveyed her contents to the neighbouring rocks. Then commenced such a drying as probably had never been witnessed on the Mazaruni before. Tarpaulins were laid, and the wet rice, soaked biscuit, and drowned peas spread over them.

The flour was not much damaged, as the water had made a cake round the inside of the barrel which kept the rest dry. The greatest loss we sustained was in the brown sugar, as not more than half was saved, and that in a semi-liquid state. This was a misfortune, as the Indians were intensely fond of sugar, and it formed part of their daily rations; indeed without it their wretchedly made coffee would have been barely drinkable. Knives, forks, and spoons were swept away, and had I not had a small travelling case with another set we should have been badly off. Our guns, clothes, and hammocks happened to be in the boat, and all were in a sad plight, but the sun shone so hot and strong that, though it drove us from the rocks to the shade of an island, everything gradually dried, and after a detention of about four hours we were enabled to proceed. Our camping ground that night was near some rocks whose formation was more extraordinary than that of any we had hitherto seen, resembling the bones of mammoths, and the fossil teeth and jaws of gigantic animals of the old world.

The following day, after ascending a few rapids and traversing the wide stretches of almost still water that lay between them, we stopped for breakfast at a pretty spot where a dry water course between two islands formed a dark cool lane, overhung by the meeting branches. Wandering up this I disturbed a beautiful Ara humming-bird,[44] which I recognised by its two long tail feathers, and the flash of red and golden green. He flew from a dead tree—which had been split down the middle, probably by some wandering Indians to obtain honey, as I found the glutinous remnants of an enormous comb—and then returned to it, but I could not catch another glimpse of him, although I searched long and ardently, as I was anxious to obtain a specimen of this gorgeous little creature.

Near this place we shot some fine macaws, whose long scarlet and blue tail feathers were quickly made into head-dresses by the crew. With the exception of parrots and cranes, we had not seen up to the present time a great variety of birds; the most numerous were orioles, trogons, and toucans. The latter were a never-failing source of amusement, as, with slow and jerky flight like that of a woodpecker, the ungainly birds crossed and recrossed the river, uttering their monotonous cry, "Tucáno, tucáno." The commonest of this species was the large one called by the Indians "bouradi," whose enormous bill is of the most brilliant and variegated tints of red, yellow, blue, and black. The crested cassique[45] was another common bird, and the only one which uttered musical sounds; it was very delightful to hear one of them pouring forth his rich and ventriloquial notes, and with raised crest and outspread golden tail singing love-songs to his mate as she swung in her aerial hammock.

Some of the pouch nests of these birds that we saw must have been nearly three feet in length, and, as they are invariably suspended from the ends of most slender boughs, they are safe from the rapacious maws of monkeys and other marauders. As a further precaution against danger, it is said that they always build on trees where the dreaded marabuntas have their nests, and in return for the protection thus afforded feed their young on the larvæ of their patron insects.

We were now approaching what we had heard were the most formidable cataracts in the river, namely, those of Yaninzaec, and hardly had we with difficulty dragged the boats up one set of rapids before we heard a roar of water that betokened a great fall. A turn in the river then brought us in full view of a most picturesque scene. Forming a crescent were five separate cataracts, fifteen or twenty feet in height, and divided from one another by wooded islets. The river rushed with great force over the rocky barriers, and the foam flakes were carried past us in large white masses, or before reaching us were caught in the back eddies and lay like snow-banks under the green bushes.

When we first appeared, a great jabiru[46]—or negro cap, as it is sometimes called on account of its black head and neck—was stalking about under the falls; and above, on a ledge of rock overhung by the golden flowers of the cedar-bush, three white egrets stood and looked in amazement at our unexpected intrusion, then gathering up their long legs flapped off to a distant tree.

After a lengthened investigation as to how we could reach the top of the falls, we discovered the Indian "portage;" so, after landing, we unloaded the boats, carried the baggage over the rocks for a distance of about one hundred yards, and then camped. That night I was awakened by the patter, patter of heavy rain on the leaves overhead, and discovered that McTurk—who always provided for my comfort before he thought of his own—had stretched the only available tarpaulin over my hammock, and that he himself was crouching under a tree trunk trying to keep his hammock dry. On these journeys a dry hammock is of the utmost importance, as, if it once gets wet, it takes a long time to dry, and fever is the inevitable result of sleeping in a damp one.

The rain forced us to commence our day's work even earlier than usual, and so by seven o'clock we had carried the boats over the "portage" on our shoulders, had loaded them, and were again wading through the rapids above the falls of Yaninzaec. Shortly afterwards we passed on our left the Cabuni River, which here empties itself into the Mazaruni, and then another baggage portage became necessary. Then two more cataracts were overcome, and on the following day we arrived at a fine stretch of river comparatively free from rapids. On that day we were gladdened by the first sight of hills, but still the scenery remained tame and monotonous. Only here and there was the all-pervading green, stained by the young dark-crimson leaves of the wallaba trees, and but for the slim matapolo palms scattered in places, and the hot sun, we might have been anywhere rather than in the tropics.

Only when we landed and on penetrating the forest could we appreciate the strange forms and luxuriant growth of the tropical vegetation. Then we saw the great moras and Bertholletias strangled in the folds of some gigantic creeper, and with their branches laden with arums and the curiously indented leaves of the pothos family; twisted bush-ropes and lianes of all descriptions linked the trees together and chained them to the earth, and while the ground was free from heavy growth, a chaos of intermingling plants and foliage formed a dense canopy overhead. In many places on the river, and especially near the rapids, we had seen the dams which the roving Indians had made for the purpose of catching fish, but we had not seen any of the natives; now, however, we knew that we were at last approaching them, for on the rocks around one of the dams we discovered some freshly beaten hai-arí roots which had been used for poisoning the water.

Fishing with poison is a favourite method with the Indians, as they thereby obtain the greatest quantity of fish with the least possible exertion. Dams are built on the rocky ledges with loose stones, and with spaces left open for the fish to enter; the roots of the hai-arí—a leguminous creeper—are beaten on the rocks with heavy clubs until they are in shreds, which are then soaked in water; the yellow acrid juice thus obtained is finally poured into the ponds after the inlets have been stopped. In a few minutes the fish appear on the surface, floating aimlessly about as if intoxicated, and are either shot with arrows, or knocked on the head with clubs. Enormous numbers are sometimes killed in this manner. The flesh of the fish so destroyed, receives no more deleterious qualities than does that of the forest game which the natives shoot with arrows poisoned with the deadly "wourali." For preservation, a barbecue is erected, and the fish are smoked over a fire.

In the open river, other means have to be adopted for obtaining fish, and the usual method is with the bow and arrow. Indians are not only wonderfully quick in seeing fish, but also possess great skill in shooting them, and, when it is remembered that allowance has to be made for refraction, the resistance of the water, and the movements of the fish, it is surprising how successful some of them are. McTurk, who was no mean performer himself with the bow, told me of most extraordinary shots that he had witnessed. Amongst our crew we had no very brilliant marksmen, and we had to depend in a great measure for our supplies on the Indians whom we chanced to meet. Seven or eight different kinds of arrows are used, and each has its own particular name. One of the most curious has its iron or bone point only slightly fixed to the shaft, and to it is attached a long string which is neatly wound round the stem. When the fish is hit the point detaches itself, the line runs off, the floating arrow shows the position of the fish, and the Indian at once gives chase. All the arrows are very long, some that we used being between five and six feet in length, and made from the stem of a certain reed.[47]

Several delicately flavoured fish are found in the Mazaruni, but the most delicious of all is the pacu,[48] which feeds on a species of lacis that grows abundantly near falls and rapids. They are very shy, but their red gold colour renders them easily discernible in the clear pools. Owing to the extent of water-poisoning which had preceded our ascent of the river, we had only obtained one of these fish, but now, as we were approaching the Indian camp, we hoped to obtain a good supply of both fresh and smoked.

Suddenly we espied a solitary Indian paddling with might and main to get away from us; we gave chase, but in his light woodskin he speedily distanced us. Then at the end of a long stretch of river we saw what appeared to be a line of animals swimming across. It proved to be a string of canoes, whose occupants, frightened at the appearance of the white men's boats, had left their fishing ground and were making all haste to their camp. This we soon reached, and found about twenty men, women, and children squatting on the rocks like brown monkeys, and evidently very nervous about the strangers. They proved to be Acawais, and could certainly not be complimented on their good looks. They were short of stature, had olive complexions, and hair like a black mop. The women added to their charms by a few pot-hooks tattooed into the corners of the mouth, and by staining their limbs with blue stripes, which at a distance gave the idea of tight-fitting drawers. But their dress was strictly one of imagination, a few square inches of bead apron— queyou—taking the place of the old original cestus. The men were attired in the buck-skin suits in which they were born, with some pieces of straw in their nose and ears, and instead of a bead apron they wore a strip of calico called a "lap."

The poor things looked very thin and half-starved, and we learn that owing to the drought the cassava crop had been a poor one, and they had been reduced to eating a wretched sort of bread made from the grated nuts of the green-heart, and now had descended the river on a fishing expedition. Moore in one of his poems asks:

"Know you what 'midst such fertile scenes
That awful voice of famine means?"

To such a question these Indians might answer "yes." A more improvident race does not exist; as long as they can satisfy their immediate wants they are content. They seldom live on the banks of the large rivers, but build their huts—two or three of which often constitute a village—near some retired creek. There they plant a little cassava, and when that is exhausted they pack their household goods on their backs, and, as they express it, "walk" *i.e.*, they wander about wherever fancy leads them, pitching their camp sometimes for a day, and sometimes for weeks in one place. In an indolent fashion they will hunt and fish, and, when they have no game, live on wild berries; occasionally when they have anything to sell they will paddle leisurely down to the Settlements and paddle back in the same easy manner. Time is no object to them, except when a paiworie[49] feast and dance are on the *tapis*. To be present on such an occasion they will travel great distances, in an incredibly short time, they will ascend and descend rivers, cross mountains, penetrate forests, and die from exhaustion rather than forego the effort necessary to obtain a drink of paiworie. Our friends had no fresh fish, but we obtained a few dried pacu, averaging five or six pounds each, and some fish arrows, of which we were in want, in exchange for fish-hooks and a little salt. Indians are very fond of salt, and as they can only obtain it in trade it forms a good article of barter.

We did not camp that evening until we had placed some distance between ourselves and the natives, as, when the latter think that anything is to be obtained from white men, they will follow and keep near them as long as they can, although the direction may be the opposite to that in which they themselves were originally travelling.

The next day the river was freer than usual from rapids, and we were enabled to replenish our larder, which up to the present had been sadly deficient in fresh meat. Some golden red howling monkeys—baboons the men called them—were our first acquisition, and the chase they gave us through the forest, though very amusing, covered us with garrapatas—large ticks—and the equally annoying bête rouge. The latter insect is of a bright scarlet, and so small as hardly to be distinguished, but it causes great irritation, and if the skin is scratched it ulcerates, and like all other sores and wounds in the tropics is difficult to heal. Then we shot two young alligators each about three feet in length; it was strange that although on the Mazaruni we saw several baby alligators, yet we never saw any large ones. Of game birds we bagged a paui, curassow,[50] and two maroudis, a species of wild turkey. The Indians say that the maroudi obtained its bare red throat by swallowing a fire-stick which it mistook for a glow-worm.

Two sorts of water-birds, were very plentiful, namely: ducklars[51] and curri-curris.[52] We did not often fire at the former, unless we were very badly off for fresh meat, as, irrespective of their ability to carry off an incredible amount of the largest shot, they are fishy, ill-flavoured birds. But the curri-curris, so called from their peculiar cry, are by no means to be despised, and probably being aware of their eatable properties generally disappeared into the thick bush, just out of range. These birds are of an olive and bronze colour, feed snipe-like on worms, and have a heavy flight, similar to that of an owl.

Sometimes we startled a little sun-bittern, and occasionally we crept near enough to watch him in his motions whilst fascinating an insect; then his body would writhe and twist, his slender neck undulating like a serpent's folds, but all the time with head quiet and eye steadily fixed on his victim; finally there was a quick darting movement, and there was no more insect. Our day's sport was brought to a conclusion by spearing a very large electric eel. It was Saturday night, and according to custom McTurk's cry of "Grog-oh" speedily brought the crew to receive their weekly glass—dose they called it—of brandy, and this well-earned medicine infused such life into their tired bodies that we were kept awake for a long time by the monotonous strains of an old fiddle with which they were "making dance."

The next day we remained in our camp below Turesie cataract, and as somebody shot a deer, and somebody else a maroudi, we had a grand Sunday dinner consisting of:

SOUP.
Macaw.

FISH.
Smoked pacu and Electric eel.

SIDE DISHES.
Curried monkey, Maroudi à la Turesie.

JOINT.
Haunch of Venison.

BAKES.
Dumplings, Sea biscuit.

Coffee and Eno's Fruit Salt *ad lib.*

CHAPTER XV.

THE BUSH-MASTER—LABARRI—CAMOODI—WOOD ANTS—
TURESIE—A PACU HUNT—CASHEW TREE—WOODSKINS—
PIRAI—SINGING FISH—INDIAN DANCE—BEADS—FASHION—
A RIVER BEND—VIEW OF HILLS—SNIPE—INDIAN
MYTHOLOGY—WANT A DOG—TABLE MOUNTAINS—
MERUME RIVER—COURSE OF THE MAZARUNI.

Towards midnight I was aroused by a low rustling sound in the bushes; as I glanced around, my eye fell on an old mora tree just opposite, and at the foot of my hammock, there on the grey trunk I plainly saw the shadow of a snake's head and neck. From its position, there could be no doubt that it was close beside me, and almost over my head, its body being half hidden by the branches of one of the trees in which it was coiled. As I watched, the head and neck moved towards me and drew back in slow undulating movements, the forked tongue shot out and seemed almost to touch me. I did not dare to move, and hardly to breathe, as the reptile seemed only waiting for my slightest motion in order to strike. The minutes that I lay there with my eyes fixed on the horrid shadow seemed like hours; all sorts of thoughts passed across my brain; had I the nightmare? could the curried monkey have disagreed with me? I was wet with perspiration and at last could stand it no longer, but, slowly disentangling my feet from the blanket, threw myself forward and sprang to the ground. Seizing my gun, I pointed it to where the snake must have been, but there was no appearance of one, and a careful search revealed nothing. Then I went to bed again, and there in front of me, on the tree, was the same writhing form and shooting tongue. I put up hand, and its shadow almost grasped the neck of the creature; then I raised myself, and looking up saw my enemy. A projecting twig and a few leaves gently swayed by the breeze were all that remained of my snake, but the shadow they cast was so exactly that of a serpent that when I pointed it out to McTurk he fully believed for a moment that it was one.

The forests of Guiana are well furnished with everything that a traveller can want in the shape of beast or insect, and in snakes they are especially prolific. Of these, the "bush-master"[53] is the most dreaded, and as its name implies, is lord of the woods. In colour it is as brilliant as its bite is venomous. The "labarri"[54] is equally poisonous, but is not so aggressive as the "bush-master." The "camoodi"—a boa-constrictor—is the largest of all the snakes, and the stories of their enormous size and strength would be incredible to any one who had not travelled in Guiana. A gentleman in Georgetown solemnly assured me that once when he was out shooting in the interior, with a party of seven others, they stopped to rest after a long walk and all sat down on a falling trunk; all at once it began to move, and what they had imagined to be the trunk of a tree proved to be an immense "camoodi," which glided slowly into the forest without being fired at by any of the amazed spectators. The "water-camoodi"[55] is even larger and more dangerous than the land species.

It was destined that our night after the shadow-snake incident should not pass wholly destitute of the pleasures of camp life, as, on putting on my hat before starting, I found that it was wreathed round and round with the clay tunnels of the wood-ant, thousands of which had taken advantage of its position, at the foot of a tree, to erect on it their covered ways before they climbed up aloft. Charlie was highly amused at the appearance of the hat, but soon rid it of its inhabitants by holding it over a fire.

After ascending the falls of Turesie we noticed a long reed performing strange evolutions in the water; this the Indians knew to be an arrow with a pacu at the end of it, which had been shot and then lost by a native. We at once gave chase, and a most amusing hunt followed. Whenever we approached it, one of the crew plunged into the river, and immediately the arrow disappeared to come up again fifty yards off in another direction. This was repeated until the poor fish was tired out and at last landed. Another excitement was in store for us, as hardly had the pacu been caught before we saw in the distance a deer swimming across the river. Away went the three boats in full cry, but the light canoe soon led the chase, and it was a pretty sight to see her shoot through the water amidst a shower of rainbows raised by the splendidly sweeping paddles. Now she gains on the deer, no, the animal will reach the shore; to shoot would be useless, as the body would sink; now he flags, as the distance he has already swum is great, the "Akoora" flies through the water, the crew are near enough to hear the panting of the victim, and the next minute is his last. He proved to be a fine young buck, and was a great acquisition to our stores. I am afraid I did not want him to escape, until he had been captured; but I did then, it seemed so hard that he should have chosen the moment of our arrival for his swim.

Soon after our deer chase we saw a splendid cashew[56] tree loaded with purple-red fruit. This was a treat not to be neglected, and so in a quarter of an hour the tree was down and stripped. The fruit was tart, but extremely refreshing and of a pleasant flavour. Near this place I took a shot at a parrot, and brought him down so little hurt that by the evening he had quite recovered his spirits, and in two days was perfectly tame. He became a great pet, and, as he called himself "Pourri," we christened him so. Later on, when one of the boats was sent back to the settlement, he accompanied it, and there I found him well and happy on my return.

The river now was freer from impediments than it had been hitherto; the islands were fewer, and occasionally we were in sight of both banks. Owing to its shallowness, sandbanks were numerous, and we frequently were obliged to get out of the boats and push and lift them over. We camped that evening in sight of a range of hills near the Issano river. An Indian who had been following us at a distance in his woodskin,[57] since the previous day, here came up to us. He was skinny and shy, but as berries and cashews had of late formed his chief support, hunger overcame his timidity, and he was thankful for some venison. A few matches pleased him highly, as he had never seen any before, and the small fire which was burning in his boat must have been a continued source of trouble, as if it went out, the relighting of it was a laborious process.

Before sunrise next morning we were afloat on a beautiful clear expanse of water, with a white sandy beach under the trees on both sides. A silvery haze lay over the silent river, and the western hills were seen as if through a filmy veil. As the sun rose, the silver changed to gold in a flood of light that touched the hill crests, and then pouring over the strange, peaceful land, cast rare tints and shades among the drooping trees and into the forest depths. Our painted boats were quite in accord with the bright scene, and the gay feather ornaments of the crews and the gleam of the paddles were strikingly effective. The sky was of a frosty blue, unrelieved by a single cloud.

Near where we stopped for breakfast was an Indian shed—banaboo—and there we found numerous jaws of the pirai, and we were thankful that in our morning bath we had escaped these voracious fish. The pirai[58] is not large, but its jaws are so strong and teeth so sharp that it can take off a finger or a toe at a bite. It will attack anything, even an alligator, and ducks and geese seldom have any feet where this species of fish exists, but a man bathing is an object of peculiar attraction to it. Its flesh is coarse and bony, but the Indians eat it.

Several times that day our attention was directed to a peculiar humming noise, like the distant burr of machinery in motion, proceeding from the water over which we passed. McTurk and the Indians, who had heard similar sounds on the Pomeroon and other rivers, said that they were uttered by singing fish. That it was fish-music there was no doubt, as the nearer we placed our ears to the water the more distinct were the sounds, and on dropping a stone they ceased for a moment and then recommenced. The tone was by no means inharmonious, and resembled the hum of a busy city heard from a high church steeple, or the voice of Saint Francis reading prayers to the fish, to which they were repeating the responses.

As we approached the Teboco hills, one of our Acawais said that he had an uncle who lived in a village not far from the river, and asked permission to visit him. This was readily granted by McTurk, and on finding the landing we all went ashore, and the Indian, quickly dressing himself in a clean shirt and an old hat, evidently with the intention of astonishing the natives and showing them what civilization had done for him, started off with two companions on a two-mile walk through the forest. On the high bank near where we had landed we found an old shed, and near it, not in it, as it probably contained a rich entomological collection, we prepared breakfast, and then awaited the arrival of the absentees.

After a delay of nearly three hours our Indians arrived, and they were quickly followed by the strangest procession I have ever seen. Along the narrow forest path, which led from the clearing in which we were seated, stalked in single file, noiselessly and solemnly, the whole of the inhabitants from the Indian village. There were only twelve or thirteen altogether, men, women, and children, but their slow march and the long intervals between each gave magnitude to their number. As they arrived they touched our hands, and then retired to a short distance, the children trying to hide themselves behind their mothers, but with little success. It was with the utmost difficulty that we could refrain from loud bursts of laughter, so utterly ridiculous was the appearance of the natives. The men were short, but stoutly proportioned, and wore the customary "lap" and bright feathers in their hair. A few had little patches of white fluff stuck about their faces, and all were freshly painted. Their heads were got up in a very elaborate style; the parting of their long black hair was dyed vermillion, and a Vandyck pattern of the same brilliant colour ran round the forehead. Through the nose and ears of each were passed yellow straws or strips of wood, those of the ear resting on that of the nose, and giving a most humorous expression to their pathetic countenances. Some carried a blow-pipe, others a bow and arrows. In addition to their bead aprons, the women wore broad armlets and anklets of beads, and their bodies and limbs were stained and painted in stripes with crimson "arnotto"[59] and blue black "lana."[60] They were tall in proportion to the men and had well-turned limbs, but in features were coarse and plain.

We were anxious to secure the services of a man who was acquainted with the river and its tributaries; so, selecting the strongest, we found he was willing to accompany us, and at once sent his son for his hammock. In the interval, the ladies and gentlemen entertained us with a dance. Placing their hands on each other's shoulders, they formed into line, and advanced and retreated in a kind of jig. As there were only two or three steps in it, it became monotonous to all but the dancers, who continued their amusement until the arrival of the hammock. The wife of our late acquisition then bitterly lamented the departure of her husband, and seemed inclined to accompany us herself, but as there was no room for her we had to decline her offer; then she burst into tears and would not be comforted. As a last resource we produced some beads, and immediately tears were dried and the mourning wife was changed to a merry coquette, whose only anxiety was concerning the colour of the ornaments. Shakespeare says:—

"Win her with gifts, if she respects not words,

Dumb jewels often in their silent kind,

More than quiet words, do move a woman's mind."

Fashion reigns in the wilds of Guiana as it does in the regions of civilization, and it is of no small importance to a traveller that his *negotia*—beads, knives, &c.,—should be of the proper colour, shape, or description.

We christened our new hand "Mazaruni," not because his name was William—he said he had been called William during a visit he had paid to the settlement—but because we already had most of the common Christian names among our crew. Paiworie and fresh cassava had been the cause of our delay in the first instance, and a bowl of that unpleasant beverage was brought for the entertainment of our Indians, who thoroughly enjoyed it. Two woodskins, containing friends of Mazaruni, accompanied us as far as the Teboco hills, and there left us, as our course was deflected due south for some distance. This part of the river was very pretty, as from each bank numerous points ran out, all thickly wooded with trees of various shades. Before we reached the southern extremity of this river-bend we obtained a beautiful view of the Karanang Hills, and beyond them, to the south, we saw in the far distance a high table-mountain, and behind that again a lofty peak, dim and hazy, but standing out in clear outline against the pale blue of the evening sky. This sugar-loaf peak was said by Mazaruni to be that of Illuie, but on our return another native who was with us gave it a different name.[61] After passing the mouth of the Semang River on our left, we rounded the Teboco promontory by ascending the pretty falls of Teboco, and continued on our way in a northerly direction. That evening we camped, during a rain storm, on the left bank of the Mazaruni, opposite the Karanang River. Next day we varied our game-bag by shooting some snipe, and the numerous fresh tracks of tapirs gave us hopes of obtaining large game, but a small accourie[62] was the only four-footed creature we got. This little rodent figures prominently in Indian mythology.

One of the legends runs thus; the inhabitants of the sky once peeped through a hole that they had been told not to approach, and on looking down saw another world. They therefore cut down long bush-ropes and let themselves down. After wandering about they became frightened and began to ascend the ladder, but an old lady of too ample proportions stuck in the hole, and, during the fighting and scrambling that ensued the rope broke and many had to remain on earth. Then, as they had no provisions they became very lean, but noticing that the accourie was always plump they set the woodpecker to watch its feeding ground. But the woodpecker betrayed himself by his tapping. Then the alligator was told to watch, and he found out, but came back and told a lie, so they cut out his tongue.[63] Then the rat was sent off, but he never returned and the people starved. They wandered off and left a little child behind, and when they returned after a long time, having lived on berries, they found the child alive and well, and surrounded by Indian corn cobs that the accourie had fed it with. Then the child followed the accourie after its next visit and discovered the maize field, and the people were saved. In gratitude, they kill and eat the delicate little animal whenever they have the opportunity.

In their tradition of the Deluge, maize takes the place of the olive branch. They say that only one man was saved in his canoe, and when he sent out a rat to discover land, it brought back a head of Indian corn. The Caribs, in their account of the Creation, say that the Great Spirit sat on a mora tree, and picking off pieces of the bark threw them into the stream, and they became different animals. Then the Great Spirit—Makanaima—made a large mould, and out of this fresh, clean clay, the white man stepped. After it got a little dirty the Indian was formed, and the Spirit being called away on business for a long period the mould became black and unclean, and out of it walked the negro. All the Indian tribes of Guiana—Acawais, Arawaaks, Arecunas, Warraus, Macusis, &c.—rank themselves far higher than the negro race, and the Caribs consider themselves the first of the tribes, calling themselves "the" people, and their language "the" language.

Ever since our departure we had regretted that we had brought no dog with us, as without one it was almost impossible to drive the labba[64] or the great pig-like water haas[65] from their lair amongst the reeds and moco-mocos[66] that lined the banks. The labba and tapir being nocturnal in their habits were hardly ever seen by us, and it was only occasionally that we chanced to see the day-feeding animals. We frequently tried to buy an Indian dog from the natives, but they invariably declined to part with them.

After leaving Teboco, we encountered no more falls or rapids of any importance, having up to that time ascended about thirty and gained an elevation above the sea of about two hundred feet. Continuing our northerly course, we saw towards the north-west a long table mountain known as the Comaka, which was much broken and very jagged at the northern extremity. On our left was the precipitous hill of Tamanua, wooded far up its sides and then presenting a massive face of rock, seamed and scarred in places with ravines and crevices. Over the strange mountain crests rain clouds continually came and went, and storms which never failed to deluge us in their progress hurried past on their way to the hill regions.

At last from north our direction changed to west, and after about six miles of this westerly course we arrived at the mouth of the Merumé river. Twenty miles to the south lay the Merumé mountains, in which the Mazaruni has its source. The course of this river is a very singular one, completely enclosing a great area of country, with the exception of the narrow strip of land, twenty miles in breadth, between its source and the mouth of the Merumé.[67]

It had been our intention to ascend the Merumé as far as possible, then, striking across the mountains, to cross the head waters of the Mazaruni, and reaching the Oweang river, down which we could travel in woodskins, again meet the Mazaruni in its course westward. Owing to the shallowness of the Merumé, we found it would be impossible to ascend that river in our boats, and there were no woodskins to be obtained. We therefore determined to continue our course up the Mazaruni, until we reached the Curipung river, which our new hand, Mazaruni, assured us would have a sufficient depth of water as far as the commencement of the overland path. Within three days we expected to arrive at the mouth of the Curipung.

CHAPTER XVI.

A FISH HUNT ON LAND—STINGRAYS—THE "CARIBISCE"—
TABLE MOUNTAINS—A RIVER GOD—DESERTED VILLAGES—
CURIPUNG RIVER—INDIAN ENCAMPMENT—INDIAN
SUPERSTITION—THE "PEAIMAN"—DURAQUA—EATING
CUSTOMS—ARRIVAL OF LANCEMAN—TRIANGLE OF
MOUNTAINS—MACREBAH FALLS—START ACROSS COUNTRY.

It has been well said that mountains are privileges, blessings; Ararats whereon
the dove of thought may alight when weary of the deluge around. And truly
after the level country we had been traversing, it was an unutterable relief to
gaze on the strange forms and picturesque colouring of the cliffs and crags
that rose up around us. Though in height they did not approach the sublime
order of mountains, yet their forest slopes, broken with clefts and chasms,
and their perpendicular flat-topped walls, streaked here with clinging shrubs,
and there glistening with falling water, were more suggestive of the wonderful
land changes, yet more mysterious than the rounded and lofty forms of some
grand Sierras. They resembled Cyclopean monuments scattered through the
graveyard of a universe.

On the day after passing the Merumé river, we saw two natives carrying some
large fish; as soon as they caught sight of us, they took to their heels and fled
over the sandbank on which they had been walking towards the bush. As we
were in want of fish we called to them, but the more we called the faster they
ran. Then Mazaruni gave evidence of his value, as with a grunt of indignation
at the silly fear of his countrymen, he jumped into the water and speeded
after the fugitives. It was a most laughable chase and won eventually by
Mazaruni, who returned triumphantly with his heavily-weighted captives.
They gladly sold us two of their pacus, but would not part with more, as they
required them for their own camp, which was pitched somewhere up the
Cabeparu creek, near which we were. Shortly afterwards, we captured two
more pacus that had lately been shot, and they afforded us a more amusing
hunt than even those of the previous week.

On account of the number of electric eels and stingrays it was dangerous
work jumping carelessly out of the boat, and in the last hunt one of the crew
touched a ray with his foot but fortunately without receiving any injury. In
appearance a ray is rather like a frying-pan, and its lance-like tail, fringed with
a series of barbs, is a most terrible weapon. The wound it inflicts causes great
agony and is always followed by severe inflammation. It frequents shallows,
where it lies half buried in the sand, and its yellow colour renders it difficult
to distinguish. The flesh is eatable, when you can get nothing else, and we

speared many of them with a bayonet fastened to a long pole, or shot them with arrows. Some were of enormous size and defied both arrow and spear.

The next day we met a party of Indian hunters dressed in the costume of the chase, *i.e.*, in feathers, and armed blow-pipes and bows, but they had no game. We found out from them where we could obtain a certain liane called "mamurie," which we were in search of in order to make "quakes" for our overland journey. We therefore camped early that day on the left bank of the river, and the men were sent into the woods to look for the required vine. As we ascended the river from Teboco, we had noticed in some distant hills a remarkable rocky peak which is called "the Caribisce," from the legend stating that it is an Indian hunter who was turned into stone for daring to ascend the mountain. To-day from our camp, we saw in the direction from which we had come, east, another curious peak rising like a gigantic thimble from a flat table-mountain. The name of this is Sororieng, *i.e.*, Swallow's Nest, and it is an object of much dread to the superstitious Indians. Not far from it was the rugged outline of Ishagua, and far away in the south-west we saw the misty range of the Curipung mountains.

We had chosen a pretty spot for the camp, where on the high bank big moras and solemn ceibas cast a pleasant shade over rocky pools, deep and clear, in which small and large fish played near the surface. Among them McTurk thought he recognized a lucanani[68] and fished zealously for a couple of hours, but without success. I suggested that perhaps the fish saw him; he was dressed in scarlet flannel knickerbockers, and in his Scotch cap he wore the macaw's tail feathers, that even the greediest fish could hardly have mistaken for a fly—at all events we got no lucanani that day. But the fisherman was delightfully picturesque.

Then we strolled through the dark forest, where great butterflies, with wings whose outer side was of a dull brown, whilst the under part was of metallic blue, flapped heavily along. Blue morphos, too, of a most lustrous sheen glanced here and there, and danced through the foliage like the will-o-the-wisp. Besides these there were not many other species, some pretty swallow-tails and heliconias being the chief representatives of the diurnal lepidoptera.[69]

Under the fallen trees were several species of brilliant beetles, and occasionally a great golden green buprestis[70] whizzed past us. This beetle is very common, and its wings are used by the Indians for armlets and anklets. The few flowering plants that we saw were yellow; an oncidium, the mahoe, cedar-bush, ginger-wort, and other cannas, all were yellow. The prettiest leaf was that of a crimson-veined caladium, the bulb of which had probably been dropped by an Indian on his way through the forest. The natives are fond of this plant, often bringing it back with them from their journeys to the settlement and using it medicinally. When the crew returned they brought a good supply of "mamurie," and in addition one had a large land-tortoise, another had some toucans, whilst a third had seen some wonderful animal or other, but of course had no gun with him. The rest of the day was spent in basket-making.

Just before sun-down the noisy monkeys commence their usual chorus; cranes and egrets betook themselves to their resting places; macaws and parrots crossed the river, uttering their harsh good-nights, and were answered by "pourri," who had not forgotten when they, too, wended their evening flight over the waters; and finally, with a rush of wings and with weird minor cries, the green ibises—curri-curris—flew by and disappeared in the gloom—

"And far away in the twilight sky

We heard them singing a lessening cry,

Farther and farther till out of sight,

And we stood alone in the silent night."

When we left next morning, the Giant's Thimble was just touched by the rising sun, and after we had crossed a fine reach of river, we had a fresh mountain view. In the distance it looked like a single mountain, much broken and castellated in the centre, and with table ends. Mazaruni informed us that the central position was called Tapusing and the flat Aricanna; so probably they were two mountains, one standing in front of the other.

Soon afterwards we passed a peculiar rock in the middle of the river, somewhat resembling a human figure; the Indians thought it was a river god watching for pacu. Strange rock formations had been the rule rather than the exception in all parts of the river, and owing to its unusual shallowness, we had been able to notice the action of the water on the various developments, such as granite, porphyry, green stone, gneiss, &c., below the ordinary low-water mark. Hitherto we had seen no Indian village on the banks of the river, although we had passed the sites of several deserted settlements, which were easily to be recognized by the forest-clearing and the new growth of bush. To day we were glad when Mazaruni told us that we were approaching the village of Masanassa, and soon, on the left bank of the river and opposite a small island, we saw a number of woodskins and evident signs of habitation. Long before we reached the landing we had been descried by the natives, who flocked to see us and escorted us to the principal house, which stood on a high bank, with a neat approach of flowering shrubs, plantains, ochro, peppers, papaws, cotton, and fruit trees. The house was merely a large shed with wattled walls. From the beams were suspended twenty-five hammocks, so that it was evident that three or four families occupied the same house. In the centre were two large paiworie troughs, and scattered about the floor, or resting on a platform overhead, were the various cassava-making implements, calabashes, tastefully fretted "pegalls"—covered baskets in which the women keep their paints and knick-knacks—quaint, low stools, parrots, accouries, and a few snarling dogs.

In appearance and dress the inhabitants were the same as we had before seen, only the men had put on their finest and largest necklaces, made of the teeth of monkeys and peccaries, and of wild-boars' tusks. To some of these necklaces were attached long cords with tassels of toucans' breasts, and various bird-skins. Some of the women were engaged in chewing cassava, whilst others were occupied in the pleasanter employment of cotton-spinning and hammock-weaving. The villagers were not particularly enthusiastic in their reception of us, and one man, with a fierce countenance horribly painted in red, lay in his hammock in an open shed outside the house, and scowled ferociously at our intrusion, but it was plain that his enmity arose from a too copious indulgence in paiworie. The chief of the house was named Lanceman, and though his knowledge of speaking English only amounted to "yes," yet he understood a few words, and seemed an intelligent man. To his care McTurk confided the baggage—tin boxes, &c.,— that would be troublesome to carry during our overland journey, and also sufficient provisions to last us on our return from his house to the settlement. He also promised to accompany us himself to Roraima, and on the following day to bring to our camp, on the Curipung, as many men as were willing to assist us as carriers.

In two hours after we left we arrived at the Curipung River, in whose broad mouth the water had shrunk to one narrow channel, just deep enough to admit our boats. Just above, however, it widened out into a stream of about fifty yards in width, and on its left bank we camped. On the other side of this creek, and bordering the Mazaruni, was a large stretch of white sand, and on its edge a number of Indians, who had come down on a fish-poisoning excursion, were encamped. Above all other localities, an Indian is fond of an open, sandy beach whereon to pass the night. In the ground he sticks a few poles from which to suspend his hammock, and if the weather is rainy, a few palm leaves form a sufficient shelter. There in the open, away from the dark, shadowy forest, he feels secure from the stealthy approach of the dreaded "kanaima;"[71] the magic rattle of the "peaiman"[72] has less terror for him when unaccompanied by the weird rustling of the waving branches; and there even the wild hooting of the "didi"[73] is bereft of that intensity with which it pierces the gloomy depths of the surrounding woodland. It is strange that the superstitious fear of these Indians, who are bred in the forest and hills, should be chiefly based on natural forms and sounds. Certain rocks they will never point at with a finger, although your attention may be drawn to them by an inclination of the head. Some rocks they will not even look at, and others again they beat with green boughs. Common bird-cries become spirit-voices. Any place that is difficult of access, or little known, is invariably tenanted by huge snakes or horrible four-footed animals. Otters are transformed into mermaids, and water-tigers inhabit the deep pools and caves of their rivers. Yet with all their superstition, I doubt whether any of them would object to set out on a journey on a Friday, or whether any would place faith in "lucky numbers," and I am sure none would refuse to join a dinner party of thirteen.

We passed a whole day at our camp on the Curipung, and completed as many "quakes" as we could out of the material, in all numbering forty-two, each capable of holding about fifty-five or sixty pounds. Here we shot a "great mâam,"[74] whose flesh proved superior to anything we had tasted. The anatomy of this bird is peculiar, as it may be said to be nearly all breast; the flesh before cooking is of a light green, and when cooked is white and delicate. In size it is about the same as a pheasant, and its shrill plaintive whistle, which gradually increases in volume, is a never-failing forest-sound both night and morning. There is another but smaller bird of the same species. We also bagged two or three "duraquauras"[75]—partridges—which were almost as good on the table as the "mâam." The notes of this bird, from which it takes its name, are usually the first heard in the morning and frequently before dawn.

In spite of repeated assurances from Lanceman that he and his Indians would be ready to accompany us early on the following morning, they failed to appear at the appointed time. Some of the natives from the sandbank encampment were willing to join us, so we accepted their services and loaded one of their woodskins, so as to lighten our own boats, and then started. Soon after we left the river widened considerably, but became so shallow that for over an hour we had to walk and drag the boats, and even the woodskin. Then it became deeper, and maintained an average breadth of sixty or seventy yards. The banks were thickly clothed with a jungle growth, above which locust and cork-trees reared themselves. Here and there a great Brownea,[76] with brilliant red flowers or fiery legumes, stretched out, Briareus-like, a hundred arms wreathed with deeply cut arums and parasitical plants, and over the water drooped the feathery foliage of an amherstiæ, with beautiful rose-tinged flowers having long crimson stamens. Sport was easier to be obtained here than on the large river, and we had plenty of amusement spearing rays and shooting sun-bitterns, hanuras,[77] white egrets, and sometimes a beautiful Quaak heron.[78] The latter is a very graceful bird with plumy crest, and curly neck and breast feathers of a lovely lavender colour.

Nothing was wasted, for most of our civilized Indians found no flesh amiss, and apparently enjoyed the leg of a heron as much as they did the breast of a mâam. But two of our Acawais would not eat the delicious pacu, although they did not refuse the ray, or the electric-eel. In North America, too, the Comanche Indians will not eat fish that have scales, but are fond of those that have none.

The different tribes of Guiana have various ideas regarding what food is fit and what food is unfit to be eaten. For instance, the Caribs will not touch large fish, nor will they eat pork. The Macusi consider the flesh of cattle unclean, but do not object to that of peccary and wild boar. The Warraees think roast dog a great delicacy, therein resembling the Cheyennes of North America. On this river we missed the little silver fish running swiftly over the top of the water, the bats that flew out of every dead tree near the water's edge as we passed, and even the bumble bees that had been our constant companions on the Mazaruni. But their place was supplied by sociable king-fishers, many of which kept in our society for hours, awaiting our approach on some bare bough, and then skimming over the water just ahead of us. Ducklars, too, and curri-curris stood less on ceremony, and scarcely waited for an invitation to dinner. We stopped for breakfast near a village—two houses—where fifteen or twenty people assembled to look at us. A successful wild-pig hunt had just provided them with a quantity of meat, a small portion of which we wished to purchase. They, however, declined to part with any of it, unless we gave in return a much larger supply of salt than we could afford; so we had to go without it. "Gentle hospitality," quoth the Sanscrit sage, "dwelleth not in palaces. Rather seeking, shall ye find her in the tent of the desert." Before we left, a woodskin, containing Lanceman and six other Indians caught us up, and we proceeded together.

The river scenery was now more picturesque, and mountain forms, with outlines ever changing as we moved, gathered round us. Our course was so winding that sometimes the same mountain appeared on one side of us and sometimes on the other. Towards evening we obtained a very pretty view. Beyond where the river narrowed a little, two mountains stood almost together, the nearer—Wattaparu—flat-topped, and with bare, perpendicular walls, loomed up grandly and in striking contrast with the other—Aricanna—whose rounded base was crowned with a curious pinnacle, the whole being thickly wooded from top to bottom. The one was all shining silver-grey, the other of a rich purple bloom. But with the mountains had come the rain, and it was as much as we could do by perpetual bailing to keep the boats above water. At length we camped on a sandbank, and for the first time since we left Georgetown built a house.

As we might now expect constant rains, in all our future camps the building of a shelter was our first care. The huts were necessarily substantial, in order to sustain the weight of our hammocks. Four stout forked poles were worked into the ground, and formed the corner posts; these were connected by strong poles, and in the centre of the narrower ends of the parallelogram two more thick forked poles were erected high enough for the tarpaulins, which were thrown over the connecting beam to form a sloping ceiling. All the fastenings were made with bush-rope, which was as pliable as cord. Rafters placed across the connecting side-beams formed a dry platform in wet weather for the "quakes," guns, &c. After a little practice, it was astonishing how quickly the shelter was set up. In spite of our house the night was not a pleasant one, as owing to our exposed situation the rain beat in terribly through the open sides. It passed though, and before daybreak the tarpaulins were down and the boats reloaded. The course of the river was more tortuous than on the preceding day, and it seemed as if we should never reach the other side of Wattaparu, so frequently did we pass and repass it. In some places fallen trees obstructed our passage, and these had to be cut away; and in others enormous boulders, formed of coarse conglomerate and diorite rising from the bed of the river, gave us but scanty space to squeeze through.

At last we reached a mountain triangle. In front was Wairinu, a splendid table-mountain with bold perpendicular wall, and castellated like some gigantic fortification of the most perfect stone masonry. On our left was Pacaru, surmounted by a high cone and with massive slabs of rock jutting out from its side. On the right rose Wuruima with its outline similar to Pacaru. Everywhere there was a beautiful blending of rock and forest, the rocks varying from red overhanging buttresses to grey perpendicular heights, furred at intervals with shrubs, and the forest which covered every available spot with dark green foliage was brightened in places with a few patches of colour, and the lighter tints of palm and wild plantain leaves.

On reaching the Seroun creek, near which the Indian path leads across the country, we found the water too shallow for an ascent, so crossing to the right bank of the Curipung, we camped on some high ground below the falls of Macrebah. Nowhere had we found so picturesque a camping ground. Under the trees was a broad beach of the whitest sand, at whose foot ran the dark river, foam-flecked from the beautiful falls over which the water rushed in three successive cataracts, flanked and broken by enormous boulders. Mountains surrounded the little valley through which the river flowed, and their wonderful precipices and curious forms were a never failing source of attraction. As this was the terminus of our river travel in boats, we soon set to work filling and weighing the "quakes;" the weight assigned to each man being forty-five pounds of provisions, which together with his own bundle and a few et ceteras altogether amounted to about sixty pounds, no inconsiderable weight to carry, when the temperature and the difficulties of the route are considered.

For our future progress McTurk arranged the following plan. All the hands, except two, who were unwell and were to be left at Macrebah in charge of the boats, were to take part in the overland journey to where we rejoined the Mazaruni. Then all the original crew, except six of the best men, were to return to Macrebah, and with the two sick ones make the home journey to the settlements in two of the boats. The other boat, "the Adaba," was to be left on a raised platform, which was built under the trees, to take us back on our return from Roraima. As we had forty-two quakes and only twenty-two men to carry them, Lanceman started off in a woodskin to a neighbouring Arecuna village, to try and get more. He succeeded in obtaining five, so we saw that we should be compelled to make short daily journeys, and after each to send back relays of men to bring on the extra quakes.

Our preparations occupied us for a day and a half, during which time our Indians also cut a short track through the woods from the opposite bank of the river to join the Seroun path, thereby avoiding a tedious and rock-encumbered walk up the shallow creek. As it would require two trips to remove all our baggage to the first day's halting place, McTurk started early in the morning with the intention of sending back the necessary number of men for the remaining quakes on the following day. I remained behind, so as to superintend the departure of the second detachment, and guard against any unnecessary delay.

CHAPTER XVII.

A "DACANA-BALLI"—STRANGE ROCKS—A ROOT PATH—
INDIAN SUPERSTITION—THE CRY OF A LOST SOUL—NEW
CARRIERS—A FEATHERED COSTUME—CURIOUS TREES—
COCK OF THE ROCKS—CAMP ON THE LAMUNG—A BOA-
CONSTRICTOR—STENAPARU RIVER—THE CARIAPU—A
BURNING TREE—THE MAZARUNI—CAPTAIN DAVID—
PICTURESQUE CAMP.

It was a dismal morning when McTurk set out on his tedious march; the rain
fell in torrents, and I congratulated myself on being under shelter, and hoped
that by the morrow the weather would have cleared. At intervals during the
day the rain ceased, and I was able to ramble about the falls, where there were
many botanical treasures in the various agaves, yuccas, and ferns. Wherever
a gleam of light shone across the forest border, there the little sun-hairs—as
the humming-birds are well named by the Aztecs—darted among the
blossoms, and often poised themselves for a minute at a time close to my
face, as if wondering to what class of vegetable I belonged.

Under our house was a fine dacana-balli tree, whose large white blossoms lay
strewn on the ground, and weighted the green foliage like a snow-fall; in the
forks and on the branches were some orchids and pretty pink and white
euphorbias, and amongst these flowers, also, humming-birds loved to revel.
In the white sand were numerous tracks of wild animals that daily came from
the forest to drink, but none ever appeared when I was on watch. Towards
evening the atmosphere had cleared, so that I anticipated fine weather, but
one of the Indians said it would surely rain again, as the toucans cried so
loudly. The birds were weather-wise, as in the night the rain recommenced,
and when the carriers arrived next day it was still pouring. There was no time
to be lost, so after the men had breakfasted we set off.

After crossing the river, the first part of our journey was to ascend the slopes
of the Seroun mountains. As soon as we joined the old path above the creek,
difficulties commenced. The narrow trail wound in and out, and up and
down, and over and under enormous masses of conglomerate rock, whose
smooth and shapely sides, rising perpendicularly for sixty or seventy feet,
were crowned by grasses and ferns. Under some of these were flowers and
green branches that had been offered to the rock spirits by the superstitious
natives; others, with their overhanging crags, formed natural shelters which
had served for a night's resting-place to the less timorous Indians. Between
these boulders were deep pits, which were hard to avoid, and into which a
false step would have given a drop of thirty or forty feet.

Over rocks and streams, and through quagmires, we made our varied way, and at last caught sight of the Curipung River above Macrebah, far below us. Soon after we reached the top of the hill range, having ascended nearly one thousand feet. Here the path ran through a level forest, but, instead of by boulders, the walking was henceforth made exceedingly fatiguing by the countless roots which composed the track. No ground was to be seen; it was simply a network of roots from which all earth had been washed away, and which varied in size from a sharp thin blade that cut like a knife, to a rounded, full-sized limb, over which you slipped, with every probability of straining your ancle even if you did not break your leg. I wore a pair of moderately-sized shooting boots, but to my unaccustomed soles the proceeding was most painful; a pilgrimage on peas to Rome would have been nothing in comparison. The resemblance to a pilgrimage was rendered all the more striking by the perpetual tolling of the bell-birds,[79] which in spite of the pouring rain uttered their wonderful notes from every part of the forest. Sometimes the ringing sounds produced by these birds resemble "quâ-ting," at other times you hear a drawling "kóng, kóng, kóng" at intervals, and then the full notes "kóng-kày." In each case, the last syllable is a note higher than the first, and the tone is more that of an anvil when struck by a hammer than that of a bell. The sounds are remarkably clear and resonant.

The campanero is pure white—strange colour for a tropical bird—and from its forehead extends a long tube which it can inflate at pleasure, and which is covered with small white, downy feathers. Its belfry is generally the topmost dead bough of some lofty tree, and even if in spite of its ventriloquial notes you have discovered its whereabouts, yet its colour renders it extremely difficult to distinguish. Our Indians, and others that we met, did not object to shoot one occasionally, but in Brazil the campanero is greatly dreaded, as its toll is believed to be the cry of a soul condemned to perpetual torments. The American poet Whittier has made this belief the subject of one of his poems, entitled

THE CRY OF A LOST SOUL.

"In that black forest, where, when day is done,

With a serpent's stillness glides the Amazon,

Darkly from sunset to the rising sun,

A cry as of the pained heart of the wood,

The long despairing moan of solitude,

And darkness and the absence of all good,

Startles the traveller with a sound so drear,

So full of hopeless agony and fear.

His heart stands still and listens with his ear;

The guide, as if he heard a dead-bell toll,

Starts, drops his oar against the gunwale's thole,

Crosses himself and whispers 'A lost soul!'

No, Señor, not a bird, I know it well,

It is the pained soul of some infidel,

Or cursed heretic that cries from hell.

Poor fool! with hope still mocking his despair,

He wanders shrieking on the midnight air,

For human pity and for Christian prayer."

After six or seven hours of the weariest walking we arrived drenched to the skin—by the way it does not take much to wet the Indians to the skin—at our camp. There I found McTurk footsore, but energetic as usual, and happy in the addition of a few more Indian carriers who were "on the walk," and willing to accompany us. The chief of the party was an old fellow with streaming black hair and of fierce aspect. He did not know his proper name, but produced a small package in the folds of which was a card with "Isaac" written on it. As there was already one Isaac in our party, we christened the new man "the Pirate." Among his most cherished treasures was a large parcel, which he opened with much ceremony. It contained five or six other palm leaf packets, from the last of which he drew a printed tract in the Acawai language, which he had obtained from one of the missions near the coast. The tract was composed of a few prayers and Bible extracts, which he requested McTurk to read aloud. It was a curious scene; a few fires threw a glare over the dark forest outside, and clustered round the shelter, under which we lay in our hammocks, were the Indians listening with the deepest attention to the reading, and now and then repeating to each other in a low tone some word that was better understood than the rest.

The Pirate, although he could not read, knew many of the lines by heart, and made an admirable clerk, although I much doubt whether his knowledge was more than that of a parrot. Our friend lived on the Cako River, and together with the rest of his party was on his way down the Mazaruni to sell birds and hammocks. Thinking that on our arrival at the Cako the assistance of these men in obtaining woodskins might be valuable, we easily induced them by the promise of food and a few knives, &c., to retrace their footsteps, and aid us in carrying our quakes.

When we started next morning it was still raining, but the ludicrous appearance of the Pirate made us forget all discomfort. On his head, shoulders, back, and perched all over his quake were a number of parrots; we saw nothing of the man but his legs, he was literally clothed with parrots. These birds were not in the least alarmed at the brown-skinned Indians, but whenever McTurk or myself approached they uttered their harsh cries, and whilst some in terror ran their claws deep into the poor man's flesh, others fluttered off into the bush and caused much loss of time before being recaptured.

Our path differed but little from that of the preceding day; we hardly ever touched the ground, but limped painfully over the matted roots. We continually crossed small streams and creeks, whose water ran fresh and sparkling over the stony beds, except when we were hot and thirsty, and then it generally lay in tepid, stagnant pools among the rocky basins. These Indian paths are not always easy to follow, so little do they vary in appearance from the surrounding bush. The original picking out of such a path must have been of considerable difficulty, as in the dense forest there are few landmarks to steer by, nothing in fact but the sun. A track once made, however, even by a single Indian, is easily recognized by the sharp-eyed natives, to whom a broken twig, or a scratched root, tells the story of a previous traveller. So exactly do they follow the narrow trail—always in single file—that often for miles the very footsteps of the explorer are trodden by his successors. I think paiworie has much to do with the generally true direction of these paths, as if you were to place a trough of that liquor on one side of a trackless forest twenty miles in breadth, and an Indian on the other, the two would meet in a very short space of time.

The vegetation which surrounded us was not of a very interesting nature, as the soil was often poor and stony, and frequently covered with a carpet of selaginella or other lycopods. A pretty little dark blue and white gloxinia was very abundant, and in swampy places grew yellow lilies and various cannas. The dakama trees strewed the ground in every direction with their brown nuts, of the size of an orange, and having a pink and white core. These are uneatable, and it was only occasionally that we found the delicious Souari nuts, whose finely grained kernel rivals the most delicate almond. Besides the buttressed forms of the bombaceæ, there were strange-looking trees whose trunks were made up of a number of thick stems joined together at a height of ten or twelve feet from the ground. One that I measured had eight separate supports, and above where they united the trunk had a circumference of over twenty-five feet. We saw no game birds, although we sometimes heard the drumming of a "pani"—curasson—or the shrill notes of a mâam. In addition to the tolling of the bell-birds, we frequently recognized the harsh peacock cry of the "cock of the rocks"—Pipra rupicola—and near one of their dancing places we shot three specimens. The colour of the Guiana species in the male differs from that of Ecuador and Peru in being much lighter; instead of crimson it is a splendid orange on the body, and the wing feathers are brown instead of black and silver grey. The short square tail is ringed with reddish yellow, and the orange crescent-shaped feathers placed on the head like a cocked hat are edged with black.

In Australia the bower-birds—Chlamydoderæ—build their galleries and cabins, and in New Guinea the gardener-bird[80] not only builds a house but also arranges pleasure-grounds around it, and here in Guiana the "cock of the rocks" has his dancing place. The spot chosen is a mossy level, which is cleared of stones and sticks, and surrounded by low bushes. The assembled birds form a circle, and presently an old cock walks into the ring and with spreading tail performs a series of steps, which from the Indian account of them must vary from those of a stately minuet to those of the "Perfect Cure." When he is tired, he receives the applause of the hen-birds and retires, another taking his place. Some of their upward leaps are said to be astonishing, and are repeated in rapid succession until the bird is exhausted. It is during these antics that the natives shoot them or capture them alive, as so absorbed are both the spectators and the performers that they pay no attention to the stealthy approach of the Indian. In captivity these delicate birds soon languish, and out of two that I sent home from Georgetown, one died on the passage, and the other only lived about a month in spite of great care and attention. The dancing grounds of the "cocks of the rock" are unadorned with flowers, fruit or shells; as long as they are smooth and free from stones, the birds are satisfied and apparently believe that their own bright plumage is a sufficient ornamentation, and that they can afford to turn their attention to the study of graceful accomplishments. Also among the birds of Paradise, the beautiful plumaged species do not construct bowers or gardens, a gift which is possessed only by their more intellectual but less ornamental brethren.

We camped after our second day's tramp near a stream called the Lamung, and at once sent back to the old camp a sufficient number of men to bring on the remaining quakes the following day. The good temper and cheerfulness with which all the carriers, and especially the new contingent, performed their double journeys was really remarkable; and, though these forest journeys were to most a natural part of their lives, yet we could not help feeling sorry for the great but unavoidable labour. We remained in camp all next day, but sent forward a number of quakes, the carriers returning, so that the entire number might be ready to depart with all the remaining baggage when we again set out. Besides the palm-leaf covering of each individual quake, those that were sent forward or left behind were ranged by the side of the path on poles, and well protected from the weather by broad leaves and branches. Naturally they formed very conspicuous objects, and though they must continually have been noticed by several parties of Indians that passed on their way to the Curipung River, yet nothing was ever touched or in any way disturbed.

In one of our rambles around the camp we killed a beautifully marked boa-constrictor, about nine feet in length and very thick. Another disagreeable visitor we had was an enormous hairy monkey-spider (araña monos) six inches long and with two formidable nippers like a bird's talons. On touching it with a stick it threw itself back into a fighting attitude, clashed its nippers and twined its long legs about the wood in its efforts to break it. We saw no wild beasts, but the Indians reported having seen a large tiger,[81] which walked slowly along the path in front of them, close to the camp, and disappeared in the bushes. One of them had a gun, but he was too frightened to fire.

A circumstance, trivial in itself, here very nearly put an end to my journey. Charlie, whose zeal had outrun his discretion, in drying my boots had placed them so near the fire that they were roasted; consequently when I put them on the following morning, they literally came to pieces in my hands, and during the day the heel of one of them dropped off. As I knew that without them it would be impossible for me to reach Roraima, for with our limited luggage one pair of thin canvas shoes was all I had besides, my future occupation whenever we arrived at our camping ground was that of a cobbler. McTurk and Charlie first of all cunningly re-attached the heel, and ever afterwards I managed by the aid of string and bush-rope to keep the different parts together. So carefully did I nurse and mend them, that they actually brought me back to Macrebah, which was as far as necessary, but the anxiety caused by so simple an accident can hardly be imagined.

During that day we shot a pani, for which we were duly thankful, as good fresh meat had of late been very scarce. Game was not plentiful, and as McTurk was extremely anxious to complete the expedition as quickly as possible—as the men were paid by the day—we wasted but little time in looking for it. In many parts the bush growth was ill adapted for game of any sort, and in the likely places, though we heard panis and duraquaras, yet we could not get a shot at them. Seldom had the truth of the old proverb "a bird in the hand, &c.," been more forcibly presented to us.

We passed through one very pretty silvan scene, where the path came out on to an open mossy glade surrounded by a perfect circle of grand old trees, whose grey buttressed trunks contrasted vividly with the green-robed stems of the slender plants in the background. In other lands it might have been a temple grove dedicated to the old Druid worship, and Hellenic belief would have peopled it with Dryads and Oreads, but to the Indian mind no dancing fay or wood-nymph would step from the opening trees, and only the terrible Didi could inhabit the mysterious circle. Soon afterwards we crossed the Stenaparu River, and then commenced a very steep ascent, which we climbed by the aid of rocks and roots.

When we reached the summit we were at an elevation of 2,600 feet above the sea, and the forest plateau extended for miles before us. The fatiguing ascent had made us very thirsty, and from passing Indians we heard that we should not find water for a long time. The sight of several "swizzle-stick" trees added to our thirst, and recalled the iced pepper-punches and cooling drinks of Georgetown. At length, after passing a branch path on our right which led to Camarang, on the Upper Mazaruni, we arrived at the brink of a great precipice. At first it was difficult to imagine how we were to descend, but by following a zig-zag trail, and aided by bushes and stony juttings, we gained a ravine about 700 feet below, through which flowed a delicious stream. From here the path ran along the mountain side, and though we should have been glad to halt, the absence of water prevented our doing so. At length we saw a few Manicole palms, a sure sign of the vicinity of water, and in a few minutes we found a small rivulet, where we erected our house.

The night was wet and stormy, and when we started next morning in the rain, one of the Indians who was lame and feverish had to be left behind, with the understanding that he was to overtake us with the rest of the party, who had gone back for the extra quakes. On this day the path gave signs of being almost untravelled, and in many places we had to search diligently before we could pick up the lost thread. By continually bending a twig here and slashing a branch there, we left sure indications of our line of travel for those who were behind, but in order that all should overtake us, we shortened our arduous day's march over hill and creek, and camped near a stream called Cariapu, *i.e.*, mora. From the father of an Indian family encamped near, we found that we had followed an unused trail, but that by retracing our steps for a short distance we should be able with his assistance to strike the new path, which would bring us to the Mazaruni by the middle of the next day. Our party was now at three different points, but as our new friends had of course established themselves beside us, we formed a small though very picturesque camp, under the fine moras from which the stream took its name.

As the rain never ceased to pour, one of the men thought he would improve the occasion by setting fire to a gigantic mora, whose trunk was hollow throughout. From the inclination of the tree, we thought that in the event of its falling the direction would be away from the camp. Still, as it looked dangerous, McTurk gave orders that the fire which, apparently, grew less and less, should not be relighted, and after our usual game of euchre we stretched ourselves in our hammocks quite ready for a good night's rest. Before midnight there was a cry that the tree was falling, and springing up we found that the draught had so fanned the flames that the entire tree was ablaze, sheets of fire and smoke rushing from all the apertures, and from the very summit. It was a magnificent sight, but from that moment sleep was banished, as had the mora fallen towards us, we should inevitably have been crushed. As the rain fell in torrents we could not change our shelter, so we had to pass the rest of the night staring at the burning tree, and ready at a moment's notice to rush to a place of safety.

Dawn found us still watching, but the mora had not fallen, and as far as we know never did fall; still it had caused us to pass a very uncomfortable night. When we departed the rain ceased, but the dripping bushes supplied us with abundant moisture, and we soon forgot that the storm was over. The new path was but little better than the old one, and was very intricate, now crossing swamps, or running over steep hills, and now making us wade through creeks, or traverse a slippery bog for fifty or sixty yards.

Snakes were plentiful, but two duraquaras were the only birds we obtained. Owing to our anxiety to reach the big river, this last day's journey, although the shortest, seemed longer than any previous one, but at length we arrived at a dry creek called the Asimaparu, and after following its muddy bed for a short time we again found ourselves on the banks of the Mazaruni. We had left it flowing east, at an elevation of less than 200 feet above the sea; here it was flowing north, at an elevation of 1,300 feet. On the high bank we made a clearing, cut down the trees that intercepted our view of the river, and built the usual shed. Before night the Pirate, Lanceman, Mazaruni, and the rest of the Indians had all arrived with the baggage, and the tired party enjoyed a well-earned rest.

The next day our original crew, with the exception of the six best men, set off on their return journey to Macrebah on their way home, accompanied by the other Indians, with the exception of Lanceman, Mazaruni, and two Arecunas, who remained with us. In order to send news of our progress to our friends at Georgetown, McTurk loaded an empty cartridge shell with the letter he had written, the novel envelope ensuring its arrival in a clean and dry state, if ever it reached its destination. The Pirate went away in a canoe to obtain woodskins for us from the Indians who live near the mouth of the Cako, from which we were only a few hours distant; but long before he returned our arrival had been discovered by natives whilst passing up and down the river, and we soon received a number of visitors.

When the Pirate returned, he brought with him the chief inhabitant of that part of the river. He called himself Captain David, and having once been to the coast, understood yes and no, wore a shirt and an old black hat, had only two wives, and considered himself a white man. He graciously accepted a cigarette, and after critically examining our baggage promised to send woodskins on the following day to take us to the Cako, from which river we had determined to find our way across country to Roraima. He himself had never been to Roraima, and thought we were insane for wishing to go there, but said that perhaps he might find somebody who could guide us. Owing to the influx of visitors, who as a matter of course established themselves in close proximity to us, our narrow camping limits were inconveniently crowded. But want of space was atoned for by the picturesque scene, which, when darkness fell, was very curious. Our own white-roofed habitation overlooked the silent river, and behind it were slung the twenty red[82] hammocks of the Indians, some under palm-leaf shelters, some covered with broad uranias, and others merely suspended from tree to tree. Here and there little fires were scattered about—as Indians are particularly fond of sleeping close to or over a fire—and from one nook a burning lump of the hyawa[83] resin sent up a fragrant smoke. Through the dark background of trees the fire-beetles flitted, and the occasional nocturnal forest-sounds only rendered the silence more complete. Once a loud rustling overhead brought some of the Indians to their feet, but it was only caused by a species of the harmless lemur, and the camp was soon wrapped in sleep.

CHAPTER XVIII.

AMATEUR BARBERS—AN INDIAN EXQUISITE—MOUTH OF
THE CAKO—CAMP ON VENEZUELAN TERRITORY—
TRUMPETERS—MOUNT CAROUTA—REASON FOR
ASCENDING THE CAKO—MARIMA—INDIAN GUIDE—
GLIMPSE OF RORAIMA—THE ARUPARU CREEK—COTINGAS—
SAVANNA INDIANS—A WATER LABYRINTH—AMUSING
SCENES—END OF NAVIGATION.

As the Captain did not arrive at the appointed time with the woodskins, we amused ourselves with some amateur hair-cutting, which so delighted the natives that many of them insisted on being shorn of their long black tresses. These they carefully gathered, and after wrapping them in leaves buried in some retired part of the forest, so that no Kanaima should get hold of them and exercise his incantations to the destruction of their late owner. Here we discovered that Mazaruni, who was extremely plain, was excessively conceited, and was never tired of gazing at himself in a small hand-glass, and arranging the straw ornaments in his nose and ears in what he considered the most becoming fashion. Whenever a woodskin appeared in which there were any ladies, he would immediately retire to his hammock and change his dress, *i.e.*, take out the old straws and insert new ones, carefully placing them at the proper angle. Then with a few fresh touches of blue and vermillion he brightened himself up, and felt that he was a dandy of the first water. By the time the barber's duties were completed the Captain arrived with his woodskins, which were quickly loaded, and we proceeded up the river.

Stepping into a woodskin for the first time is a delicate undertaking. If the foot is placed on one side a capsize ensues, and in the exact centre the bark bends so that the feeling is that you are trusting yourself to a sheet of brown paper. The only safety is in stepping in lightly and quickly, and at once sitting down in the bottom of the boat, breathing only when you are perfectly balanced in the middle of it. A little practice, however, soon gives confidence, and you are able to use your gun as well as in an ordinary-sized craft. The paddlers sit one at each end, the man in the bows having to keep a sharp look out for rocks or snags, which would pierce or upset the frail shell in a moment.

In about three hours we reached the mouth of the Cako, and looking up that river saw in the distance a fine table-mountain called Carotipu. We found the Cako to be a fine river, about one hundred yards in width, and with moderately high banks. We ascended a short distance, and then camped on the left bank—the Venezuelan[84] side—in order to be free from several Indian parties who had erected their "banaboos" on the opposite shore. But our precaution was of no avail, as when we were comfortably settled and had cleared the bush around, over came the Indians and quietly established themselves in our midst. One or two of the women had pleasing countenances, but their striped and too sturdy limbs and sack-like forms entirely destroyed the first impression of feminine beauty. I think it was Alphonse Karr who said, "La nature a fait la femelle, et la civilization a fait la femme!"

Most of the men were powerfully made, but their painted and unintelligent faces were not improved by the black pellets which, according to custom, they all held between their lips. This vegetable pellet—I do not know what it is composed of—is the Indian substitute for the betel-nut of the Malays, the cocoa-leaf of the South Americans, the opium of the Chinese, the tobacco of Europeans, and in outward appearance is not an improvement on any of them. When the natives heard that we wished to buy provisions, they brought us all they could, but it only amounted to a small quantity of cassava bread, a few pumpkins, and three or four roots of sweet cassava.[85] The latter not being poisonous require no special preparation, and when the roots are roasted they are very palatable. Our next object was to buy some woodskins, as the owner of those that had brought us from the Mazaruni did not wish to part with them. On the day after our arrival five were offered to us, and these we purchased for four small flasks of powder. As ten shillings was not much to give for five boats, we promised the natives that on our return they should receive them back again.

Powder is eagerly sought by the Indians, as many of them have long single-barrel guns—buck-guns they are called in Demerara—that they have obtained in trade, and their opportunities of getting ammunition are exceedingly limited! They are very fond of fire-arms, and our breech-loaders were a never-ending source of wonder to them. Of late, we had heard the most appalling sounds issuing from the forest; sometimes they resembled the bellowing of a cow who had lost her calf, and at others were like the howls of a wild animal. At last one of the perpetrators was shot, and it proved to be a small bird known in Guiana as the "calf bird," which has a bald head and plumage of an olive colour.

McTurk told me that these birds are common on the Pomeroon River, and that once a newly arrived Englishman, who had been out shooting one day, returned in haste to camp, with the intelligence that he had heard such a terrific bellowing and roaring that he was certain a band of tigers were fighting with some other animals. McTurk and others hastened to the scene, and shot three calf-birds. Considering that it comes from a bird, the noise is certainly the most astounding I have ever listened to. We shot some trumpeter[86] birds, which also make a very peculiar sound. They live in flocks, run swiftly over the ground, and look like a number of diminutive ostriches.

They are graceful creatures, with long velvety necks, beautiful blue and purple breast-feathers, and back and wings of a silver grey. The Indians call them Waracabas, from a fanciful resemblance in their notes to the cry of the Waracaba tigers, which hunt in packs.

Having spent nearly two days in camp, with the vain hope of securing a guide to Roraima, we determined to start early on the following morning. The natives promised to bring more cassava on the morrow if we could only wait another day, but with an Indian the morrow is as indefinite a period as "mañana" with the Spaniards, or "bookra" with the Arabs. The five woodskins—the two largest each containing three persons, and the smaller, two—were loaded down to the water's edge when we set out, but we soon reached Captain David's house, and there we left the three quakes of provisions for our return journey. The course of the river was pretty and very winding, continually opening out fresh views of distant mountains. We rounded the northern extremity of Mount Carouta which was thickly wooded, except under its high central dome, where the precipitous rock was quite bare. Nearly all the mountains that we had hitherto seen, were extremely precipitous on the northern and eastern faces, but on the western side there were generally patches of heavy forest even where, to the eye, it looked most perpendicular. We hoped that Roraima would present the same forest growth, and by ascending the Cako River we thought we might arrive opposite the western slope of the mountain.

We knew little about the course of the river, as no information could be obtained from the Indians, and we were probably the first white men who had ever ascended it. As it was probable that the river rose in the mountain range near Roraima, we intended to follow it as far as we could, and then strike off across country. From what Captain David told us, we were much afraid that owing to the scant population along the river banks we should be unable to find a guide. Still we determined to push on, and in the event of failure, to return to the mouth of the Cako and make another attempt to reach Roraima by the Cukuie River.

After passing Carouta, we saw in our front the flat-topped mountain of Ibropu, and soon after we camped on the right bank of the river, opposite a path leading to Camarang, on the Mazaruni. We erected our shed on a high jutting promontory above a white sand beach, and after unloading the woodskins carried the quakes up the bank. It was fortunate we did not leave them below, as in the morning there was no sand to be seen; the river had risen, and the beach was covered to a depth of three or four feet. As we approached Ibropu, we caught sight of a fine waterfall that descended from its eastern slope, and the stream which it formed entered the Cako near a very pretty island. Here, two fine Muscovy[87] ducks flew over our heads, and, as they ran the gauntlet, each boat in succession greeted them with a volley, but unsuccessfully. Shortly afterwards, I discovered five more swimming near the shore, and by dint of quiet paddling and taking advantage of a bushy point we crept within range, and with two barrels I bagged four of them. They were very large and heavy birds, differing from the tame Muscovy only in having less coral about the bill. They are difficult to approach, and though we frequently saw them alight on the high trees, and from afar distinguished them by their white wing-coverts, yet by the end of the day we had only obtained six. It is said that these ducks build their nests on lofty trees, and, when the young ones are sufficiently grown, the parents carry them down to the swamps to educate them. Those we shot were uncommonly tough, but duck and pumpkin were such rare delicacies that, had the former been of cast-iron, I think we should have enjoyed them.

We passed along the east side of Ibropu, then the ever-winding river turned south, and we saw a high table-mountain which we fancied must be Roraima, but the view was only for a moment, and then a veil of clouds concealed it. Afterwards we found out that the mountain we had seen was Marima, which is situated to the north-east of Roraima. We paddled along fine stretches of river, here getting a snipe, there a duck, and sometimes a curri-curri, and at last camped on the left bank. Before it was dark we heard the sound of a horn blown lustily from the river, and soon a woodskin appeared containing a man, woman, and child. It turned out that they lived near Roraima, and having heard from Captain David that we wanted a guide had hastened after us. The man's name was Abraham, which was about the only common biblical name that we had not encountered among our various crews at some time or other. He declined to camp with us, but preferred going farther on, as he said that close by was the cave of a celebrated "water-māmā," near whom it was dangerous to sleep.

The Indians firmly believe in the reality of these mermaids, or "water-māmās," as they are called in Dutch Creole; and where they are supposed to have their caves or nests, there great danger awaits the traveller. Some are related to be extremely beautiful and possessing long golden hair—like the Lorelei—and whoever casts his eye on them is seized with madness, jumps into the deep water, and never returns. Others are hideous, snakes being twined about them, and with their long white talons they drag boats under the water and devour their occupants. On the Orinoco and Amazon similar creatures are supposed to exist, but these are capable of drawing their prey into their mouths at a distance of a hundred yards. In order to avoid such a calamity, the natives always blow a horn before entering a creek or lagoon in which one of these monsters may be living; if it happens to be there, it will immediately answer the horn and thus give warning to the intruder.

When we awoke in the morning it seemed as if the "water-māmā" had indeed bewitched us. The river, which on the previous night flowed quietly beneath the bank on which we were encamped, had disappeared. The woodskins were high and dry on a ledge of rocks that extended for some distance up and down the bed of the stream. There, on the other side of the rocky plateau we discovered the lost river, which had fallen three feet during the night, and had lost nearly the same volume of water that it had gained after the recent rains. About a mile farther on we found Abraham waiting anxiously for us, and glad that we had survived the perils of the night. On this day we caught some beautiful views of Roraima whenever the clouds lifted, and towards noon we left the Cako and turned into a broad creek on its right bank called the Aruparu. By so doing we feared—as eventually proved to be the case— that we should not reach Roraima from its western flank, but as our guide assured us that it was the only way he knew of, we thought it best to follow his advice.

The creek scenery was pretty, but monotonous; the clay banks were clothed with thick bush, with here and there masses of yellow blossoms and the pink tassels of the Brownea. There were also many shrubs known as the "witê," whose long velvet pods contain beans covered with a very sweet but insipid pulp. A drawback in picking them was that every pull brought down showers of stinging ants, which, as well as parrots, are very fond of that fruit. Sometimes we passed an Indian banaboo that had lately been occupied, and at others the new jungle growth showed where a small village had once existed. At the mouths of the smaller streams, which flowed into the creek, there was generally a barricade of sticks and poles made by the natives for securing fish, but most of the streams were dry and the barricades of ancient date. In the mud and sand were endless tracks of tapirs and the "water-haas"—capybara—and occasionally a splash and rustle told where we had disturbed one of the latter, but we were seldom near enough for a shot.

Ducklars were very numerous, and as we turned each corner, there they would be sitting in rows on the branches of fallen trees awaiting our approach; then a dive and an ungainly flutter to start them, and away they would go to the next bend in the river. But after the Muscovy ducks the men looked with disdain on the fishy ducklar, and those that were shot that day remained uneaten. On many subsequent occasions they looked back with regret on the despised and wasted ducklars. Now and then we heard the "kwet-kwet" of the beautiful scarlet cotinga, and once the brilliant but harsh-voiced pompadour[88] flew across in front of us. Not seldom the narrowing stream was over-arched by the bending trees, and under their dark shadows the splendid blue morphos and still more lovely butterflies of a sparkling violet hue floated lazily. At one place where the forest seemed clearer we ascended the bank, and were gratified by the sight of a savanna, which with a diversity of wood and hill stretched off to some distant mountains.

Owing to the muddy nature of the banks and the thick bush, it was late that night before we could find a camping ground, but at last we came to a spot where some Indians had already erected their sheds. They were wild-looking creatures, hideously painted and stained, and the hair of the men was longer than that of the women. They were stalwart and tall, and had come from their homes in the savanna country to this fashionable watering-place for fishing and bathing. They shook their heads and groaned when they heard that we were going to Roraima, and recommended us to turn back and not act foolishly.

An amusing incident occurred here. Our primitive acquaintances kept us awake for some time with their monotonous sing-song talk, and shortly after I had dropped asleep McTurk awoke me with the intelligence that he was going to have his bath, as day was breaking. I got up at once, as it appeared to be getting light, and we bathed and dressed, and sat in our hammocks waiting coffee. After some time day did not appear to advance much, and to our astonishment we saw the moon slowly rising over the trees. In our anxiety to make an early start we had mistaken moonrise for daybreak, and had got up at about half-past twelve a.m.

Hitherto the creek had been free from all impediments and was deep enough to float large boats, but soon after we left our sleeping quarters the ominous stroke of an axe told us that Abraham was cutting a passage through a fallen tree. For the rest of the day our journey was like going in a canoe through a forest that had been cut down and left. Here, a great tree trunk permitted the passage of the woodskins underneath, but without their loads; there, an enormous limb necessitated the unloading and lifting over of the boats; in some places a sunken log had sufficient water flowing over it to float the woodskins, but only after their contents had been discharged; in others an opening had to be cut through tangled branches and stems. We were never in the boats for five minutes at a time; it was a perpetual jumping in and out, loading and unloading, lifting and hauling, pushing and carrying, cutting and squeezing. Frequently, the arch formed by the overhanging trunk seemed high enough to allow the woodskin and its contents to pass under, but when well in the centre a jam would occur, and we would find ourselves crouching in the bottom of the boat unable to move hand or foot, and water rapidly coming in over the sides. It was most amusing, and I never enjoyed a good laugh at McTurk's expense without immediately finding myself in a similar position. The great strain on the woodskins caused two of them to split, and only by rapidly conducting them to shore did we save them from sinking. By filling the cracks with bark, linen, and paper, they were soon made serviceable again.

The windings of the creek were extraordinary; often after following a southerly direction for a mile or more, we would turn north for the same distance, and come out on the other side of the narrow promontory only a few yards from where we had started. The same thing would be repeated east and west, and the patient stream seemed never tired of twisting itself into a hundred folds and then untwisting.

Just before dark, we arrived at a place past which it would be impossible to proceed, and Abraham informed us that we had reached the end of the creek journey. So we landed and built our house.

CHAPTER XIX.

OLD GRANNY'S DESCRIPTION OF THE PATH TO RORAIMA—
TREE-BRIDGES—MONKEY-POTS—BUSH-ROPES—CASHEW
COTTAGE—SAVANNA INDIANS—MAZARUNI—MAGNIFICENT
PALMS—BIXA ORELLANA—COTENGA RIVER—FALLS OF
OOKOOTAWIK—VILLAGE OF MENAPARUTI—MARIKA
RIVER—THE SORCERER AGAIN.

About half a mile higher up the creek lived Abraham's mother, and there we intended to leave sufficient provisions for our return journey and whatever articles we could not carry with us.

Our first care on the day following our arrival was to hide the woodskins in the forest, so that they should not be appropriated by any passing Indians. Then we followed a trail through the bush which brought us to the hut. A very old lady with long white hair received us, and began to moan and beat her breast wildly. We asked what she was doing, and discovered that she was relating the difficulties of the path to Roraima. Over level country she travelled smoothly and in low tones, but when she came to the mountains that had to be crossed, then her voice rose, she shrunk to the ground, raised herself on tip-toes, waved her arms, struck her chest, uttered strange cries, and the higher and steeper the mountain the louder and shriller became her screams.

Already our superstitious carriers had lent too ready an ear to the terrors of Roraima as depicted by the son, and now the mother seemed disposed to add her store of legends and tales of witchcraft for general information. We therefore arranged our quakes as quickly as possible, rethatched her crazy shed so as to preserve from the weather the numerous articles we deposited on fresh rafters and were ready to start. Before we left she made the entire party blow three times on her back for good luck, but whether the luck was for her or for us we never found out. It was an odd farewell, but as it pleased old granny—as we called her—we were content.

Our path did not differ much from that of our previous foot-journey, but the creeks and streams were more numerous and the crossings often extremely difficult. Our bare-footed and trained carriers walked easily enough over the narrowest logs, but for us, with boots and weighed down with gun, bag and cartridges, it was different. Generally the water was too deep to wade through, and the only way of crossing was by means of a slippery trunk as narrow as a tight-rope, and many feet above the stream. Sometimes when the slender bridge was suspended at an angle, the crossing was more dangerous than amusing, as a fall would probably have been on to the sharp snags and branches that threw their points out of the deep pools underneath. As in our former walk, the ground was covered with dark blue gloxinias and a pretty creeping plant whose glossy leaves were delicately veined with pink; near the streams grew cannas and thick masses of the umberilla grass[89] varied with soft-textured marantas. Palms were more plentiful than before, and we saw varieties that we had not previously met with. We saw also the curious "monkey-pot" tree[90] with its strange bowl-shaped fruit and wooden covers. Purple-heart and the crab-oil tree[91] were not uncommon and strange nuts constantly fell around us.

Many of the bush-rope forms were very curious, differing in size and shape from a boot-lace to a ship's cable. Here, like the strangling serpents of Laocoon, they hold a great tree in their huge folds, and there a delicate vine had formed a complete network around some forest giant until it was as helpless as a fly in a spider's web. Very terrible are these lace-like parasites which cling at first in their helplessness to some lordly trunk and then slowly extend their treacherous embrace until their support is shut up in a living grave. The poor tree dies, and its destroyers live and thrive on the dead body of their benefactor. Few flowers relieve the monotony of these dark forests, and it is strange that here, where birds have such brilliant plumage, flowers should be almost unnoticeable. Nor do they atone by perfume for their want of colour, as with the exception of a faint breath of vanilla, or of the fragrant blossoms of a lecythes, no odour of flowers greets the senses.

The forest was not dull, as besides the tolling bell-birds, numerous kites and hawks added their harsh cries; nearer at hand little humming-birds were perpetually lisping "tweek-tweek" or a gay fire-bird calling out "quark."

Once we heard a flute-bird,[92] whose mellow ventriloquial notes were of wonderful sweetness, and as they floated around the sound was that of an Æolian harp struck by the wind on the tree tops. The exquisite tone reminded me of the "Siffleur montagne," which I once heard singing in the woods of Martinique. But in the forest all birds' sounds are pleasing, and even the harsh-throated parrots and macaws are pleasant to listen to. What does the bell-bird say when he tolls out "quiâ-ting" or the pompadour cotinga when he screams "wallababa" or the duraquara when he greets the dawn with his own name? Something surely, and though we cannot understand it, it is clear to the initiated. Those two parrots holding such confidential intercourse must understand one another, and that touching monologue of the flute-bird cannot be uttered in vain! Forest music must be, like Tzigane music, without laws and dogmas, and though subtle and mystic, yet distinct and easily comprehended by those who utter it.

After some hours of steady walking, during which we had been gradually ascending, we arrived at a small clearing in the centre of which stood a circular house, thatched and wattled. A fine cashew tree shadowed it, and in a twinkling we were enjoying the refreshing fruit which an agile Indian who had climbed up, shook down for us. Cashew Cottage was unoccupied, the family being in town or at some watering place, or more probably "on the walk." Abraham conducted us to a point which was a little way off the path, but from which we obtained a fine mountain view.

We were facing the west, and close in our front ran the Marima[93] range, sloping and forest-clad for the greater part, but towards its southern extremity was an enormous square pile of sheer rock without even a shrub on its smooth sides. Behind this and in the far blue distance another perpendicular wall of rock was just visible; this was the northern end of Roraima. Stretching far away to the north were other mountains, the most conspicuous of which were the dome-shaped Serāpi and the flat-topped Ilotipu. As far as the eye could reach the violet tinted ranges rose one above the other, and threading its way between them we could trace the course of the Cako River. As usual Roraima only showed itself for a moment, for the white clouds fell slowly down and hid its sharp profile. Then we resumed our journey, whose direction was now towards the south-eastern end of Marima.

From Cashew Cottage two paths branched off into the forest. Abraham chose the one to the right, and in about four hours we emerged on to a high savanna plateau. In the centre of it were two conical huts, old and deserted. Close to them lay several large troughs hollowed out of tree trunks, but whether they had originally been intended for canoes or to hold paiworie we could not determine. Not far from here we built our shelter, as Abraham said that a stream ran through the forest below us. When we sought it we found it was dry, but as McTurk was unwell and feverish, owing to the numerous cuts, bruises, and sores gained during our hard tramps, we thought it better to remain where we were and send back for water to the nearest brook.

From the savanna we had a fine view all round. On one side were the Marima mountains, and a picturesque fall which proved to be the head waters of the Aruparu; and on the other, from the foot of a steep precipice, a broad valley bounded by wooded hills extended far away to the east in one unbroken surface of foliage.

In the evening a party of Indians arrived. They were on their way to the Mazaruni, but some of them agreed to accompany us, and others said that if we waited for a day they would bring us some cassava from their home in the forest. We therefore promised to wait, and early next morning despatched three men to bring some more quakes of flour from old Granny's house. Like other Indians we had met and questioned, these people beat their breasts and uttered various cries when they told us of the mountains to be crossed, and added their testimony to the spirits of Roraima. Besides cassava, they brought us some cobs of Indian corn and green plantains, which we paid for in small silver coins, as they said if ever they went to the coast they should require money. They were an inquisitive set, and our clothes and shoes astonished them beyond measure. I admit that at that time my boots certainly were curiosities. When we went to perform our ablutions in the rain water that the troughs held, we were always followed by a squad of sight-seers who had never seen soap or sponges, and who stood at a distance and laughed.

At this period Mazaruni was in his glory, for besides Sarah—Abraham's wife—three more women were added to our party by the arrival of the new comers, and as they carried burdens as well as the men, he was always on hand to assist them in any difficult places. And the difficulties were many, for we found that the hardest part of our journey was before us. Directly after leaving camp the path descended through the forest, over the usual terrible but unavoidable roots, and in the course of time we arrived at the Owtaro River, which we crossed just above a splendid set of falls that were precipitated over a rocky wall, between two hundred and three hundred feet in depth, into the valley below.

Soon afterwards we reached the foot of the Opuima Mountain,[94] and commenced an ascent which fully accounted for the breast-beating and wild outcries of the natives. By root-ladders and with the aid of trees, which were themselves clinging with difficulty to the precipitous side, we slowly wended our way to the top. The ascent seemed interminable, and from sheer exhaustion I was frequently on the point of throwing away my gun and cartridges. At length the struggle was over, and we sat down on the summit to await the arrival of the plucky carriers. I should not have been at all surprised if none of them had reached the top, as I am certain that with the same weight they carried I should have been totally unable to make the ascent. But they all arrived safely, not quite so light-hearted as when they started, but ready to proceed after a short rest. In many places the ground seemed covered with snow, from the whiteness of a pretty lichen[95] which was specked here and there with a yellow flower growing from the end of a long stalk.

On the hill slopes were many magnificent palms, one species of which was finer even than the royal palm. The shapely stems were of great height, and the beautiful fronds were over twenty feet in length. McTurk had never seen the species before, but probably it is the Ceroxylon Andicola, which is found high up on the Andes. Scattered about at their feet were delicate ferns whose tiny pinnules quivered at the least breath, whilst the huge fronds above them were unmoved by the passing breeze. It was a rare treat to behold these two singularly contrasting examples of the most exquisite grace and beauty known in the botanical kingdom. Here were also shrubs of the Bixa orellana, whose seeds furnish the "arnotto" paint so much used by the Indians.

At length we came to the Cotinga River, or, as the natives call it, the Quiâ-ting. It is curious that both the English and Indian name of this river should have reference to the bell-bird, although it is common in the locality. Here the stream is deep and about thirty-five yards broad, and a canoe which we fortunately discovered took us over in relays. On the opposite side was an unoccupied shed and a provision ground, which gave evidence that the desertion of the house was only temporary. Here were some blocks of red jasper of a very smooth and delicate grain.

On re-entering the forest, our path ran parallel to the river, but at some distance from it. Presently a bend in the river brought us to the side of a very pretty fall, where the water swept over a long and deep dyke, whose stones were as smooth and regular as if chiselled by hand. The name of the fall was Ookootawik, and there we intended to camp, but Abraham assured us that a large village was very near. So on we went, terribly fagged and tired, and at last reached a scene of desolation. In North America a similar scene would be called a "windrow," for the appearance was that of a forest overturned by a whirlwind or tempest. Tree lay piled on tree, the roots of one interlaced with the branches of another; there were ladders of trunks stepping up and up, and topped by the gnarled branches of some great tree, which seemed to have been whirled down from a height and to have lodged there. Many were black and charred, and others snow-white and barkless, throwing up their scraggy arms like skeletons. Of course all signs of a path had vanished, and over this forest wreck we had to scramble and pick our way, trusting to the horn of Abraham for the right direction.

Horn-blowing was a very useful accomplishment of our guide, as it kept us straight and frightened away the various evil spirits, from a water-māmā to a wood-demon.

Another stretch of forest and then we came out on to a savanna, across which we saw the dome of Waëtipu—the sun mountain. Four hours after Abraham had told us the great village was close at hand we arrived there. The first house that we came to belonged to the head of the village; he seemed highly delighted to see us, said his name was Captain Sam, that he had been to Georgetown, that his house and everything in it was at our disposal, but that we would be more comfortable in the stranger's house, which was on the other side of the savanna. Thither we hastened, and found a very large, lofty, and well built open shed, and we were soon more comfortably housed than we had been since our departure. Around us were a few more houses, but they all had wattled walls, and none looked so cool and clean as ours. Close by, at the foot of a sugar-loaf hill, flowed the Quáting, and never was bath more enjoyed than ours that night in its cool, clear water. The name of the village was Menaparuti, and numbered probably about fifty souls.

Next morning we only waited long enough to buy some cassava, and then started off again. On clear days Roraima is in view from the village, but the morning was wet, and clouds covered all the mountains. We commenced with a short but very steep ascent, and after following a wretched path came to a mountain called Marikamura. Then we had a climb which, in length, far surpassed that of the previous day; the rocky steps were steeper, the root-ladders longer, the trunks which here and there formed the path more slippery, and the ascent altogether more fatiguing. About half way up we met an unpleasant-looking Indian who informed us that he was a great "peaiman," and the spirit which he possessed ordered us not to go to Roraima. The mountain, he said, was guarded by an enormous "camoodi," which could entwine a hundred people in its folds. He himself had once approached its den, and had seen demons running about as numerous as quails. We asked him if they would be good broiled on toast, and though he did not understand, he made an angry gesture and soon disappeared. The tale of this monster carried us back to old classical days, when the famous python hindered the march of Regulus.

From the summit we descended a considerable distance, and at length camped on the right bank of the Marika River. This was a pretty stream, the water foaming here among great boulders, and there flowing dark and smoothly over slabs of stone. The high banks were clothed with helianthus and cannas, and some beautiful ferns threw a green mantle of the most delicate point-lace over the moist earth. Away from the streams the soil was stony and poor, and the trees, instead of taking root, balanced themselves by great buttresses and numerous stilted stems of the most fantastic forms.

In the course of the day we had crossed many little savannas, strewn with small hard pebbles, which so hurt the feet of our Indians that most of them were compelled to make and wear bark sandals. On these savannas grew a very peculiar grass which bore a strong resemblance to miniature mops, as from the top of each stem fell a thick crop of hairy fibres. There was also a very pretty flowering grass, like a half-opened snowdrop, with its white outer petals extended to a long pale green point.

A wet evening made us retire early to our hammocks, and soon after, a few shrill cries were heard issuing from the forest, and presently with hair streaming wildly and shaking a rattle, the old sorcerer, whom we had met on the mountain, passed hurriedly along the path towards Roraima. He looked neither to the right nor left, and quickly disappeared in the gloom. Then Abraham once more dilated on rock spirits and sorcery to the timorous Indians, and the night passed slowly away in storm and rain.

CHAPTER XX.

SAVANNA—RORAIMA AT LAST—APPEARANCE OF THE
MOUNTAIN—WATERFALLS—HEAD OF THE QUATING—
TRIBUTARIES OF THE AMAZON AND THE ESSEQUIBO—
KUKENAM—ITS FALL AND RIVER—THE "PEAIMAN" AGAIN—
FALLS OF EKIBIAPU—A CELEBRATION.

The sun was fiercely bright when, after an early start from our camp on the Marika, our straggling party issued one by one from the dark, shady forest on to an open savanna. A glad shout from the foremost announced that our goal was in sight. Hastening up an intercepting hill we looked down on an undulating savanna country, streaked here and there with forest belts. On our right towards the north were the craggy heights of Marima; on our left, beyond the terraced side of Waëtipu, the table-land faded away in the silver-blue mountains of Brazil; and in front of us, at the distance of a few miles, "walled round with rocks as an inland island," stood Roraima.[96]

At the foot of the mountain the hilly ground lay in patches of yellow stony savanna, and dark strips of woodland rising in elevation as they approached its base. Then came a deep forest-clad ravine whose farther side sloped steeply up to a distance of about three thousand feet, and springing directly out of this sea of green rose a perpendicular wall of red rock, fifteen hundred feet in height. Hardly a shrub broke the sheer descent of the shining cliff; scarcely a line of verdure marked where clinging grasses had gained a footing on its smooth face. The south-eastern corner was slightly rounded, and its tower-like appearance increased its general resemblance to a Titanic fortification a few miles in length, rising from a forest glacis.

The glancing rays of the sun struck the red sandstone layers which shone like glass, and stood out in bold and bright relief above their green base. A fly could hardly have rested on the slippery slabs, and this was the mountain we had come so far to scale! The level summit-line was backed by forest trees, which to us appeared like bushes, and from their feet, like skeins of floss silk swaying in the wind, three waterfalls descended and were lost in the woods below. But towards the northern end of the mountain, a magnificent cascade, whose lip seemed to be below the summit, sprang in a broad silvery arch right down into the green depths, barely touching the rocky wall in its descent. This is the source of the Cotinga River, or as the Indians call it Quáting-yama, i.e., head of the Quáting. Eventually this river falls into the Amazon after mingling with the Rio Branco and Rio Negro. Still farther north was another fall whose waters formed one of the principal tributaries of the Cako River.

To the north-east of the mountain, and close to it, was a miniature Roraima, and towards its south-western extremity was another mural precipice, apparently just as impregnable. The mountain was Kukenam, and from our position it seemed to be part of Roraima, but afterwards we found that they were separated by a wide and wooded valley. From this mountain, too, a splendid waterfall makes a clear leap of fifteen hundred feet before it disappears in the green wilderness at its base. It issues from the forest as the Kukenam River, and after joining the Yuruarti, which also rises in the Kukenam mountain, forms the Caroni River, which flows into the Orinoco below Ciudad Bolivar. Thus this extraordinary group of mountains becomes the watershed of some of the tributaries of three great rivers, viz.; the Amazon, the Orinoco and the Essequibo. No wonder that the Indians named it "the ever-fruitful mother of streams." No wonder, too, that such a spirit-dreading race should regard the weird and mysterious mountain with an awe which might almost be called reverential, were it not entirely inspired by fear. They believe that the magic circle which encompasses their "red-rocked night mountain," cannot be approached without danger, that he who enters it will never return, and that the demon-guarded sanctuary on the summit will never be gazed on by mortal eyes.

It is impossible to behold these smoothly chiselled mountains without wondering how they have been shaped and moulded by Nature into their present uniformity of feature. It could not have been by fire, as no trace of volcanic action exists in them. Were it possible that the present equatorial regions had passed through a glacial period, one would think that by the polishing and grooving of glaciers alone could the planed and sculptured rocks have attained their massive and perpendicular outlines. But it is supposed that South America, in ages long past, was divided into island groups, indicated as Wallace says, "by the great area and low elevation of the alluvial plains of the Orinoco and Amazon. A subsidence of less than two thousand feet would convert the highlands of Guiana and Brazil into islands separated by a shallow strait from the Andes."

Hence it must be that the action of water has carved the island sides into smooth perpendicular walls. For my own part, the idea would cling to me that in the untold past the surrounding region was a high plateau which by earthquakes and convulsions had been so shattered and broken that nothing was left in its original position save these mountain-monuments that lie scattered over its surface. It is also a matter of no little surprise that in a country of almost perpetual rain and moisture, which usually tend to produce rounded and broken hills and mountains, the predominating features should be the perpendicular cliffs and plateaus of dry and arid climes.

Our first full view of Roraima did not last long, for thick fleecy clouds gradually rolled over its flat top, and then slowly unfolded themselves down the red sides until they rested on the green slopes, presenting the appearance of a carefully spread damask table-cloth. Near where we had halted, we found the "peaiman" looking very disconsolate under the shelter of leaves. For a consideration, he offered to charm away the evil spirits that would beset us, and declared that without his assistance we should be unable to cross the river that we saw below us. Not desiring his society, we declined his aid and continued our walk.

In an hour we reached the river, and crossed it just above some fine falls where it was about forty yards in breadth. The water was not deep, but its red sandstone bed was as slippery as the smoothest ice, so that it required much caution to avoid falling, and being swept over the cataract, which was between forty and fifty feet in height. Where the river was dry, a curious appearance was presented by the sandstone which lay in perfectly even blocks like large red bricks. Abraham said that the name of the river—Eki-biapu—was derived from these singular slabs which are supposed to resemble the stones on which cassava is baked. In the savanna, on the other side of the stream, we erected our shed, a neighbouring grove supplying poles and the necessary fire-wood.

We celebrated our arrival by a grand clothes-washing, Charlie being chief washer-man, whilst I did the ironing by placing the articles between flat-stones and sitting on them. The day was finished by a grand banquet, consisting of rice, "Worcestershire" sauce, and "bakes." In bumpers of sparkling "Eno's Fruit Salt," we drank to the successful issue of our undertaking, and retired soberly to our hammocks for our first night's rest under the shadow of Roraima.

CHAPTER XXI.

CLUSIAS—A MELASTOMA—FOREST TREES—FRESH CAMP—A
FLORAL TREASURY—BRAZILIAN MOUNTAINS—A COLOUR
SYMPHONY—RORAIMA'S EASTERN WALL—NO MEANS OF
ASCENT—GOAT-SUCKERS—SOUTHERN WALL OF RORAIMA—
FALL OF KAMAIBA—KUKENAM FALLS—WESTERN SIDE OF
RORAIMA—REASONS FOR RETURNING HOME—SAVANNA
FIRE—A STORM.

From the ridge above our camp, we saw a long tongue of savanna running up through the forest belt, almost to a level with the base of the mountain wall. To this clear spot we bent our footsteps, taking with us provisions for three days, and leaving all the men except two in camp. To avoid the wooded ravines, we followed the undulating savanna for a long distance in a south-westerly direction. The path was well trodden and distinct, but there were no signs of habitations, and, indeed, the arid appearance of the country gave but little promise of support. The exceptional drought which prevailed in the lowlands of Guiana prevailed also in the mountains, and no water flowed over the beds of many of the rivulets that we were constantly crossing. Wherever streams ran, the hollows and ravines were clothed with a bright green foliage; beautiful ferns grew on the banks, and among them was a grand species, which, in growth, resembled the sago palm. There were clusias too with pure wax-like flowers, and innumerable trees of a species of Melastomacea, whose large white blossoms unfold themselves with a rare tinge of pink which fades as day advances.

In the larger forest belts, the trees were chiefly of the chinchonea[97] and laurus; but their pale flowers were varied with yellow gomphias and crimson befarias. Slender palms and quaint cecropias added their beauty to the woodland edges, and the rough-leafed curatella mingled with the fragile mimosas. Over the savannas large kites hovered, and occasionally small parrots flew from one grove to another; white-throated swallows, of a reddish brown colour, dashed here and there, and a few long-tailed fly-catchers[98] balanced themselves on the thin stems of a rubus whose berries we often found very refreshing. I recognised some old friends, too, in meadow larks,[99] with their pretty black horse-shoe marked throats. But birds were not numerous, with the exception of a little brown species like a linnet which was continually rising from under our feet, and settling again a few yards off. In the wooded dells and ravines were pigeons, and from the thick bush came the unceasing frog-like croaks of the fringed chatterer.

On all parts of the savanna were dotted pyramid-shaped ant-hills, many of which had been freshly torn open by the great ant-eaters.[100] These curious animals as well as the smaller tamanduas are very common in Guiana, though on account of their nocturnal habits they are not often met with in the day time. They are slow clumsy creatures, peaceable and harmless, but formidable when attacked, as their hug is almost as deadly as that of a grisly bear. Their skin will resist the bite of a dog; but the snout is their weak point, as a sharp blow on it from a stick will kill them. When an ant-eater throws itself back and extends its powerful claws, it will seize the first object within reach and hold on to it, so they are often killed by throwing some article into their embrace, and then tapping them on the proboscis. The tongue of the animal is very long and round, and can be lubricated at pleasure from two large glands below the roots; when with its strong claws it has opened an ant-hill, it thrusts in its tongue which sweeps around and is quickly covered with the insects which must, one would think, be swallowed in enormous quantities to afford sustenance for so large a body. The wonderful mechanism of an ant-eater's tongue calls forcibly to mind the extraordinary muscular flexibility of all tongues, from that of a giraffe, or snake, or bird to our own. The tongue is so familiar an organ that we are apt to overlook its varied offices, and its power and motion.

At last we turned off the Indian path, and soon reached a delicious mountain stream which flowed at the foot of the slopes, directly below Roraima. A thick grove on the other side of the rivulet formed a sheltered nook, and as the position seemed an admirable one from which to attempt an ascent, McTurk sent back one of the men with instructions to move camp to the present site. We then continued our climb towards the south-eastern extremity of the mountain. The higher we mounted, the more tedious became the walking, owing to the boulders and débris which lay hidden under the long grass. Sometimes a ravine had to be crossed, or our way pushed through a narrow belt of woodland.

On all sides were flowering shrubs and trees whose blossoms were not only brilliant but extremely fragrant. A more sweet-scented region than that around Roraima cannot be found. Eugenias, aromatic lantanas, ericas, genipas, a species of salvia, gesnerias and many other plants were as abundant on the mountain-savanna as the bignonias and passion-flowers which draped the forests.

After copious rains this district would be a perfect El Dorado for botanists. Even after the drought which had preceded our visit there were still many rare blossoms to be seen, and, though often faded or withering, we could form from them some idea of the floral wealth of Roraima. There were orchids, too, both tree and terrestrial, and of the latter a lovely crimson cleistes[101] bore off the palm. Wherever it was damp panicles of golden oncidiums drooped from the tree branches, but they as well as the odontoglots and epidendrons were dead or dying. One species—a

Stanhopea[102]—seemed to set the dry weather at defiance, and its dark purple cup and bright green petals always looked as fresh as though they had been watered daily.

At length we arrived at a point almost on a level with the perpendicular wall of Roraima, but with a vast forest-clad gulf intervening. It had been evident to us from the first that our best method of proceeding would be to choose from one of these open savanna ridges any point in the straight-cut rock that appeared at all practicable for an ascent, and then by the aid of a compass to make our way direct to that spot across the wooded ravine. We afterwards found that the passage of this deep and precipitous ravine presented difficulties which were second only to those of the wall itself. The north wind swept so keenly over our elevated position that we were glad to seek shelter for a time under one of the great black boulders that lay around.

Our climb had made us thirsty, but we had to content ourselves with the water contained in the sheath bases of the leaves of the wild pines,[103] which grew in great numbers on the surrounding trees. These natural reservoirs contained a good supply of rain-water, but it was very old and full of insects.

Looking back over the country we had traversed, we saw a picturesque landscape of mountain and plain. Far below, the undulating yellow savanna was pierced at intervals by tongues of green forest; beyond, a few silver flashes marked where a stream ran through a narrow valley, and on its left towards the east rose the Sun mountain—Waëtipu—in a series of wooded terraces, and with its southern extremity crowned by a high sugar-loaf. From here, far away to the south, stretched a chain of blue hills with flickering spaces of shadowed sunlight between them, and on the edge of the horizon towered the great table mountains of Brazil, which, like colossal monoliths, contrasted with the peaks and domes of the adjacent ranges in Guiana. The scene was by no means grand but acquired a certain charm from the variety of colour diffused by the western sun. The arid savannas which had seemed so barren and dreary were now tinted with a soft green paling to silver-grey; the purple film of distance, which we knew was only the parched foliage of some forest belt, was streaked with golden lines, and the hard red rock shingle over which we had painfully trudged, gleamed and sparkled like early dew. Colour brightened the landscape, but life was wanting. No bird sang, no hut was visible, no wreath of smoke curled up from wood or plain, no moving object caught the eye as far as it could reach. Cows in the green valley by the river, a goat clambering about the rocks, or even an Indian banaboo would have relieved the loneliness of the picture. Once we thought we could distinguish a cluster of huts in a distant vale, but the sweeping shadows hindered any close observation.

From the open country we turned to the giant fortress which rose sternly above us. The contrast was sharp and decided. From the heights on which we stood, the wide-stretching savanna land seemed a grassy country over which a good horse could galop, jumping with ease the narrow forest belts which intersected the plains like hedges. But nothing less than a winged Pegasus could expect to attain the summit of the bare red wall that raised itself for hundreds and hundreds of feet, unrelieved by aught save a few tangled bushes and tasselled bunches of some wild grasses. Carefully we scanned every ledge and crevice, seeking some practicable spot to which we might direct our steps on the morrow. At the southern extremity of the eastern side, which we were facing, a ravine near a rounded tower-like rock, draped with grass and lichens, which recalled to my mind the Metella Tomb of the Roman Campagna on a gigantic scale, gave better promise of a foot-hold than anywhere else. But a closer examination showed that this fissure only separated the rounded mass, at about two-thirds of its height, from the rest of the mountain which then rose as perpendicular as in other places.

The following day when we resumed our explorations the results were similar. Near one of the falls an angle in the rock, and a fringe of shrubs running up for some distance along a deep crack, held out hopes of a practicable ascent, but they vanished in a plumb-line of wall without ridge or chink. Upon the elevated ridges we were not troubled by animal life, as besides a large rattlesnake, which one of the men killed, we found nothing except two goat-suckers' nests, each containing a young one. But down on the savanna we were so plagued by a small black fly that life was almost insupportable. These insects attacked the eyes and ears, and bit severely, leaving a bright red mark with a black centre. Even the Indians were obliged, when in camp, to sit all day surrounded by dense volumes of smoke.

It was therefore with no regret that, after finding the ascent of the eastern side of Roraima impracticable, we left camp one day with hammocks and provisions—the latter now unfortunately reduced to little except flour, of which we had far too much—with the intention of exploring the south side. The nights were very cold, as the thermometer generally fell below 60 degs., but the days were intensely hot, and in walking over the open savannas we were much blistered by the sun, a circumstance which rendered the incessant attacks of the black flies more aggravating. As we crossed over the ridges, before turning towards the mountain, we passed a very pretty tree-filled hollow with precipitous sides and very deep. At one end of this chasm a fine stream emerged from underground, and after falling over the rocks in a picturesque cascade, wound round the base of the cliff and disappeared through a narrow outlet.

To reach an open point suitable for a survey, we passed over ground very similar to that on the eastern flank. There were the same steep spurs, the same widths of jungle, and the same black boulders, grass-covered and so slippery that the greatest caution was necessary in placing the feet, for a sprained ancle or a broken leg would have been of serious consequence in these wilds. At last we stood above the great ravine that surrounds the mountain, and commanded a near view of the southern wall. This side of Roraima is, if possible, even more precipitous than the eastern. The outline is similar, except in the centre, where it is wonderfully turreted and shaped with battlements. Here and there enormous black slabs appear to be let into the red stone as smoothly as if by hand, and in other spots quaint mosaic patterns can be traced. There were no waterfalls from the summit, but in three or four places the dark shiny lines showed where water had only recently ceased to flow. A fine cascade issued from the forest slope near the smooth western extremity, but we could not tell whence the water came. This we imagined must be the second fall of the Kamaiba, mentioned by Schomburgh as having a breadth of seventy yards. Although when we saw it we estimated its width at barely that number of feet, yet its diminished size could readily be accounted for by the exceptionally dry season.

From this point we had a splendid view of the eastern side of Kukenam, which projects beyond, and runs up parallel with the western flank of Roraima. Its steep wall, though seemingly perpendicular, did not present the same inaccessible front that Roraima did. North of its great waterfall, we could trace ledges covered with trees and bush, which to us seemed contiguous and continuous enough to reach the top. But Roraima was our goal, not Kukenam, and even to reach its base across the broad, dense forest valley that intervened, would have been the work of days. These southern slopes are actually more prolific in floral treasures than the eastern. The great fantastic black rocks which lie scattered about in infinite variety, are all clothed with agaves, cactuses, bromelias, gesnerias, mosses, and orchids. Every step reveals some new charm, every breath of air seems laden with a fresh sweetness; now it is the delicate fragrance of a yellow melastoma, and now the heavier odour of a chocolate-tinted odontoglot.

The soil on the southern side of Roraima was more moist than on the eastern, the plants were brighter, and the blossoms more abundant. In one place, which in our excursions we continually had to cross, there was a broad swamp, which was the last thing we expected to find on such elevated ground, traversed apparently by no stream. Here, grew a beautiful utricularia with dark blue flowers, a nepenthes, and various cœlogynes. There were also numerous sobralias,[104] but none were in flower, which was a great disappointment to us, as Schomburgh has pronounced this variety of orchidea to be the most fragrant and beautiful of its class. Near this swamp and hovering over the bell-blossoms of a thibaudia[105] we saw the only humming-bird that we met with in the locality; from the quick glance we obtained of it we could see it was not one of a very brilliant species, the plumage being of a reddish bronze.

It was always a relief to emerge on to this flowery marsh from the thick forest entanglement of the craggy ravine, and one day, after repeated failures to trace out the smallest likelihood of a possible ascent, we sat down on a rock near its edge, and agreed that the southern flank of Roraima was as impracticable as the eastern. One thickly-bushed crevice near the south-western end had cheered us with a prospect of success, but alas! between the wooded ledges were impassable walls of sheer rock, which neither man nor monkey could ascend. At another place the bush connection up to a certain point was only interfered with by an overhanging slab, but that projection was an insuperable impediment. Gradually the conviction was forced upon us that the Indians were right, and that Roraima was impregnable. That the north side, even if it were approachable through the wide-stretching primeval forest, was impossible of ascent we had no doubt, on account of the stupendous wall of rock we had seen—though at a distance—from Cashew Cottage. So now it only remained for us to see what we could of the western side. Of this flank we could only get glimpses by retiring towards Kukenam, and from savanna hills obtaining our view up the dividing valley.

Owing to the clouds which almost incessantly filled this gorge, it was seldom that we could enjoy a satisfactory view, but what we did see only convinced us that the western side was a repetition of the others. To thoroughly examine that side of the mountain, it would have been necessary to make a journey round Kukenam, with the hope of finding high, open ridges, from which we could have made a close inspection. But this would have been a work of many days, and, as we felt, a fruitless labour. Irrespective of my expressed opinion—when asked by McTurk—of the futility of further efforts to ascend Roraima, I was influenced by two other unexpressed considerations. One of these was my firm conviction that my unfortunate boots would not stand a longer sojourn in the neighbourhood, and I did not wish to pass the rest of my days in the wilds of Guiana, and the other a desire for something to eat. For the fact was that our provisions had run short; rice, bacon, coffee, sugar, mouldy biscuits, all had vanished except several great quakes of mildewed flour, and it was beyond human nature to return to camp day after day, hungry and tired, and sit down with any enjoyment to cold water and "bakes" or dumplings. In theory the carrying of a great quantity of flour may have been good, as I suppose—although I am by no means certain of it—it would have warded off actual starvation, but in practice it was bad. May future visitors to Roraima take plenty of flour, but also may they take other things to render it eatable!

On the day after our last view of the western wall we turned our steps homeward, that is to the camp under the eastern slopes, where our Indians awaited us. Before dark, we arrived at a circular hut which stood alone on the top of a barren hill. It was deserted, so we took up our quarters in it for the night. As daylight faded, the mountain fortress loomed more and more mysterious; the battlements were touched with a light rose colour, and the clear-cut summit was sharply defined against the purple sky. For a short time the mists rolled away, and this great "sermon in stone" stood out in vivid, faultless accuracy, all the more impressive from the perfect stillness of the scene. Then darkness fell; but presently the moon arose, and lo! the recent rich colouring gave place to a fretwork of pure frosted silver. The edges of the woods and the pencilled lines of the delicate foliage were burnished with the soft rays, and then, indeed, Roraima looked weird and solemn.

We were destined to see the mountain under many aspects, as whilst the clouds were enveloping it for the night, a pink reflection in them made us look for the cause. Then we saw that all the country to the south and east was illuminated by fire. We knew that probably the savanna grass around our camp had been set on fire by the Indians, but had the design and direction been arranged by an experienced pyrotechnist the effect could not have been finer. As if by art, the flames kept in accord with the hill outlines, here rising in long lines one above the other, and there encircling the oval peaks as with coronets of fire. The exhibition did not last long, for a storm, whose approach had been signalled by a few thunder-claps, broke with great fury and a deluge of rain descended. It continued all night, and we were very thankful that we had a roof—although a leaky one—over us.

Next morning the face of the country had changed, the parched appearance had disappeared, and all was green and fresh. The great Kukenam Fall, which of late had been growing more and more attenuated was now a splendid body of water, and three or four fine cataracts dashed down the side of Roraima where previously there had only been the faintest indications of moisture.

On our way back to camp, rivulets whose thread of water we had before stepped over, were so swollen that we were forced to wade through them, and in one or two cases we had to seek a place where a ford was possible. Our Indians were rejoiced to see us back again, as they had not expected that the mountain-demons would allow us to return. They were very glad to hear that on the following day we should prepare for our departure towards home. During our absence, they had transformed an open shelter into a picturesque little house with door and walls formed of palm leaves; a similar one, but made entirely of boughs, gave them a comfortable lodging. Thus warmly housed, our last nights at Roraima were pleasanter than the previous ones, and the smoke-filled apartment proved a successful remedy for the poisonous flies.

CHAPTER XXII.

INDIAN VISITORS—A REWARD TO ASCEND RORAIMA—LAST
VIEW OF RORAIMA—HOW TO ASCEND RORAIMA—
MENAPARUTI—A HUNTING PARTY—CASSIREE—INDIAN
PASTIMES—RUMOURS OF WAR—AMARYLLIS—QUATING
RIVER—CASHEW COTTAGE AGAIN—THE ARAPARU—FALSE
ALARMS—OLD FRIENDS.

When engaged in repacking our diminished baggage, we were visited by a
hunting party of Arecuna Indians. They were taller and fiercer looking than
our Acawais who shrunk timidly away, and it was with difficulty that we could
induce our own Arecunas to approach the strangers and interpret their
language. Their long black hair was cut short and combed over the forehead,
and the part thus "banged" was painted red. Their feet and knees were also
painted red, and their faces were striped. Some of them wore cross pieces of
steel wire as a lip ornament, and one was contented with a couple of common
pins crossed in the same way. The chief wore a peculiar bell-shaped and
tasselled ornament in his under lip, which he gave to me in exchange for two
or three charges of powder. For his necklace of teeth I offered him a very
good hunting knife; this he declined, but intimated his willingness to part
with it for an old cutlass whose value was about one-third of the knife.

McTurk offered them two guns if they would show us how to reach the top
of Roraima, but they beat their breasts, grunted, and with wild gesticulations
declared that there was no way of ascending to the summit of the cloud
mountain. If they had known of any way, the promise of a gun would
certainly have induced them to point it out. The chief had a miserable "buck"
gun, but the rest carried only bows and arrows and blow-pipes.[106] The only
bird they had shot was a duraquara which they had obtained near their own
village, that was a few miles off in the savannas towards the east. We had
noticed a few deer tracks, and once McTurk had seen a large animal cross
slowly over an opening in the high ridge on Roraima, but he was unable to
make out what it was. But game was scarce, and the Indians said they could
not get any before we left next day, but they would return to their village and
meet us on our journey with vegetables and cassava.

True to their appointment, we found them waiting near our former camp at
Eki-biapu Falls, but the provisions they brought only consisted of some old
cassava as hard as rock, and a few unripe plantains. We had started before
sunrise in order, if possible, to reach the village of Menaparuti on the same
night; it was a long march, but with our lightened loads we hoped to
accomplish it. Before entering the forest we turned for a last full view of

Roraima. "Parting looks," says the old Welsh proverb, "are magnifiers of beauty," and to us the grand red walls looked more perpendicular, stiller, and more solemn than ever. Against the pure blue sky the sharp outlines of the softly-coloured mountain stood out in perfect relief, and the atmosphere was so clear that we fancied we could hear the roar of the falls. What messages were those waters carrying to earth? They alone knew the secret of Roraima, but their language, like that of the birds, is understood only by themselves. They could tell what we had vainly tried to find out, for we most assuredly failed to tear the veil from the head of this mysterious Sphinx. We were disappointed—who would not be?—at the time. But we did not regret those Roraima days; to others, perhaps, we had apparently laboured fruitlessly; but not to ourselves, for we had learnt far more by Nature's lessons than can be taught by books, had witnessed scenes that well repaid some weariness of body, and had so enjoyed them that the spell of the mountains lingered long after we had left them. It is far from an unpleasant reflection to think that there are still a few unvisited spots in the world, and as the summit of Roraima is one of them, it may be that before long the fascination of travel will induce some toil-loving mortal to again attempt its exploration.

If I have dwelt too long on the various points of our journey, it has been with the idea that a knowledge of the difficulties to be overcome and the assistance to be gained *en route* may be of use to future travellers. I do not think it possible to make the ascent of Roraima except by a balloon, and the novelty of such an exploring tour would give additional zest to the undertaking.

And now let me atone for my tiresome details by a quick journey home. We reached the village of Menaparuti late at night, after a very long day's walk, and once more slung our hammocks in the fine open shed. Here we rested a day in order to obtain a supply of cassava, which the villagers prepared for us in abundance. They had no fresh meat, so a hunting party went off to the woods in search of game. All they brought back was a small mâam, and a large striped coatimundi,[107] whose flesh was so pungent that it completely spoilt the bird which was cooking in the same pot. The favourite beverage among the inhabitants was a disagreeable-looking compound called cassiree; it was of a pink colour, and being prepared in the same way as paiworie it was highly appreciated by our men.

We were much amused by a number of village children who used continually to pass our house on their way to the river. Slowly, in single file, they marched past, the tallest leading, and the sizes diminishing until the last was not the height of his bow. They never smiled, and were so grave that they impressed one with the idea that they were little old men starting on some dangerous expedition. Once we followed them, and directly the small troop was out of sight of the houses, its members changed immediately into children. They shouted and laughed, pushed each other into the river, jumped into their tiny canoes and raced one against the other, swam about and were as happy as schoolboys on a half holiday. After their fun had lasted some time they all crossed the river, resumed their solemn air, and disappeared in single file up a forest path on a shooting foray. About an hour afterwards they returned triumphantly, dragging another coatimundi which the little imps had managed to kill, probably with a poisoned arrow.

From childhood to old age male Indians are seldom without a bow or a blow-pipe in their hands, peccaries, pumas, and panis falling as easy a prey to the man as toucans, pigeons, and small birds to the boy. To get food is their principal object in life. They have few pastimes, but enjoy a dance, or the "ha-ha" game.[108] In some tribes, when a youth wishes to show his courage and powers of endurance of pain, he is shaken up by his friends in a bag filled with Monouri[109] ants, which are the most dangerous of their kind, the sting of one being sufficient to cause fever. This is almost their only amusement. I do not think they were much impressed with the intellectual recreations of the white men, as when McTurk and I were playing our usual evening euchre, they could not understand the object of throwing down pieces of painted paper only to pick them up again. They thought the picture-cards were wonderful, and that they were the portraits of foreigners.

We obtained a good many teeth necklaces from them, as they were inclined to sell anything they possessed for powder or knives, but they had no other curiosities worth the trouble of carrying. There was great competition amongst the women as to who should dispose of the most cassava; in fact they brought a great deal more than we could take, and much of what we did pack soon became mouldy and uneatable, in consequence of insufficient sun-drying.

The evening before we left, some natives from the Mazaruni spread a report that we were to be attacked and killed by the Cako Indians, as soon as we reached that river. We paid no attention to the rumour, but our men were evidently much disturbed. We thought it highly improbable that the timid and peaceful people we had seen should suddenly become hostile; still the idea of an ambushed river and poisoned arrows was not a pleasant one. It was just possible that traders in Venezuela, hearing of our expedition, and being ignorant of its import, had instigated the Indians to take offensive action, but it was very improbable, and we soon forgot all about it.

Before dawn we were up and away, and ere the last house in the village had disappeared, we heard the crowing of a cock. Had we heard it sooner what a dinner we might have had! Indians never eat eggs or poultry, and only keep hens as pets. On leaving the savanna, Abraham conducted us by a different path from that by which we had come, stating that it was a much shorter one, but he had not known of it before. In an old cassava field, there were some beautiful golden red blossoms of an amaryllis, evidently a garden-flower run wild.

We crossed the Quáting much higher up than previously, near a small village called Nimapi. It was a pretty place, the houses being perched on the side of the high hill on the left bank of the river, and surrounded with plantains and fruit trees. There were also a few huts on the right bank, and as in one of them there was a trough of paiworie, we had to sentinel the door until the last man had crossed in the cranky canoe which we used as a ferry-boat. From this village commenced an ascent which equalled, if it did not surpass, in steepness any that we had accomplished. The damp and slippery ground made it all the more difficult, but in time we reached the summit. The path afterwards branched into our old one near the Opuima mountain, which we descended in wonderfully quick time. So long and rapid was that day's march that we slept that night at Cashew Cottage, having made the distance in half the time that we had previously taken.

A large family party was assembled at the cottage, and from them we received the intelligence that three of our woodskins had been taken from their hiding place. This was worse news than the other, and when about the middle of the next day we arrived at old Granny's, a man was at once despatched to find out the truth. He returned with the joyful intelligence that all the woodskins were perfectly safe. Several parties of Indians had stopped at the old lady's hut during our absence, but nothing that we had left had been touched, and the rice and coffee were very acceptable to us.

After the late rain, the water in the Aruparu creek was deeper and our descent was not so much impeded as our ascent had been. On the way down, we replenished our larder with a fine water-haas, which was as large as an ordinary pig. At last we arrived at the house of Captain Sam on the Cako River, and there found that the story of the attack was an entire fabrication, probably invented to induce us to remain longer at the village, or to proceed by another—the Cukuie—route. Then again we entered the Mazaruni River and landed at our former camp. Our old friend the Pirate, who was cruising about in his canoe, came to bid us farewell, and in his charge we left the woodskins to be returned to their owners.

Before starting on our last walk through the forest, we saw a woodskin approaching, its paddles being plied vigorously by a man and a woman. Mazaruni, at the prospect of another conquest, immediately began to adorn himself, and as the boat drew near, our amusement was great at recognizing old Granny and her son, Abraham, whom we had left at their home on the Aruparu creek. The paddles, under the strength of the skinny arms of the old lady, swept the water as powerfully as did those of her robust son, and she did not appear to mind in the least the physical exertion for which we pitied her. Indian women, although well treated by their husbands, are so accustomed from their girlhood to the exercise of physical endurance that what we consider must be a sad strain on their powers is but a second nature to them even in old age.

Our friends had brought with them much of the flour and salt, and some of the various articles that we had given them, and intended to proceed farther down the river on a trading expedition. We gently blew on the old lady's back for good luck, and with a farewell to Abraham set off through the dark forest.

CHAPTER XXIII.

A PAINFUL WALK—BIRD'S NEST FERNS—DOWN THE
CURIPUNG—VOICES OF THE NIGHT—AN INDIAN FAMILY—A
QUICK JOURNEY—SHOOTING THE FALLS—TIMBER SHOOTS
IN CANADA—A LOST CHANNEL—ANTICIPATIONS OF A
FEAST—CAPSIZE—A SWIM FOR LIFE—TEBUCU FALLS—HOME
AGAIN.

In order to reach Macrebah before our hands and feet were quite worn out,
we determined to waste no time but to proceed by forced marches. Poor
McTurk, in addition to injured limbs and feverish attacks, was worse off as
regards foot covering than I was, as he was reduced to three pair of india-
rubber shoes, which he wore one over the other on account of the holes.

With our thin soles, the sharp-ribbed roots made our movements as delicate
as walking over eggs, and it was very ludicrous but rather painful to find
ourselves now on one leg and now on the other, vainly endeavouring to
escape the knobs and pointed projections which thrust themselves against
our bruised feet. I could not help thinking of the grasshopper when he said
to the bee;

"There's a time to be sad,

And a time to be glad,

A time both for working and stopping;

For men to make money,

For you to make honey,

And for me to do nothing but hopping."

During this walk we saw for the first time the great "bird's nest" fern, adapted
for the purpose its name implies. Numbers of these plants grew on the trunks
and low branches of the trees, and in many instances they had been made the
nesting places of ground-doves. No other species of bird occupied them, but
we invariably discovered one or two eggs of the dove, and in one instance
the mother allowed us to look at her as she sat on her nest.

Concerning the rest of our foot-journey, it suffices to say that in three days
we arrived at Macrebah and there found our boat, the Adaba, all safe. My
wonderful boots would certainly not have lasted another day; but I had no
further need of them, and in gratitude I hung them to a high pole driven into
the sand, and after tracing underneath the well-known words

"Whoever dare these boots displace

Must meet Bombastes face to face!"

I abandoned them as an offering to the Spirit of Macrebah Falls.

The large dacana balli, which we had left covered with white flowers, had now fruited, and the great green nuts fell heavily to the ground. The Curipung River was but little affected by the recent rain, and its claret coloured water reflected the white sand in as clear a purple as when we first saw it. Here we rested for a day and dismissed all the Indian carriers, with the exception of our own six, who formed the crew of the Adaba, and Lanceman and Mazaruni, who accompanied us, when we departed, in a woodskin. "Master will no take boot," said Charlie with a mischievous grin, as he pointed to the two skeletons swinging near the water's edge, when we started.

A long day's journey brought us down to the Mazaruni River. There was little current in the creek, and in some places so little water that there was scarcely sufficient to moisten the throats of the disconsolate herons which, like lone fishermen, moodily gazed at the shallow stream from the pebbly shore.

The sun was just setting when we arrived at the mouth of the creek, and never before had the scenery of the great river appeared to us so picturesque as it did then. The black water stretched away north and south-east to the wooded hills, whose sides were first a rose colour, then crimson, then purple. Above the dark forest, across the river, a golden green haze expanded itself up and up until it touched the pink and pearl clouds in the east. The sharp promontories of silver sand sparkled as they caught the expiring rays, and stood out so clearly that even on the most distant could be seen the shadowy forms of the egrets or cranes. Then, as the colours all faded into a slowly darkening purple, a mysterious silence prevailed; the cries of the monkeys ceased, the toucans had called "tucáno" for the last time, and the ibises no longer screamed "curri-curri" as they flapped by. The sombre jungle grew blacker, the sky clearer and the thin vapour which stole up from the water's edge crept along the forest-crest and spread a film over more distant objects. Then on noiseless wing the night-hawks floated past looking like great butterflies, bats skimmed through the forest openings, and fire-beetles suddenly started into life.

Presently the breeze brought faint sounds from the river, a frog croaked, again we heard the fog-horn notes of the howling monkeys, and then the "brief twilight in which southern suns fall asleep" was over. When the full moon rose, the scene might have been in Greenland. The river changed to a sheet of silver-blue ice, the vapour-clad trees sparkled like dew, the sky and stars were brilliantly clear, and the great sandbank was a drift of the purest snow. On this white bank some travelling Indians had encamped, and their dark figures stood out in as bold relief as those of Esquimaux on a snow-field. The illusion was heightened by the sleigh-like appearance of a woodskin which had been drawn up from the water, and at whose side three dogs were lying asleep.

The night sounds which issue from the forests of Guiana are singularly strange and weird. Whether on broad river, narrow creek, or out in the lonely woods, the traveller is greeted with unearthly sounds that utterly banish sleep. Scarcely had we ensconced ourselves in our hammocks, which had been slung to the trees bordering the sandbank, when the "voices of the night" broke forth. First, the night-jar ran down its scale "ha, ha-ha, ha-ha-ha," each note lower than the preceding, and each the acme of the most hopeless sorrow. The utter misery told in this bird's voice must be heard to be believed. Next a mâam uttered its shrill plaintive whistle, whose volume increased until the whole forest resounded with it. Then, as if a warning to the noisy reveller, a loud rattle, like that of a night-watchman, sounded close by. This was the music of a night-hawk. Immediately after came the melancholy cries of a pigeon, like a human voice calling for aid. These sounds were hushed by the dismal wail of a sloth, which, in its turn, gave place to a series of sharp clucks like those of a hen, and which were produced by some winged creature of darkness. After a moment's stillness a stealthy rustle in the leaves betokened the neighbourhood of a snake or lizard, and, farther off, a breaking branch told where a larger animal was pushing its way.

These sounds continued until nearly midnight, that hour when, as Cotton says:

> "The goblin now the fool alarms,
>
> Hags meet to mumble o'er their charms;
>
> The nightmare rides the dreaming ass,
>
> And fairies trip it o'er the grass."

Suddenly the Indians commenced to whisper, for even their sleep had been aroused by the wild screeching of the terrible didi, whose dreaded notes ended in a prolonged and mournful crowing. This unearthly sound seemed to be the climax, and soon the real silence of the night settled down.

> "Now night it was, and everything on earth had won the grace
>
> Of quiet sleep; the woods had rest, the wildered waters' face;
>
> It was the tide when stars roll on amid their courses due,
>
> And all the tilth is hushed, and beasts and birds of many a hue,

And all that is in waters wide, and what the waste doth keep,

In thicket rough, amid the hush of night-tide, lay asleep."

For three or four hours the silence lasted, only broken occasionally, and for a few minutes at a time, by the moan of a jaguar, or the fierce snappings of the small hunting tigers on the track of some peccaries, or of the night-loving tapir. Before dawn the concert was renewed; the monkeys howled, the mâams whistled piercingly, the honoquas and duraquaras gave endless repetitions of their own name, and with the first streak of daylight the parrots chattered from the tree tops. Day broke, and the camp was again alive.

Bird cries are imitated to perfection by Indians, and we not unfrequently obtained a pani, or a duraquara, by such means. At night they would note the position of the roosting bird by its notes, and then in the early morn proceed in its direction, attract it by their imitative cries and shoot it.

Amongst the Indians encamped on the sandbank was a family which was on its way to Georgetown, with hammocks and birds for sale. We christened its members the Cowenaros, i.e., cocks of the rock, as they had a fine specimen of the bird in their possession. They were good-looking people, and as the father was the only one who had ever visited the coast, there was considerable excitement with the younger members, especially on the part of Miss Cowenaro, who was going to celebrate her début into society by a new dress—the first she had ever worn. By some means she had obtained some pink calico, and out of it she had manufactured an extraordinary robe which she was always trying on, or, perhaps, accustoming herself to wear. At any rate, on our way down the river we never arrived near a prominent rock without seeing the young lady perched on the top of it, and evidently lost in admiration of herself.

After leaving Lanceman's house at Menaparuti where we found all that we had left, the rain, which we could see by the heightened river had been falling heavily in the mountains, burst upon us. The fine weather which had favoured us for so unexpected a length of time, broke up and rain set in. Sometimes the squalls were so severe that the waves almost swamped our boat, and the woodskins, containing Lanceman and Mazaruni, who accompanied us to the Settlement, were only saved by a quick run to shore.

Our journey up the river had by no means been a slow one, in spite of the delays at the cataracts and rapids, but now with the swift current in our favour and the speed with which we shot the falls, up which we had toiled wearily on foot, our progress was extremely quick. Shooting the falls was splendidly exciting, and not unaccompanied by danger. I had once employed a spare afternoon in Ottawa by accompanying the rafts in their descent of the "timber shoots," and great amusement it was, but devoid of the inspiring element of danger. There the descent was swift but smooth, steerage was unnecessary, and no impediment barred the narrow, wall-edged current. Here it was different, conflicting currents seethed in all directions, broken rocks and half-hidden projections cropped up all around, and nothing but the strong arm and steady eye of both the man at the prow and the man in the stern could save the boat from being dashed to pieces.

To those unaccustomed to it—as I was—the novel sensation of fall shooting is delightful. Choosing the long smooth tongue of water which indicates the safest passage, the words "Give way all!" are spoken, and though the paddles work with intense vigour, and the foaming water is pouring madly at your side, the boat seems to stand still; the rocky walls rush up to you, the waves dash at you instead of from you, the roar increases, the drop looks perpendicular, and still you are apparently not moving; there is a plunge, a wave or two shipped perhaps, and the next moment the boat is floating quietly in the smooth back-water below the falls. Sometimes the difficulties of the descent are much increased by the twists and turns which have to be made in the very middle of the fall itself. Our Indians, who had been rather nervous at the first few cataracts, soon recovered their self-possession, and were so elated at their skill that once or twice their valour almost overcame their discretion.

When we reached the Falls of Yaninzaec, the rising water had so altered the appearance of the river that we could no longer recognize our old landmarks. In the island labyrinth we lost the channel which led to the "portage," and it was in vain that we tried to regain it. All our efforts only brought us to one or other of the great falls, a safe descent of which could no more be accomplished than that of Niagara. Darkness at last came on, and we had to encamp on a small island.

Next morning we were fortunately discovered by the two woodskins— containing Lanceman and the Cowenaros—and under their guidance we reached the portage; passing on our way a curious rock called "the Cabuni"— near the mouth of the river of that name. After carrying the boat over the portage, and reloading it, it was McTurk's intention to proceed a short way down the river and camp early, so as to replenish our larder with fresh meat. It was many days since we had tasted meat, and our appetites told us that game would be very desirable.

"I shoot and eat one pani," said Sammy.

"Pani!" said Charlie indignantly. "I eat one maipurie myself."

Now as a pani is nearly as large as a turkey, and as a maipurie, *i.e.*, tapir, is about the size of a small donkey, the speakers must, indeed, have been hungry. For ourselves we had arranged quite a little banquet with the remnant of the provisions that had been left at Lanceman's house. There was a tin of mullagatawny soup, a pot of marmalade, a tin of biscuits, and besides a bottle of brandy which we had been treasuring for weeks, there was still a small supply of Seidlitz Powders, which had of late superseded Eno's Fruit Salt on occasions of great jollification. In order the better to enjoy our intended repast, we had refrained from breakfast on that day, but "*l'homme propose, Dieu dispose.*"

Having safely descended several cataracts after leaving Yaninzaec, we saw in the distance a pleasant spot for camping, and from the same direction heard a great howling of monkeys which promised sport. We rapidly approached a fall, the roar of whose waters seemed unnecessarily loud. This we descended, but a sharp turn that had been hidden by a high rock revealed another and steeper fall, which it would be madness to attempt to shoot. But it was too late, no power could stop us; we were already in the long swift current which swept down to the deep drop. "Give way!" shouted McTurk, as a glance showed that there was no chance of escape except by the mere possibility of speed; then there was a sweep of paddles, a plunge, a wild swirl of waters, wave after wave rushed over us, and the boat went down. The whole affair had happened so quickly that, almost before I could realise it, I found myself under water and powerless to rise to the surface, as my legs seemed to be entangled in something—probably the framework of the awning we had lately put up as a shelter from the rain. The idea flashed through me that this surely could not be the end of my long looked for Roraima expedition, and giving a great struggle up I came to the surface.

The first thing I saw was the Adaba, bottom upwards, floating down the river, and McTurk and two of the crew clinging to her. I soon reached them, and in about thirty minutes, by gently guiding our support towards a rocky island, our feet touched the ground. Higher up the river, in a different direction, we saw that what we thought were the remaining four of the Indian crew, standing on another rocky islet. Almost immediately afterwards the woodskins appeared; having descended on the opposite side of the river, where there was a moderately easy passage unknown to us. They at once unloaded, and pushed out into the river to try and save whatever happened to be floating.

Suddenly the cry was raised "Where is Charlie?" Then we saw that only three men stood on the far rock, and that what we had at first taken for a figure was only a barrel. We never saw him again. Sammy, who sat next to him in the bow, said he saw him spring clean out of the boat before she went down, and strike out for land. No cry was heard; we on the boat thought he was with those on the barrel, and they thought he was with us. As he was a very strong swimmer, we could only suppose that he had been sucked down by the terrible undercurrent, or that he had been dashed against a rock. It was very, very sad, and for a time we could not believe that he was really drowned. For the rest of that day and next morning we searched long and carefully in the hopes of recovering the body, but uselessly. The Indians said that two years ago three natives were drowned in the same place, and their bodies were never found. The poor fellow had only been married a month before we left Georgetown, and among the crew were two of his wife's brothers. One of these had a very narrow escape as he was not a good swimmer, and was just sinking when he caught at a pillow floating by, which supported him until he reached the flour barrel that saved the other two. Everything was lost, with the exception of a few hammocks and a tin canister of mine, which, besides Indian curiosities, fortunately contained shirts and other clothes. For the crew had divested themselves of everything when in the water, and not one of their bundles was picked up. Guns, ammunition, field-glasses, provisions, plants, boxes of clothes, in fact almost everything we had, and alas! a human life—the only thing that could never be replaced—all lay in the deep water under the falls of Tebucu.[110]

When we continued our journey, we took Lanceman as a guide to guard against any future catastrophe, and no other accident occurred, with the exception of a hole which was knocked into the side of the boat whilst being let down a fall by means of ropes. From the woodskins we had received paddles to replace those we had lost, and urged on by hunger we made rapid progress, and at last issued from the island-dotted river into the large lake-like expanse of water near the junction of the Cuyuni.

After we had passed the neat houses of the Caribs, the island church came in view, cottages appeared, people with clothes on were seen walking about, there were ducks and geese, and the different signs of civilization. We soon rounded Palmer's Point, and after a tremendous squall of rain and wind, arrived at the Settlement, where we received a hearty welcome from the Superintendent and his family. And thus ended our expedition to Roraima, a journey which we had accomplished in a little more than two months.

CHAPTER XXIV.

FROM SOURCE TO SEA—END OF THE DROUGHT—
D'URBAN—A RACE MEETING—ENTHUSIASTIC COLOURED
FOLK—ROYAL MAIL STEAMERS—VENEZUELANS—CARIBE—
CARUPANO—CUMANA—AN EARTHQUAKE CENTRE—
BARCELONA—LLANURAS—LLANERO—PLAINS—LA SILLA.

When, on our way back to Georgetown, we saw the waters of the Mazaruni mingling with those of the Essequibo, it was like parting with a human friend whose career we had watched until its close. We had seen it, or its great tributaries, at its birth, spring from its cradle in the broken mountain tops into the green valley below, and in that one great leap for life rush blindly into the big world that lay before it. Not an easy-going, quiet life—not a gentle, cared for one, but a life from first almost to last of strife and battle. Occasionally, in its school days, checked and restrained, and forced into channels that it spurns, only to dash more impetuously than ever against the rocks and crags that beset its path. Sometimes its smooth, shining, face rippled only with a smile, and the tremulous music of its voice as it flows softly over its pebbles, tell of peace and rest, but such expressions are but minutes compared with the years of its more troubled life. Not until its youth and middle age are long past, does this turbulent river exert its powers for the benefit of mankind. Wearied with strife, it now sweeps on with deep and silent current, bearing contentedly on its bosom the joys and sorrows of others, and rendering fruitful the land through which it courses. Older and older it grows, but persevering to the end, until at last it slips away from us, and the course of the tired river is ended in the grey sea.

At Georgetown, we heard that the drought had continued until very recently, and had caused much suffering among the poorer classes. The public tanks had run dry, and water brought from a long distance was sold in the streets by the bucket. But now the long looked for rain had come, much to the satisfaction of everybody—even of the planters—and as an old black lady said, "It was indeed a cause of great 'tank'-fulness." With the rains had also come the annual visitation of "hard-backs," great beetle-like insects, that flocked in myriads to the gas-light, and literally enveloped tables and chairs in a coat of living mail.

We arrived just in time for the races, and for the two days they lasted the town presented an unwonted scene of excitement. The road to the d'Urban race-course was alive with a laughing, pushing crowd of various nationalities, in holiday garb. Vehicles of all descriptions, heavily weighted, plodded to the course, or empty rattled back at full speed, eager for another load. The days were hot but the distance short, and the broad road lined with pretty gardens and cottages, half hidden in green shrubbery, formed a pleasant and animated drive. Some of the buildings, too, were worthy of notice, especially the handsome Roman Catholic Cathedral, the Orphan Asylum, and the Almshouses. A gateway and avenue of palms marked the entrance to a wide-spreading grass-land, round which the course ran. A dividing road led up to the circular grand-stand, which was not a very picturesque building, as its architecture was something between that of an umbrella and a band stand; but it was cool and suitable to the occasion. The surroundings differed but little from those of most race-courses; tents, booths, sheds, and structures of more or less pretension, varying from the well carpentered stand, admission to which was four "bits"—a bit in Guiana is fourpence—to the slender structure composed of a few boards and a roof of leaves, where the entrance fee was theoretically a "bit" but practically nothing.

Of the races themselves there is not much to be said. As nearly every event—as was expected—was won not only by the same stable, but also by the same horse, the meeting could hardly be termed an exciting one. To stimulate competition and to avoid disappointment, a certain gallant major entered his carriage horses, but as I do not think they ever got round the track, their entries were not altogether a success. Still the intention was laudable, and if others had been equally public-spirited, the racing would have been far from tame. The winning horses were undeniably good, and were the love of sport as widely diffused as cane, the Georgetown race-meetings would compare favourably with those of any colony. At present the inhabitants object to an annual presentation of cups, plates, stakes, and purses to one stable, but as long as the races are kept up, it must continue until enterprise claims a division.

To the coloured population the races were a source of unmixed enjoyment. From the rude Barbadian to the peaceable Mongol, all were bent on a day's diversion. When the inevitable dog ran down the track, they howled and screamed with delight, and when the horse of the mounted policeman ran away with its rider, joined in the race, and came in a good third, the enthusiasm was unbounded. After each race the crowd was permitted to rush into the space hitherto kept clear in front of the judge's stand. Then as many as could approach swarmed round the box, eagerly demanding a piece of paper with the name of the winner written on it. The numbers posted up were nothing to them, they had probably seen a wide difference between the first and second horses, but nothing could satisfy them except a written statement; a "bit" depended on the result, and oral testimony was valueless. Such laughter and shrieking would follow! Those who had lost would try to defer payment until the next race was over, and those who had won would loudly demand their money. Angry gesticulations would succeed to wordy warfare, and just as a free fight seemed inevitable, the band would strike up and the whole crowd, without exception, would commence to dance. Then, until the course was again cleared, nothing would be visible but a mass of parti-coloured heads bobbing up and down.

With the exception of the brilliant head-dresses, white predominated too much in dress for much effect, but here and there might be seen Indian coolies in cardinal red or mazarine blue, and others who had not been afraid to risk the union of green, orange, pink and purple. But from above, one saw only the bright turbans and twisted handkerchiefs keeping time to the music, and it was very amusing to witness the transformation when, during a passing shower, the animated poppies were replaced by a dense mass of dancing umbrellas. No drunkennness nor any unpleasant incident marred the enjoyment of the meeting, and not until the roses of the setting sun had all faded, did the merry crowd wend its way back to the duties of every-day life.

Very soon after the race meeting I took leave of kind and hospitable Georgetown, and proceeded to Trinidad on my way to Carácas. A few days after our arrival in Port of Spain, I heard that the French mail-steamer "Cacique" was about to sail for La Guaira, and so instead of waiting for the monthly English mail-boat, I secured my ticket by the former and hastened on board at the appointed hour.

As the "Cacique" lay at anchor about two miles from the wharf, and besides a heavy surf running, the rain poured in torrents, the little open boat that conveyed two or three of the passengers—myself included—was almost swamped, and we were thoroughly soaked before reaching the steamer. After the well-appointed vessels of the Royal Mail, with their disciplined crews, admirable attendance, and officers who spare no pains to make their passengers as comfortable as possible, it was with some dismay that we saw the little tub in which we were to continue our voyage. A closer inspection was not more cheering as the cabin accommodation was wretched, and the tiny upper deck unpleasantly crowded. I must add that this was not one of the regular French Mail-steamers, but only an inter-colonial vessel running between Martinique, Trinidad, and La Guaira.

Our fellow-passengers were nearly all Venezuelans; the ladies were extremely pretty and graceful, but a little over-dressed for a sea-voyage, and not being good sailors they soon presented a very dishevelled appearance. The men, as usual dreadfully vociferous, in their shouting, stamping, and gesticulations reminded me of my late friends the Arecuna Indians. They mean nothing, it is merely their mode of emphasizing their expressions, and though they shake their fists in each other's faces, and contradict one another flatly, no insult is intended or received as such. They all wore long black coats, tall hats and high-heeled boots, a dress which they thought quite appropriate to the deck of a ship. Fortunately, except for the invalids, there was no necessity to go below, as all the meals—and very good they were—were served on deck, which also answered for sleeping quarters. In the matter of ice, there was not much on board, and no one was allowed any except the captain. I once drew his attention to that fact, but he only shrugged his shoulders.

It was dark when we left the Gulf of Paria and sailed through the Dragon's Mouth, and then turned west towards the mountains of Cumaná. Next morning we found ourselves at some distance from shore, but moving parallel with the Venezuelan coast, which looked high, grey and arid. After passing Caribe there were a few signs of habitation; stretches of white sandy beach were backed by groves of palms, and in the bright green wooded ravines, which intersected the cactus-covered hills, a hacienda peeped out here and there.

Our first halt was at Carupano, which is said to be a rapidly progressing town. There is certainly room for improvement. In the centre of the bay rises a high rock covered with different species of cereus, and on it stands a lighthouse. On the beach is the custom-house, and a collection of low yellow mud huts surrounded by brown rocks and bare hills. The town itself is situated farther back, and a river flowing through the neighbouring palm groves gives a fresher aspect to that part of the withered scene. Like most ports on this coast, it is excessively hot and unhealthy.

Early next morning we entered the Gulf of Cariaco and anchored off Cumaná the capital of the State of that name. Here, as at Carupano, the town is situated at some distance from the coast, and at the foot of a brown hill crowned by an old fort. Between us and it is a broad sandy plain, dotted over with mud huts of the most unprepossessing appearance. There is little to interest the spectator in the arid scenery, except its colouring, and that is of the brightest and most varied description. The intense light, the excessive radiance of the sun, and the clearness of the atmosphere—Cumaná is comparatively healthy—produce an astonishing effect of colour that would not be possible if vegetation predominated.

Here and there glistening points of white sand run out into the water, and behind them are undulating grey hills which end abruptly in low walls of red rock. Through the yellow plain the Manzanares winds its way from the town, and its banks are covered with a growth of dark green verdure. The hill of San Antonio above the town looks white and shining. Nearer to us, a long promontory is covered with a broad belt of palms, among which some red-roofed houses are seen. Beyond, across the gulf, is a red, rocky shore, which fades away in a russet brown; and over the coast-range, which is almost crimson in its rich tints, rise the purple peaks of distant mountains. Sky and sea are of the purest blue, and the snowy sails of the fishing boats, that skim over the latter, are only matched in whiteness by the gossamer shreds of cloud that float above. To what extent modern conveniences are carried in the capital we could not tell, but the canoes that brought us Muscat grapes were only hollowed tree-trunks, and the vehicles on shore that conveyed passengers to the town were donkey-carts.

From the number of nets which we observed, it was evident that fishing was the chief occupation, and the continuous strings of pelicans showed that there was an abundance of food. These ungainly birds were a great amusement to us as we basked in the intense heat of the powerful sun. Sometimes they flew past in long lines on heavy wing, with their long necks doubled over their backs, and with no other thought than that of regulating their movements with those of their leader. At others, they approached singly or in pairs, each one attending to its own business. Here one falls like a bullet, but diagonally, and disappears under the water. In a second it re-appears, and disgorging the fish from its capacious pouch swallows it whole. That one must have missed his aim, as he sits gazing with an air of astonishment, as if such a thing was impossible; and his mate who alights behind him and slides along the water to his side, reproves him with a look as comical as it is expressive. The graceful man-of-war "hawks" appeared to be much more expert than the pelicans, and though they did not dive so frequently, yet they seldom missed their fish.

Around Cumaná the dry plains and barren rocks, the stunted vegetation, the roofless walls and shattered buildings are suggestive of the earthquakes and tidal waves which have desolated this as well as other parts of this region of South America. Only now is the town recovering from the shock of 1854, which in twenty seconds reduced it to a heap of ruins.

After leaving Curnaná the scenery was more picturesque. Deep bays ran in between rocky headlands, at whose feet were islets as white as if they had been salted. Crags and bare hills, varied with tree-clad promontories, and dainty little coves full of the bluest water and rimmed with the whitest sand. After threading our way through various islands, we passed between El Morro and the craggy islet of Borracha, and cast anchor opposite Barcelona, another State capital. The place was not attractive, and I was glad to be able to answer no when a Venezuelan asked me if I was not going to visit the great English paper-manufactory which is established in the town.

The district is interesting, for here commence the great "llanuras" which stretch away to the Orinoco, and whose inhabitants are veritable free children of the desert. The "Llanero" will not live in towns, and is only happy when with his horse for a companion he roams over the boundless grassy plains tending his cattle. Brave, hardy, athletic, and eminently patriotic, the "Llanero" is a power in the land, and has played an important part in the establishment of national independence.

Inexpressibly sombre was the vast brown savanna extending to the purple horizon, relieved only at intervals by a few hills or a flat-topped mountain. Even the sea seemed to have caught the cheerless tint of the land, and instead of sparkling blue, we tossed in dull water of a leaden grey. By degrees the level shore gave place to undulating ground, this to rounded hills, and the hills to a mountain range, above which towered La Silla, one of the highest peaks—in the State of Bolivar—of the northern Cordillera of the Andes.[111] Then we knew we were approaching La Guaira.

CHAPTER XXV.

VIEW OF LA GUAIRA—PROJECTS IN VENEZUELA—
LANDING—INDIAN PATH TO CARACAS—BRILLIANT
BEETLES—VIEW FROM CERRO DE AVILA—DESCENT TO
CITY—CLIMATE—AN EARTHQUAKE ALARM—SAD ASPECT OF
THE CITY—MYSTERIOUS POWER OF THE MOON—
PERIHELION AND PESTILENCE.

Viewed from the open roadstead where vessels anchor, La Guaira is
picturesque. Almost from the very edge of the water the land begins to rise,
so that the houses, with the exception of those that line the curved shore, are
perched on the various spurs and knolls in a gradually ascending scale. The
depth of the little town is only a few hundred yards, and straight up behind
it rises the rocky wall of the Cerro de Avila, which terminates in the peaks of
Naiguatá and La Silla. The height of the former is 8,800 feet above the level
of the sea. On the right, the cliffs which shut in the town end in an abrupt
white promontory, enclosing a low stretch of cultivated ground dotted with
palm groves and strips of forest; and on the left the coast range extends away,
casting down long spurs and spits of palm-covered land which shoot out far
into the sea. On all sides there is a blending of green hills, rugged and barren
precipices, cactus-clad rocks, fertile plains, and white houses.

To the right of the town may be traced the carriage road to Carácas, which
after endless zig-zags disappears round a mountain corner. Of the mule or
Indian path to the same place nothing can be seen, except the general
direction indicated by a steep ravine which cuts into the face of the Silla
immediately behind the town. Near this ravine, at a height of about fifteen
hundred feet, a fort holds a commanding position, and a battery on the shore
completes the defence—such as it is—of La Guaira. Landing here is effected
with considerable difficulty, owing to the tremendous swell, against which
there is no protection.

Many projects have been formed to convert this roadstead into a port, but
like all other good intentions in Venezuela, they remain projects. For some
years a small breakwater has been in course of construction, but the sea
demolishes it as fast as it is made. Lighters are used for the conveyance of
passengers from the vessels, and from one of these we were jerked on to the
jetty dripping like river-gods, as the wave which had carried us on its crest to
the landing was followed by another which broke over the boat. A capsize in
these waters would probably be fatal, owing to the number of sharks which
here lie in wait for victims. Not long ago a young negro was bathing near the
jetty and was attacked by a shark, which snapped off his right hand. He did
not lose his presence of mind, but by beating the water with his left arm

hoped to frighten away the monster. But he was again attacked, and before the boat which had put off from shore to his assistance reached him, his left hand had been cut off. The shark was harpooned and captured, and on opening the stomach of the animal, there were the two little black hands. The boy recovered, and now earns a living by showing his hands, which he has preserved in spirits, to compassionate strangers. If the sea-sharks are bad, the land-sharks are equally so, and it requires an hour's hard bargaining to have your luggage carried from the Custom House to the hotel—a distance of a hundred yards—even for the exorbitant sum laid down in the official tariff.

The Hotel Delfino is in keeping with the wretched town, and rather than sleep there I determined to start at once to Carácas. Having made arrangements that my heavy luggage should arrive there early next morning by coach, I hired a mule for three pesos—dollars—and set off for the capital by the famed Indian path. The distance from La Guaira to Carácas by the new coach-road is over twenty miles, and as the crow flies about nine, but then the great Silla has to be crossed. At the end of a narrow ill-paved street we reached the ravine, down in whose depths several swarthy washerwomen were dabbling in about two inches of water, which was all that remained of the usual mountain torrent. This we followed for a short distance, and then turned off to the right, up an excessively steep and stony path.

From the fort, the view over the town and the neighbouring village of Maquetia towards Cape Blanco was charming, and it was a relief to have left behind the insufferably hot streets. I do not think my steed was accustomed to extend his walks farther than this fort, as henceforth my time was fully occupied in persuading him to move. Before starting I had remarked to his owner that he hardly seemed up to my weight, but the reply was that, in spite of his appearance, he had many good points and his indomitable spirit atoned for all imperfections. His points certainly were numerous, but unfortunately they were all physical, as a more angular creature I had never seen—in fact he was all points, and I soon discovered that his indomitable spirit was unquestionable. After repeated efforts to make the saddle stay in its proper place, I at last fastened the girths so tightly that I was sure nothing could move it. In this endeavour I had been aided by the animal, who very kindly, as I thought, drew himself into the smallest possible compass. Hardly was I again seated when he commenced to swell, and in a second the girths were in shreds and the saddle and its occupant slid to the ground. In Guiana, tapirs are said to rid themselves of boa-constrictors in the same manner. With the assistance of cord and boot-laces I managed to patch up the broken tackle, but my future progress was necessarily very slow.

The path was ever winding up and up, and pretty scenes were continually opening. Here was a bold rock sparsely covered with prickly pears or magueys, and there in a deep ravine, through which a mountain torrent ran in many leaps and falls, the light green plantain fields were ruffled by the breeze into waves of frosted silver. Plantations of coffee and bananas fringed the path, and at the hill corners, where the ground fell steeply to the valley below, were perched the owners' houses, with their clean white walled drying grounds, which looked like little forts. Over the large gateway of one of these, which was particularly neat and flourishing, was the inscription. "Rio Grande," Señ^r. Pacheco, 1877. The proprietor, or perhaps the superintendent, was sunning himself on the doorstep, whilst his old wife improved the opportunity by a searching examination of his head.

From the back of his rancho there was a delightful view looking towards the sea. On all sides the forest was gradually giving place to cultivation, and even the steepest of the rocky angles were in many places blackened by the destroying fire. Occasionally, where the woods were thick brilliant cotingas flew in and out, and amongst the coffee trees glossy green jacamars darted about like giant humming-birds. There were only a few bright butterflies, but a great variety of gorgeous beetles. Some of the latter were of great size, and most of wonderfully metallic hue. Others were of satiny green with black spots, silvery white with red lines, black with crimson bands, brown with yellow bands; there were blues, greens and velvety browns, all touched with rich bronze, and as different in shape as in colour. Here was one clouded like a goat-sucker, there another in maroon velvet ornamented with black hieroglyphics, some with antennæ three inches in length, others with only a horn.[112]

Afterwards in Carácas I had an opportunity of inspecting a private collection of Coleoptera, and I was astonished at the amazing variety of species belonging to Venezuela, and their extraordinary shapes and strange proportions:

"Their shape would make them, had they bulk and size,

More hideous foes than fancy can devise,

With helmet heads and dragon scales adorned,

The mighty myriads, now securely scorned,

Would mock the majesty of man's high birth,

Despise his bulwarks, and unpeople earth."

The only four-legged animals that we saw were small donkeys, so laden that the legs and ears were the only parts visible, and their great bulk made it a difficult matter to avoid collision.

At last we reached the top of the ridge of Avila, on one side of which were ravines and cultivated slopes and hill spurs trending away to the blue sea, and on the other rounded hill-spurs that half concealed the city of Carácas, which was situated in the valley below. The south-western limit of the valley was bounded by the strangest range of hills ever seen; hundreds of sharp skeleton ribs formed the base, and these were of all shades of brown, green, yellow, and red. Above them rose the grey and arid slopes, cut into endless clefts and chasms, and over their summit range after range of mountain stretched away to the horizon. Soon we left the Indian path, and descended by the old military road, half-paved, steep, and winding towards the city. The descent seemed almost as long as the ascent, and I began to wonder how so low an elevation—for Carácas is less than 3,000 feet above the level of the sea—could possess a climate which has been designated that of "perpetual spring."

When we entered the city limits it was night, as instead of the usual four hours, our journey had occupied nearly eight. Trusting to my mule to find its way to its stable in the hotel, for none of the few people who were still abroad could give me any direction, we at last arrived opposite a spacious building, the Legislative Palace, which was surrounded with sleeping soldiers. There they lay in companies and detachments across the roads, on the side walks, and under the porticoes. Could a revolution have suddenly broken out? Strange that they should not have known anything about it at La Guaira! A sentry opposed my progress by pointing his musket at me, but the mule was in a hurry for the first time, and could not stop. Soon after it walked through an open gateway on the opposite side of the Palace, and I found myself in the courtyard of the hotel. There I heard that there was no revolution at present, but the military and most of the inhabitants slept out of doors, for fear of another earthquake similar to that which a few days previously had destroyed the neighbouring town of Cúa.

For a Spanish American city the Hôtel Saint Amand had fair accommodation and good living. The former was limited, as the best rooms were occupied by the English Minister, but to partake of the latter all the non-resident inhabitants of the town and the members of the Legislature used to assemble. Still there was plenty of room for improvement in the establishment, and the new hotel which is about to be built will probably supersede the old one.

From the accounts I had heard of Carácas, I had expected to find a bracing atmosphere after the heat of Guiana, but I was doomed to be disappointed. From the time I arrived until I left, neither the days nor the nights were enjoyable. No breeze tempered the heat, the air was dull and heavy, the sun was as hot as at La Guaira—which is said to be one of the hottest places in the world—and the general feeling was one of depression. Of course, I was told, it was an exceptional season, that the heat was unusual, and that the oldest inhabitant—that unfailing encyclopedia of dates and events—could not remember such weather. Where can one go in the present day without finding exceptional weather, and changes that are always astonishing to the oldest inhabitant?

After leaving Bermuda—and, indeed, whilst we were there—we had met with nothing but exceptional seasons. At St. Thomas it was said to be exceptionally cool with the thermometer at 89.° At Martinique such rain had never been known. At Trinidad it was extraordinarily dry. In Demerara there was an unheard of drought, and here in Carácas weather-prophets foretold dire phenomena from the unusual state of the atmosphere and its unwonted sultriness.

Since the destruction of Cúa—of which I shall speak in another chapter—the alarm had increased in Carácas; nor, after two severe shocks on the 13th, was it at all diminished by a printed warning issued on the 15th of April by Señor Briceño, a scientific gentleman of the city, who had made the study of earthquakes one of his principal pursuits. In it he wrote to this effect: "Be watchful! humanity compels me to place the inhabitants of Carácas on their guard, for I believe there are causes for fear, and the situation is alarming." He then showed how in former earthquakes the shocks corresponded with the different phases of the moon, and affirmed that "it was much to be feared that at full moon on Wednesday the 17th of the month (April), at 1° 29′ 0″ at night, a tremendous shock would be experienced." It was in vain that men of great scientific attainments refuted the arguments of Señor Briceño, in vain that they asserted that all the combined intellect of the world could not foretell earthquakes, and that regarding such phenomena nothing could be affirmed and nothing denied, a panic had seized the people of Carácas, which increased as the prophesied time approached. To have turned a river with a book, or have stayed an avalanche with a wise saying, would have been as easy as to have stemmed the tide of the general alarm by scientific discussion.

It was Holy Week, but for fear of a catastrophe the religious ceremonies did not take place, and the churches were closed. The weather was damp and changeable. A painful silence reigned in the deserted streets, and scarcely a house gave signs of being inhabited. An immense number of people had left the city and gone into the country, taking their household effects with them. Carriages and conveyances of all sorts demanded exorbitant prices for transportation, and received them. The great square—La Plaza Bolivar—was like an encampment. From its trees hundreds of hammocks were suspended, its avenues and gardens were covered with picturesque tents, its benches and seats were turned into couches, and every available spot was occupied with camp bedsteads, canvas stretchers, or sofas. To avoid a similar fate to that which befell a regiment of 800 soldiers who perished in the great earthquake of 1812, when Carácas was destroyed, all the military had left their barracks and slept in the open air. The other plazas, and even the Calvario, presented a similar appearance to that of the principal square.

To add to the sad scene which the city presented, the neighbouring heights and woods were on fire, and the heavy smoke thickened the dense atmospheric vapours. The day previous to the expected fatality passed slowly and mournfully away. As night advanced, anxiety increased. It was intensely still, the only sounds were those of coughing and crying children, and the moans of frightened women. One o'clock sounded from the cathedral, and then the quarter. Heads appeared at tent doors, pale faces grew paler, watches were examined, there was an extraordinary air of expectancy, and people only listened. The clock struck the half hour. Everyone breathed again, a confused murmur arose simultaneously, the name of Briceño was received with jeers and laughter, some women fainted and others fell into hysterics now that the tension was removed, and the panic was over. None, except the experienced, can appreciate the intense dread inspired by earthquakes; some may say they are too accustomed to them to care for them, but it is not those who live in South America, where the terrible shocks level houses, villages, and towns in a few seconds.

In 1812, there was a roar as of cannon firing, then a silence; this was followed by a tremulous motion, which increased until the ground seemed to roll in great waves, and in a moment the city of Carácas was in ruins and 12,000 people perished. Of late years there have been an extraordinary number of tidal waves, devastating storms, and earthquakes in Peru, Chili, and Ecuador; the direction of the convulsions has been more and more northerly, and since the destruction of Cúcuta in 1874 the north of South America has been widely shaken. The wise men of the south have paid much attention to the causes of these convulsions of nature, and numerous theories have been indulged in. By some they have been attributed to luni-solar attraction, by others to the transits of Venus and Mercury, to comets, and to different electric influences. Quite lately, a sensation has been created in Europe by the prediction that we are rapidly approaching one of the most pestilential periods of the earth's history. And why? Because in 1880, or soon after, the perihelia of the four great planets—Jupiter, Uranus, Saturn, and Neptune—will be coincident. The theory is that, when one or more of the largest planets is nearest the sun, the temperature and condition of our atmosphere are so disturbed as to cause injurious vicissitudes, terrible rains, and prolonged droughts &c., resulting in the destruction of crops and pestilence among human beings and domestic animals. Soon, for the first time in 2,000 years, four planets are to be against us, and we are warned that every living thing will be put to a severe and trying ordeal.

Various prophets have arisen who have foretold the advent of great convulsions within certain dates, but I think the Caraqueñan astronomer alone has been bold enough to predict the destruction of a city by an earthquake, at a given hour and minute, taking for his data the changes of the moon. It is strange that, for so long a period, a mysterious power should have been attributed to the cold, peaceful moon, or its phases. Superstition has assigned to it great influence over health, over the weather, over the tides, over the ascent of sap in trees, over vegetation, &c., and we all know how dangerous it is said to be to sleep with the moon's rays falling on the face. Eminent men of science have declared that these ideas have no foundation whatever, and that neither theoretically nor practically have they ever been proved true in the smallest particle. Yet on account of their antiquity and the firm hold they have established on public belief, it is probable they will exist for a much longer time yet. Regarding the periods at which earthquakes occur, Humboldt has said that, if it were possible to notice the daily state of the earth's superficies, one would soon be convinced that the earth was always being shaken at some point or other. For the inhabitants of Venezuela, it is an alarming fact that the intervals of time between the great earthquakes are growing less and less. In 1766, a great earthquake occurred at Carácas, and in 1812, Carácas was totally destroyed, as were Cumaná in 1853, Tocuyo in 1868, Cúenta in 1874, and Cúa in 1878.

CHAPTER XXVI.

EL PASEO—HISTORICAL RENOWN—RESERVOIRS—VIEW OF
CARACAS—RIVERS OF PARADISE—COMPARED WITH
MEXICO—PLAZA DE BOLIVAR—STATUE OF THE
LIBERATOR—ENTRY INTO CARACAS—FUNERAL CORTEGE—
A NATION'S GRATITUDE.

For a view of Carácas and its neighbourhood, no better point can be chosen
than the summit of the "Calvario," or, as it is now called, the "Paseo-Guzman
Blanco." The hill lies to the west of the city, and has been changed from a
barren waste into a very pretty garden, with winding carriage-drive and walks.
It has an historical renown, as it was here that the old Indian rulers of the
country made their last fight against the Spanish invaders, and from its
summit, where now stands the statue of the late President, the Cacique
Paramaconi defied to single combat the leader of the Spanish host.

On the side nearest to the town the slopes are laid out with flower-beds,
rockeries, fountains and miniature cascades. The shrubs and plants are of
hot, temperate and cold climes; there are lichens and ferns, lilies, sunflowers,
two or three kinds of hybiscus, gardenias, dahlias, verbenas, sago palms,
roses, heliotropes, lantanas, honeysuckles, and various brilliant creepers. In
the centre of the beds on the summit were two magnificent clusters of one
of the commonest yet showiest orchids—Cattleya mossix—in Venezuela.
The large flowers were of a rich rose colour and the lip delicately spotted; in
each cluster I counted over two hundred blossoms, and they formed most
attractive centre-pieces. Near by are the reservoirs which supply the city with
water from the river Macarao. They are cut out of the solid rock and are of
fine proportions; the distributing pipes are of iron, but it seems a mistake
that the aqueduct itself should have been made by open trench-work instead
of by piping.

From our elevation, Carácas looks like all other Spanish American towns;
low houses with brown and red roofs, among which stand out conspicuously
numerous cupolas, domes, spires, towers and the white façades of the
churches. The city divides the valley of Chacao into two parts, that towards
the east looking fresh and green with coffee and sugar plantations, thick
groves and forest; and the other, towards the south-west, fertile and
cultivated but without the rich woodland which marks the opposite side.
Winding about through rows of poplars and willows, the river Guaire flows
through the valley in a south-easterly direction, being joined in its course by
three little streams called respectively El Caroata, El Catuche, and El Anauco.
These three streams divide the town into four parts and have broad, deep
beds, but in the dry season would hardly rank above gutters; yet a national

writer, taking them, I suppose at the flood, has recognised in them—together with El Guaire—the four rivers of Paradise, and taking into consideration its climate of perpetual spring, has compared the situation of Carácas to that of Eden.

Still, small as these streams may be, their green banks clothed with orange, quince and avocata trees with here and there plantain, or sugar and coffee estates, give a bright smiling aspect to the valley which contrasts with the arid range of the southern hills.

The northern sierra, with its domed Silla, is also barren and grim for a considerable portion of its lower half, but above it is crowned with fine trees and foliage. I tried hard to be impressed with the scenery so highly praised by Humboldt, but I failed. Perhaps it was because I could not shake off the remembrance of another valley view, viz: that of Mexico from the hill of Chapultepec, which I had seen the previous year. In the two panoramas, there were just sufficient points of resemblance to cause a comparison. The green plain, the poplar rows, the magueys, the weeping willows, the cypresses, the ruined habitations, the white city and the mountain frame were in both pictures, but the view of modern Carácas was only a diminutive shadow that faded almost out of sight with the memory of the Mexican landscape. In the latter, everything is on so magnificent a scale, and all is enshrouded in the glamour of history.

From Chapultepec, with its giant cypresses and sad associations, the eye wanders over the garden, villages, cultivated-fields and swamps, avenues of poplars, and great aqueducts to the city itself, with its innumerable churches and convents. Beyond it sparkles a silver lake and canal, and the whole is enclosed by lofty mountains, above which tower the snow-covered heights of Popocatapetl and Iztaccihuatl, the volcanic guardians of the city of Montezuma. Though externally Carácas presents a similar appearance to other Spanish American towns, yet internally it is far brighter and more cheerful. Its streets, which intersect one another at right angles, are broad and clean, the houses are well-built, the merchants' stores and the shop-windows are quite attractive, and what with flowers, fountains and statues, the Paris of South America—as the inhabitants love to call their little town—at certain seasons looks gay and animated.

In the centre of the city is the chief Plaza—Plaza de Bolivar—which is flanked by the Cathedral, the President's or the Yellow House (Casa amarilla) as it is called out of compliment to the White House at Washington, the Archbishop's Palace, and the usual collection of small shops and "palperias" that abound in all plazas. The trees and flowers are carefully tended, and the benches and chairs are not only numerous, but, strange to say, comfortable.

When there is no moon the Plaza is well lighted by pretty clusters of oil-lamps. Once the city was lighted by gas, but the company—like other Venezuelan projects—failed, and now oil is used.

The middle of the Plaza is occupied by a magnificent equestrian statue of Simon Bolivar the Liberator. It is a work of art that must be deemed fully worthy of the great man, even by his most ardent admirers. An unprejudiced observer might ask whether the man was worthy of the statue. It is doubtful whether the true life and character of Bolivar will be known or at least acknowledged. I have lately read his memoirs by General Holstein, who was chief of the Staff of the President Liberator, and with whom he claims great intimacy. The author here says, "The dominant traits in the character of General Bolivar are ambition, vanity, thirst for absolute, undivided power, and profound dissimulation.... Paez was heard to tell Bolivar, after the action at Villa del Cura, that he would move off his own troops and act no more with him in command; adding, 'I never lost a battle wherein I acted by myself, or in a separate command, and I have always been defeated when acting in concert with you and under your orders.' ... To these brave men (here a number of men are named) Colombia and Bolivar himself owe the expulsion of the Spaniards, and the salvation of the country, if their present expulsion may be called so. The brightest deeds of all these Generals were performed in the absence of Bolivar. Abroad they were attributed to his military skill and heroism, while in fact he was a fugitive a thousand miles from the scenes of their bravery, and never dreaming of their successes.... General Bolivar, moreover, has never in person commanded a regiment, nor four soldiers. He has never made a charge of cavalry, nor with a bayonet. On the contrary, he has ever been careful to keep himself out of danger.... Bolivar has several times offered his resignation, but never unless he knew beforehand that no one would dare appear in favour of accepting it.... The great mass of the people are ignorant, bigoted and rude, to a degree not easily conceived by one educated in almost any Protestant country. Hence it is that Bolivar's speeches, proclamations, promises, conversations, are thought of so highly. These people, once getting a notion into their heads, keep it fast. They think Bolivar a great man, and believe that his monstrous faults are in fact the faults of others, because he tells them so."

Colonel Hippisly in his "Narrative of the Expedition to the Rivers Orinoco and Apure, in South America," says:—

"Bolivar would ape the great man. He aspires to be a second Bonaparte in South America, without possessing a single talent for the duties of the field or the cabinet.... He has neither talents nor abilities for a general, and especially for a commander-in-chief.... Tactics, movements, and manœuvres are as unknown to him as to the lowest of his troops. All idea of regularity, system, or the common routine of an army, or even a regiment, he is totally unacquainted with. Hence arises all the disasters he meets, the defeats he suffers, and his constant obligations to retreat whenever opposed to the foe."

Certainly his life was one of extraordinary vicissitudes; he was perpetually flying from, or returning to, his country. At one moment an outcast, at the next making a glorious entry into Carácas. In reference to one of these returns the author I first quoted, says:—

"The entry of General Bolivar into Carácas (August 4th, 1813) was the most gratifying event of his whole military career. But here I cannot omit to mention a singular and characteristic trait of that vanity of which I have already spoken. Previous to his entry into Carácas, a kind of triumphal car was prepared, like that which the Roman consuls used on returning from a campaign after an important victory. Theirs was drawn by horses; but Bolivar's car was drawn by twelve fine young ladies, very elegantly dressed in white, adorned with the national colours, and all selected from the first families in Carácas. They drew him in about half-an-hour from the entrance of the city to his residence; he standing on the car, bareheaded and in full uniform, with a small wand of command in his hand. To do this was surely extraordinary on their part; to suffer it was surely much more so on his. Many thousands were eye-witnesses of the scene."

The same year Bolivar was again a fugitive. Once more, in December 1842, the inhabitants of Carácas flocked in immense throngs with banners, pennants, oriflammes, and trophies of war, to do honour to Bolivar. But this time it was a funeral procession, as the remains of the Liberator were being brought for interment in the city. In a poem on Simon Bolivar, Whittier has written:—

"How died that victor? In the field with banners o'er him thrown,

With trumpets to his falling ear, by charging squadrons blown,

With scattered foemen flying fast and fearfully before him,

With shouts of triumph swelling round, and brave men bending o'er him?

Not on his fields of victory, nor in his council hall,

The worn and sorrowful leader hears the inevitable call,

Alone he perished in the land he saved from slavery's ban,

Maligned, and doubted, and denied, a broken-hearted man."

But the question naturally arises, how is it possible that Bolivar should have liberated his country, and preserved in himself the supreme power, without superior talents? To this General Holstein replies:—"If by 'liberating his country' it be meant that he has given his country a free government, I answer, that he has not done so. If it be meant that he has driven out the Spaniards, I answer that he has done little, or nothing, towards this; far less, certainly, than the meanest of the subordinate chieftains. To the question, how he can have retained his power without superior talents, I answer, in the first place, that the reputation of superior talents goes a great way.... The stupid management of the Spanish authorities has facilitated all the operations of the patriots. The grievous faults of Bolivar and some of his generals have been exceeded by those of his adversaries. It is not strange, therefore, that Bolivar should have been able to do all that he has done with very limited talents."

A late writer on Venezuela—Señor Miguel Tejera—has thus summed up the character of Bolivar.

"Bold and fortunate as Alexander, a patriot like Hannibal, brave and clement like Cæsar, a great captain and profound statesman like Napoleon, honourable as Washington, a sublime poet, a versatile orator, such was Bolivar, who united in his own mind all the vast multiplicity of the elements of genius. His glory will shine in the heaven of history, not as a meteor that passes and is lost in the bosom of space, but as a heavenly body whose radiance is ever increasing."

Between two such extremes of blame and praise as those I have quoted, a middle line may perhaps give a true estimate of the character of the Liberator; and, though his fame may not have been spotless, though he may have been neither a great warrior nor a statesman, yet he was a patriot, and above all, successful. Alive, he was by turns a demi-god and an impostor; dead, his beautiful monument in the Cathedral of Carácas testifies to the reverence of the nation.

CHAPTER XXVII.

THE LEGISLATIVE PALACE—A COMPLIMENT TO THE
CAPITOL AT WASHINGTON—PLAZA DE GUZMAN BLANCO—
THE UNIVERSITY—SAN FELIPE—REMINISCENCES OF
HUMBOLDT—A STRANGE DISEASE—PROJECTS IN
VENEZUELA—EARTHQUAKE AT CUA—THE LEGISLATURE—
LEAVE FOR LA GUAIRA.

From the Plaza Bolivar you pass at once into the square where stands the
Legislative Palace. This edifice of Doric architecture is graceful and imposing,
but does not impress one with the idea of the necessary solidity in so
earthquaky a country. A handsome court with a large fountain (fine as regards
its material, but feeble in its water-jets) divides it into two parts, one of which
is surmounted by a huge dome—another compliment to the city of
Washington—that will probably fall at the first severe shock. The most solid
portions of the building are the iron pillars of the corridors which came from
England.

The history of the building of this edifice is singular. The original site was
occupied by the Convent of La Concepcion. One morning the convent was
missing; it had been swept away during the night by the order of the
President, and already hundreds of workmen were busily engaged erecting a
new structure. Such were the activity and enthusiasm displayed in this work,
that within ninety days the Chambers destined for the Legislature were ready
for occupation. Whenever one of the numerous arches was finished, the
event was celebrated with music and fireworks, and when the last sound of
the hammer was heard, previous to its occupation, the occasion was made
one of general rejoicing. A pretty little garden plaza runs down one of the
sides of the Palace, and in the centre is another equestrian statue of heroic
proportions, which has been raised in honour of Guzman Blanco, "the
illustrious American and Regenerator of Venezuela," who built the palace
and the aqueduct. I do not think his successor, General Alcántara, the present
President, has built anything, but, if he would introduce ice into the Paris of
South America, a niche might be found for him in the Temple of Fame.

On the opposite side of the little garden, and running parallel with the Palace,
stands the University and the Museum, both of which have a modern rococo
façade in semi-gothic style, that contrasts strangely with the arched cloisters
and great stone patios in the interior of the ancient building. The exterior
decoration is perhaps too suggestive of the educational system that is carried
on inside. Yet in spite of teaching a somewhat superficial character, public
instruction received a great impetus during the Presidency of Guzman
Blanco, and the great increase in the number of schools and scholars

promises favourably for the progress of this Republic, whose chief city has earned from some writers the cognomen of the "American Athens." It must be admitted that the Museum is not a credit to the city; its eminent director— Dr. Ernst—has laboured long and arduously in its cause, and has hitherto vainly implored the Government to support the institution. Promises are made, but only to be broken, projects are inaugurated, but never carried out; and at present there can be no better example of a "whited sepulchre" than the Museum of Carácas.

With the exception of the cathedral, none of the numerous churches offer much interest to a visitor. That of San Felipe Neri is a fine edifice, and its exterior presents a curious appearance on account of the numerous cupolas which adorn it. Already four generations have contributed largely towards its completion, and it is still unfinished.

One day when wandering near the Pantheon I passed through an ancient doorway, and found myself in a little wilderness, in which stood ruined walls and rooms open to the sky. Trees thrust themselves through the broken pavement, moss and grasses grew on the fissured stones, vines twisted themselves about the empty window spaces, and lizards and butterflies were the only living creatures to be seen. It resembled many other of the fragments that alone recall the terrible earthquake of 1812, but it possessed a special interest, for it was once the home of Humboldt when he visited Carácas in 1800. Another relic of Humboldt is to be seen in the market-place, where, on a brick pillar, stands a sun-dial which he is said to have erected, although the inscribed date (1803) hardly corresponds with the time of his visit. The market differed in no particular from the usual Spanish American market. The geography of arrangement was just the same; stalls with imported goods, calicoes, cloths, hardware, &c.; then cordage, baskets, and native manufactures; then fruit and vegetables, poultry in eel-pot cages, and turkeys tied by the leg. Last of all, the meat-market. Here and there were some small parrots, cardinals, and mocking-birds, but not a specimen of the lovely "siete colores,"[113] a bird I was very anxious to obtain. On the Orinoco I was told I should be able to obtain them at Carácas, here they said I should only find them on the Orinoco. There was very little beauty and a great amount of ugliness amongst the market women; a few pensive Indians, with their mahogany babes slung across their backs, carrying off the palm in both instances. The most curious sight, and at the same time the most repulsive, was that of a negro who was literally covered with large round knobs from head to foot. I was told the name of the terrible disease, but have forgotten it.

To gain an idea of the celebrated Caraqueñan beauty, neither the market, nor even the Plaza Bolivar on band nights, must be visited. On Sundays it is the rude fashion for the youth of Carácas to congregate round the door of the favourite church, near the University, and there to feast their eyes on the lovely figures that have been attending mass. That it is worth their while to do so is evident from the never-failing throng of admirers. The prevailing type of beauty has very distinct characteristics. The expression of the face is spirituelle, and, in colour, white as alabaster, but tinged with a healthy glow. The eyes are dark and lustrous as the hair, and the teeth perfect. But occasionally one sees types similar to the "rubias" or "morenas" of Mexico; the former with gold or auburn hair and soft eyes of the deepest blue, and the latter with delicate olive complexion, black, poetic eyes, and brown-black hair. These beauties are by no means numerous, and beauty tinted by nature is rare, but altogether I do not think anyone could deny that the women of Carácas are worthy of their reputation.

The environs of the town are neither picturesque nor interesting; the roads are unshaded and dusty, that to Sabana Grande—a favourite drive—particularly so. On the way there, and just within the city limits, may be seen another of Venezuela's failures. This time it is a railway, which was intended to connect Carácas with Petaré. The station is there, and a short distance of grass-covered rails, but they, together with a broken engine and a mouldy carriage, alone represent the projected means of communication. Harbour improvements, railroads, gas and ice companies, and all advances in civilization seem to fail in Venezuela; nothing succeeds except revolutions and statues. And yet the lemon—which those in authority call country—is squeezed to the last drop!

Near the station is a plantation—La Guiana—whose owner must have been disgusted with the repeated failures of the city, as over his gateway is inscribed the legend,[114] "Dost thou love liberty? then live in the country." Beyond Petaré is the curious Cave of Encantado, which contains bats, stalactites, quaint rock formations, and the usual accessories of a well-appointed cavern. In the valley of the Tuy are some pretty villages, and as it was there that the severest shocks of the late earthquake had been felt, it was of more interest than usual. In the neighbourhood of Cúa, and for some miles before reaching that town by the Charayave road, the signs of desolation were especially apparent. Houses in ruins, fallen church towers, tottering walls, and deep chasms in the earth, all betokened the excessive violence of the earthquake.

For days previous to the great catastrophe of the 12th of April, the inhabitants of Cúa had suffered from the intense heat. The air was heavy with a yellow vapour, and chairs and pieces of furniture felt as if they had been exposed to the sun. Slight shocks were continually felt, and repeated detonations like distant musketry shots were heard. On the 12th the church bells were agitated by a movement, a low, rumbling sound, as of thunder, brought the frightened people from their houses, then all was quiet again.

Sand of a leaden colour burst up from the streets and patios. Hours of complete calm ensued, and it was anticipated that the worst was over. At 8.40 p.m. Cúa was a pretty, flourishing town; at 8.41 it, was a cemetery. From east to west ran the earthquake wave, and this was instantly followed by perpendicular oscillations which left no house standing. There was no time for escape, and beneath the ruins four hundred people were buried. Very few who were indoors at the moment of the shock were saved. The wife of one of the principal merchants was standing near her doorway, when suddenly she saw the walls open, and she was buried beneath the *débris*; she was not crushed, however, as a great quantity of tobacco and piles of skins prevented the mass from touching her. With her freed hand she saved herself from suffocation, and all through that terrible night she heard the groans of her husband who was buried near her. He died, but she was dug out alive.

Three days later a soldier, who was passing a ruin, heard a small voice call out "I am hungry." Search was made, and in an aperture formed by three large stones was found a child, the only one saved out of a large household. A singular circumstance occurred in one of the houses whose owner had for many years been accustomed to prepare and decorate the sacred image of the Tomb, which was carried in procession during Holy Week. This casket was in one of the largest rooms, when two of the walls fell outwards leaving the ceiling poised in equilibrium by a single beam. In this position it remained until the image was removed in safety, and shortly afterwards another shock dislodged it.

At daybreak, when the disinterment of those who had been overwhelmed commenced, the most heartrending scenes were witnessed. Mothers sought children only to find disfigured corpses; husbands discovered their dead wives pressing their babies in their arms. In many cases features could not be recognised, for fire had completed the work commenced by the falling habitations. Some lives were taken away in sleep, others when employed in various occupations. Here a hammock formed a shroud, and there an open book lay by the side of its reader. For days after the destruction of the town, shocks of earthquakes were felt and subterraneous rumblings heard, but at length these died out, and a troubled peace rested with the survivors of unhappy Cúa.

Perhaps I visited Carácas at an unfortunate time, but it certainly seemed to me to be the most stupid town I had ever seen. There was very little to see, and no amusements of any kind, unless a weekly lottery and the continual firing of rockets can be classed as such. Of the latter, the people were never tired, and day and night they were thus commemorating some civil or religious event. The perpetual hissing and explosions reminded me of the conversation once held by Ferdinand, King of Spain, and a Mexican courtier, when the news had arrived of a successful revolution.

"What do you suppose the Mexicans will be doing now?" said the King.

"Letting off rockets, your Majesty."

"Well—I wonder what they are doing now in Mexico?" said the King in the afternoon.

"Letting off rockets, your Majesty."

"What will your countrymen be doing at this time?" said the King in the evening.

"Letting off rockets, your Majesty."

Day after day I attended the demure and uninteresting debates of the Legislature, and once witnessed the official presentation of the new American Minister to the President. This ceremony, which took place in the handsome state-room of the palace, was brilliantly attended by the élite of Carácas, and was simply but imposingly conducted. The Minister was an agreeable, well-read gentleman but, unfortunately, neither he nor any of his family understood a single word of Spanish, and of all towns Carácas is the least entertaining for a foreigner who does not speak the language. I think that, after arriving, they never ceased to regret that they had left their home in the valley of the Mississippi. To a very dry manner the Minister added great quaintness and humour of expression, and his society made a very pleasant change in the dulness of the hotel life. He was fond of exaggerating his natural American intonation and quaint pronunciation, and when with grave and rather pompous air he slowly uttered his long carefully worded sentences, the effect was irresistibly comic. "My young English friend," he said one day to me, in the course of conversation, "we look upon your best men as Americans; John Bright, Cobden, Dickens and Gladstone: they air Americans. Our recent visitor, the Emperor of Brazil, ought to be an American, he had quite an outfit of intelligence, and, Sir, if Dom Pedro would come over to the States and settle, mind—I say and settle, we would make a senator of him."

On another occasion he said, "Sir, you air a traveller, if you've been to Florida you air a traveller; out of a thousand people you may meet not five have visited Florida; and even in the great American nation, which stretches from the Atlantic to the Pacific and from 49° north to the confines of Mexico, though ten may have been to Paris hardly one will have seen Florida. Sir, you air a traveller."

My only regret in leaving Carácas was bidding good-bye to my kind-hearted friend. It had been my intention to proceed overland to Valencia and Puerto

Cabello from Carácas for the purpose of seeing the beautiful lake and some of the most fertile parts of Venezuela. As the steamers which touch at the different ports only remain a few hours, and are liable to arrive twenty-fours before or after their appointed time, it is necessary for passengers to anticipate them. Not wishing to remain on the coast longer than I could avoid, I had timed my departure from Carácas so as to catch the French Mail at Puerto Cabello, allowing myself four days for the journey. Inland travel is very limited, the charge for carriages or mules is most exorbitant. After much trouble I at last hired some animals at a price which ought to have bought them and the guide. However, as they did not appear at the appointed time, I suppose their owner repented his bargain, and as it would have been too late to seek others, I was obliged to return to La Guaira.

CHAPTER XXVIII.

CARRIAGE ROAD BETWEEN CARACAS AND LA GUAIRA—THE "COW-TREE"—A VENEZUELAN SUCCESS—FRENCH MAIL STEAMER—LEAVE LA GUAIRA—PUERTO CABELLO—GOLFO TRISTE—MILITARY HISTORY—CURACOA—GULF OF MARACAIBO—SAVANILLA—EMERALD MINES—CLOUDS OF BUTTERFLIES—LEAVE SAVANILLA.

In the dry season the carriage-road between Carácas and La Guaira is by no means a pleasant one. The ricketty old coaches which perform the journey have leather flaps instead of windows; if these are down you are stifled with the heat, and if they are open you are suffocated with dust. On account of the bad springs and deep ruts, you are little better than an animated shuttle-cock for a great part of the drive, and the exercise you undergo is of the most severe description.

The scenery is wild and romantic, but when I passed through it was dry and barren. Only here and there, in the deep valley on the left, were there patches of green and cultivated spots, whilst the hills on the right were rugged and aloe-clad. For the first two hours we wound up the hill-side, and then commenced a long zig-zag descent. Every now and then we had to halt, to allow the numerous pack-trains of donkeys and oxen to pass, the poor animals toiling painfully in such clouds of dust that breathing must have been difficult.

Not far from the station where we changed horses, I left the road to visit a cow-tree[115]—Palo de vaca. It was about eighty feet in height with long, thick leaves of a deep, shining green. The milk, which is said to be wholesome, is thick and glutinous and of a yellower tinge than that of a cow. A few of these wooden cows would be valuable acquisitions in many grassless regions, but I do not think any attempt to acclimatize them has ever been made.

The first view of La Guaira and the coast recalls the "Corniche" road. Below lie green fields edged with palms, groves, and white cottages standing in gardens; and beyond the clustering houses of the town the land runs out in numberless promontories into the blue sea. Truly this is a land of projects and projections! On the right and above rise steep mountains specked with the white flowers of the Frangipanni, and its ravines green with coffee plantations, mangoes and bananas. A glimpse of white houses, and the Fort of San Carlos perched above the Quebrada de Tipe, add to the picturesque element of the scene. At the pretty little village of Maiquetia they were firing off rockets, as they had not yet finished the celebration of a great event in Venezuela, viz., the completion during the past week of a single-line tramway, connecting the village with La Guaira, a distance of about a mile. And thus the contemplated railroad between the coast and the capital has ended in a one-horse car with a mile run, and even that enterprise will probably have failed in a few months. By the advice of the agent I arrived in La Guaira one day before the French mail steamer was due; as a natural consequence it was a day late. Those three days I will pass over in silence, so utterly wretched were they on account of the heat, the bad hotel, and the squalid town.

When at last the steamer arrived, the port-captain kept the passengers waiting on the wharf for about three hours before he would allow the boats to take them off. The first remark that greeted us on board was from the afore-mentioned agent.

"Show your permits, please."

"I have no permit," I replied.

"Monsieur," said the Agent, "must be good enough to return to land, and get a permit from the port-captain."

"You must really excuse me," I remonstrated, "it is too far to return, and when I bought my ticket I ought to have been informed that it was necessary to obtain a permit."

"The steamer cannot leave until you have received your permit," insisted the agent.

"Then the steamer must remain," I said coolly.

A whispered conference between the agent and his myrmidon now ensued.

"If Monsieur will not leave, the captain will be appealed to," resumed the agent.

"Appeal to the captain," was my calm but firm rejoinder.

"Monsieur must go at once," said the agent with firmness, a decision which his myrmidon seemed ready to applaud.

"Monsieur will not go," replied the passenger with equal firmness, which was greeted with applause by the other passengers.

"Once for all, will Monsieur leave?" exclaimed the agent, now furious.

"Once for all, he will not," I replied, rather angrily.

At this moment another delinquent came on board without a permit, and as I turned on my heel to look after my baggage I heard, "Monsieur must be good enough, &c." Whether this one returned to shore I do not know; if he did, he must have lost his passage, as a few minutes afterwards the anchor was lifted and we were off.

In the saloon I heard an animated discussion between the new passengers and the stewards. I think the port-captain and the head-steward must have had an arrangement between them, not to allow the passengers to come on board until after dinner. Dinner was over, and we were refused anything to eat until tea time. Now, as none of us had dined, we were hungry and did not wish to wait for another three hours. Expostulation was useless, so I sought the captain, and as he was just going to dinner, he requested me to join him, and I fared extremely well. The others, who would not go to the fountain-head, growled angrily until tea-time. I never had been glad to get on board ship before, but after the land heat and the utter impossibility of procuring anything cold to drink, the sea breeze and ice were both refreshing.

The steamer was a fine vessel, built to carry the countless hordes who were expected to visit the Paris Exhibition, *viâ* Panama. On no mail-steamer have I ever seen better attendance or such good living. The cooking was perfection, and the viands were just suited to the tropics. Abundance of cool salads—that of the cabbage-palm being particularly well made—delicious bread and coffee, really good butter, appetizing dishes, and very fair white and red wines, *ad lib.*, were items on the daily bill of fare not often found on board ship. The price of the passage was undoubtedly high, but so it was with the other lines of steamers that touched at these ports.

Close along shore we glided past the green plains around Maiquetia and the white cape, beneath which sat a row of pelicans with the most solemn physiognomies. The high coast range was broken and ribbed, deep ravines backed stretches of white sand, and the only signs of habitation were in the few canoes which floated near the shore. The next day we were still in view of the mountains of Ocumare, and soon sighted Puerto Cabello. From a distance the town appeared to be far inland, but mingled with towers and red roofs were the tall masts of vessels. Low, bush-covered islets and white sandy beaches, on which the surf broke heavily, lay between us and the town. We rounded a long point of land, and saw the Golfo Triste curving away to the north; then we entered the strangest little harbour in the world. Passing close alongside an island fort and lighthouse, we gradually drifted into a deep, narrow channel, and were soon moored to the wharf. This inside bay affords admirable shelter for shipping, but it is small, and the islets and mangrove banks on its eastern limits seem to indicate a gradual shallowing of its still waters. It is like a small swampy lake protected from the sea by sand-bars, rocks, and bushes. The town is quaint and pretty; palms, minarets, and pagoda-like towers giving it an oriental aspect. The high mountain background is crowned by two peaks, the "Tetas de Hilaria," and on the hill of the "Vigia" is an old and useless fort. To the east is Fort Mirador del Solano, on which vast sums have been spent, and which now, when nearly completed, is discovered to be of no use whatever.

Up in the mountains is the picturesque village of San Estéban, famed for its feather flowers, and also as a health resort for the fevered dwellers on the coast. In the olden days, when Puerto Cabello was the refuge for pirates, smugglers, and criminals, it was considered the most unhealthy spot in northern South America; the terrible "vómito negro" devastated the region. It has always maintained its bad reputation with the outside world, but in reality it is comparatively salubrious at the present day. Its military history eclipses that of other Venezuelan towns, as in 1743 it was attacked by an English fleet, which was repulsed with great loss, and in 1824 its capture by Generals Padilla and Paez ended the war of emancipation. Since then it has undergone three sieges. Altogether, Puerto Cabello and its environs are interesting, but the heat is too great to render a prolonged sojourn enjoyable.

Soon after leaving, we sighted the Dutch island of Curaçoa, which, during the revolution, had been the head-quarters of the Spaniards, as, although its people were with the patriots, yet the Government and the rich merchants were in favour of Spain. As we proceeded, the high mainland grew fainter, and presently we crossed the entrance of the deep gulf of Maracaïbo. Then great rocks of a ghostly whiteness started up near the ship's course, and long reaches of sand bordered the yellow green sea which surged heavily on the hot coast of Colombia. The land scenery was flat and sombre; the coast hills dwindled away to a vanishing point, and grey savannas reached to the horizon. It was dull and sad-looking and intensely hot, too hot, apparently, for the traditional dolphins which, on the previous day, had never ceased racing with the steamer, and had entertained us by the marvellous unanimity with which long lines of them would appear and disappear, taking their graceful leaps like trained steeplechasers who had disposed of their riders, but were still determined to complete the course.

Forty hours after leaving Puerto Cabello we reached Savanilla, and anchored in a large bay at a great distance from shore, where we could see only a few cottages and a lighthouse, standing in an amphitheatre of undulating green hills. It had been my intention to disembark here and proceed up the Magdalena River to Bogotá, but when the little tug came alongside to take passengers for Barranquilla, I heard that the river was too low at present even for the small steamers that run on it. This was a great disappointment, as I had been anxious to visit the emerald mines of Muzo, not only for the sake of seeing the mines themselves, but in order to obtain some specimens of the rare "Morpho Cyprio." Afterwards, at Panama, I saw two of these wonderful butterflies, and was not astonished at the belief of the miners of Muzo that the splendid insects feed on the emeralds, and so obtain their brilliant hue. Anything more exquisite than the colour and sheen it is impossible to imagine. Unfortunately for me their owner appreciated them as highly as I did, and though I was by no means illiberal in my offer, I could not tempt him to part with one of them.

Whilst we were at Savanilla great swarms of a single species of butterfly—*Danaidæ*—hovered over the vessel, and many of them rested on the deck and rigging. They appeared to be outward bound, and flew north-east in delicate clouds. As there was no breeze to blow them from the land, it must have been their own wish to migrate. If their destination was one of the islands, I am afraid the poor emigrants never could have reached it, as before we left Savanilla a strong north-easterly wind sprang up, against which they could not have sailed onwards. The heavens were already sprinkled with silver stars when we steamed out of the bay; and where only a few minutes before, in the direction of our course, there had been a bank of rainbow-coloured clouds, there was now only a pale silvery vapour that gradually diffused itself over land and sea.

CHAPTER XXIX.

TREASURES OF THE DEEP—THE SAN PEDRO ALCANTARA—
MARGARITA—SEEKING LOST TREASURE—OCEAN MINING—
NAVY BAY, COLON—INTER-OCEANIC COMMUNICATION—
GOMARA'S PROJECT—NELSON'S SCHEME—THE NICARAGUA
ROUTE—THE ACANTI-TUPISI ROUTE—INTERNATIONAL
COMMISSION.

The dream of Clarence has occupied the waking thoughts of many since
Shakespeare's time, and in the West Indies, as well as off our own coast, it
has been the ambition of treasure-hunters to find the Spanish gold which
here and there paves the sea. Near Carthagena we passed a vessel engaged
on a diving expedition, and not far from Cumaná we had seen another ship,
which was said to be in search of the vast treasure sunk in the San Pedro
Alcántara.

The history of this unfortunate vessel is an interesting one. In 1815,
Ferdinand VIII. of Spain, dispatched from Cadiz a number of transports with
men, money, and provisions, for the supply of the fleet, which was then
stationed in the Caribbean Sea. These ships sailed under the convoy of the
San Pedro Alcántara, a three-decked line of battle-ship mounting seventy-
four guns. On board were 1,400 soldiers, under the command of General
Morillo, and in the treasure-chests were between three and four million
dollars. When the San Pedro Alcántara arrived at La Guaira, the revolution
had so far progressed that the Spanish citizens of that town and of Carácas,
fearing the loss of their personal property, transferred their gold and jewels
to the man-of-war. This act was soon imitated by the convents and churches
of Venezuela, and the vessel was laden with an immense treasure of jewels,
gold and silver altar plate, valuable pictures, coin, and costly ornaments. The
jewelled tiara of the Virgin of Guadaloupe, which was sent from Valencia,
was alone of almost priceless value.

From La Guaira the San Pedro Alcántara sailed up the coast to the island of
Margarita—now known as Nueva Esparta—where the troops disembarked
and defeated the Venezuelan forces stationed there. The brave Margaritans,
who, during the War of Independence, proved themselves to be as truly
patriotic as the Llaneros, retired to the hills and inaugurated a guerilla warfare
which harassed the Spaniards beyond measure. Still their towns were open
to attack, and Asuncion, Pampatar, Norte, and others, were sacked and
destroyed by the invaders. Thus the wealth of the San Pedro was again added
to, and, as there was much treasure in these towns, it is supposed that little
was saved from the sudden descent of the conquerors.

After the plundering of the last town, orders were received that the San Pedro should sail at once to Cumaná. To celebrate their successes a grand revel was held on board one night; casks of wine and spirits were broached, and success to the ensuing expedition was so eagerly drunk that it is doubtful whether there was a single sober man in the vessel. Then arose an alarm of fire. How the fire originated is unknown, but it speedily reached a cask of brandy, which burst, and the deck was instantly deluged with liquid fire. The flames were soon darting through the hatchways and lapping the sails, and so quickly did the conflagration spread that nothing could have checked it, even if sober men had tried to stem the danger. As it was, the wild mob, mad with drink and fear, thought only of flight. With difficulty the boats were lowered, and men sought to reach them, either by jumping into them from the deck, or battling with each other in the water to clutch their sides. Of the few boats that there were, all except one were either capsized or stove in.

In the meantime the fire made its way to the powder-magazine. Suddenly a tremendous explosion rent the air, a lucid light hung for a moment over the doomed vessel, and the air was filled with mangled corpses and fragments of the ship. The after-half of the San Pedro Alcántara had been blown to pieces, and the forward half quickly sank beneath the waves. Over a thousand men perished in the fire and ocean on that night. The magazine had been situated beneath the strong chambers wherein were stored the Spanish treasure-chests, the riches of the people and churches of Venezuela and the plunder of the towns. All was now scattered and buried in the sea.

In a paper describing this disaster, it is said that in 1816 an American Captain visited the scene of the wreck, one mile from the island of Cuagua, and succeeded in securing about 30,000 dollars in silver. Again in 1845 a company was organized in Baltimore for the purpose of seeking the lost treasure. The remnant of the wreck was easily found, but owing to the lack of proper diving apparatus the attempt proved a failure. A few months later the same company sent out another expedition. This search was prosecuted under an agreement with the government of Venezuela. During the first three months quantities of copper, huge rusty anchors and guns, were dragged up, but only about 1,500 dollars in silver coin were recovered. The search had been confined to the immediate vicinity of the sunken wreck, and the divers became so dissatisfied by the ill results of their labour that they refused to continue unless those in charge of the explorations would test the theory they formed, which was that the force of the explosion had hurled the treasure-chests some distance away from the spot where the ship went down. They were humoured, and the vessel was anchored in another place. The first time the diving bell went down on the new ground, 750 dollars were picked up in two hours, and this success continued so well that in six months about 200,000 dollars in silver had been recovered. Then the major portion of the divers and crew having surreptitiously possessed themselves of such portions of the treasure as they could secrete, stole a boat and set sail for La Guaira. The remainder of the party returned to Baltimore, having been unable to pursue the exploration for want of divers.

In 1849 another American barque recovered several thousand dollars in silver, but how much is not known, as the Captain suddenly hauled his anchor on board and set sail for the Horn, bound for the new El Dorado on the Pacific coast. In 1856, 28,000 dollars were recovered, and, in 1858, 30,000 more. In April, 1877, a Captain Folingsby went to Venezuela to obtain permission from the government to search for the lost millions, and effected a contract whereby, in consideration of the payment of five per cent on all sums he might recover, he was granted the exclusive right to drag, dredge, and dive for the sunken treasures of the San Pedro Alcántara for the period of six years. Armed with this contract, Captain Folingsby organized an expedition for the thorough and exhaustive exploration of all the ocean bed over which the treasure might have been scattered by the explosion of the ship. He has had extensive experience as a diver, and having been in the employ of the Baltimore company in 1845 and 1846 in their searches, is thoroughly familiar with the ground on which he is to work. He believes that the strong boxes which held the gold, jewels, and church plate were not burst by the explosion, but simply tossed away to a greater distance than seekers have hitherto deemed it worth while to go from the wreck. No gold has as yet been found, but simply silver, and this he accepts as evidence of the correctness of his theory. He thinks that he can go over all the ground in about eight months. His dredges and drags are of the most approved patterns, fitted with special appliances such as chair-nettings, to let sand escape, but to hold everything else. As 500,000 dollars are about all that have hitherto been recovered, he has the hope of finding at least four or five millions and, with every requisite that knowledge and unrestricted capital can supply, he confidently expects to achieve success. As he was to sail from New York early in 1878, the vessel we saw near Cumaná must have been his. With that idea we cordially wished a prosperous finale to the ocean-mining of the enterprising Captain.

From Savanilla onwards to Panama the little we saw of the coast was uninteresting. We were seldom near enough to appreciate the colour-chords on beach, hill and savanna, and the sombre monotone of the land seemed but an extension of the yellow green sea. The nights were calm and beautiful, and as we sailed on and on through the great star-chamber, the vessel appeared to plunge through a sea of fire. Long gleams of blue, green and purple crested the waves that were only raised by the vessel's bow, and the teeming phosphorescent life made the starry waters more brilliant even than the sky. But pleasant as the nights were, the French Mail Company interfered with our entire enjoyment of them, by a silly order which forbade passengers to take their pillows on deck. They might sleep there if they chose—and everyone did choose—but under no circumstances were pillows allowed. Various were the devices made use of to disguise the forbidden articles, but those who indulged in them were generally awakened by a polite reminder from one of the officers or stewards that the pillows must be taken below. Then the different *ruses* had to be repeated. The pillow-prohibition was the only fault that could be found with this comfortable vessel.

Our little voyage along the Spanish Main had been slow and deliberate, but as the old Spanish proverb says "step by step goes a long way," and at last we entered a pretty horse-shoe bay surrounded by low misty hills, and were presently moored alongside one of the fine wharfs at Colon. Here we were at the narrowest point of that narrow isthmus, to cross which by water has been a problem to the great nations of the world for three centuries and a half. The project of connecting the Atlantic and Pacific Oceans by a canal is a scheme of such vast commercial importance that it may be interesting to take a rapid glance at a few of the numerous surveys made with a view to inter-oceanic communication. As early as 1513 the Spanish explorers believed in the existence of a narrow strait leading across to the Pacific. In the following year, the Spanish Government gave a secret order for the preparation of a coast-chart to determine whether such a strait really existed. In the hope of finding such a passage, Cortez sent out his expeditions and prepared a map of the Gulf of Mexico, which he sent to Spain in 1524. Then the European Powers explored and searched the whole coast-line of the New World, and at length realized the fact that from Colon the continent extended uninterruptedly north and south. Just as the Suez Canal is only an enlargement of the plan conceived and executed by the Pharaohs 4,000 years ago, so the Panama or Darien route, when completed, will be the practical result of a project contemplated as far back as three centuries and a half.

In 1551, a Spaniard of the name of Gomara proposed that a canal should be constructed to connect the oceans, and suggested three of the same routes that have been under the consideration of modern engineers. "It is true," said the proud Castilian, "that mountains obstruct the passes, but if there are mountains there are also hands; let but the resolve be made, and there will be no want of means; the Indies, to which the passage will be made, will supply them. To a King of Spain, with the wealth of the Indies at his command, when the object to be attained is the spice trade, what is possible is easy." But soon Spain fell from her high estate, religious intolerance benumbed her energies, and the project of the canal became at last a mere legend.

In 1780 the Nicaragua route was first projected, and Captain—afterwards Lord—Nelson conveyed a force of 2,000 men to San Juan de Nicaragua for the conquest of the country, and in one of his despatches said, "In order to give facility to the great object of Government, I intend to possess the great lake of Nicaragua, which at the present may be looked upon as the inland Gibraltar of Spanish America. As it commands the only water-pass between the oceans, its situation must ever render it a principal port to ensure passage to the Southern Ocean, and by our possession of it Spanish America is severed in two." The expedition was a failure, however, and nothing came of Nelson's project.

In 1814, the Spanish Cortes decreed the opening of a canal, but the matter was deferred and the decree never executed. In 1825, after the Central American States had secured their independence, they asked the co-operation of the United States in constructing a canal. In 1828, the King of the Netherlands proposed to undertake the work, and sent over General Verveer with instructions to build the canal. The General found Central America engaged in one of its regular half-yearly revolutions, and the matter was deferred until 1830, when the revolution in his own country put an end to the plans. In 1836, Mr. John Bailey made some preliminary surveys for a route across Nicaragua, which were brought to a close by the dissolution of the "Confederation of the Centre." In 1850, under appointment from the Atlantic and Pacific Ship-canal Company, Mr. Childs, of Philadelphia, began a survey on the Pacific side, and after examining several routes chose the line which terminated in Brito Harbour, giving very strong reasons against the Lake Managua route, which have been confirmed by every subsequent survey. British capitalists were interested in this route, and would have adopted Mr. Child's plans if favourable arrangements could have been made with Nicaragua. But the Nicaraguan Government finally killed the scheme, as far as British capital was concerned, by demanding twenty-five per cent of profits.

In 1873, President Grant appointed an Inter-oceanic Canal Commission, to examine the various proposed routes and report on the most feasible. The Commission considered the following surveys: the Isthmus of Tehuantepec; the Nicaragua route, *viâ* Lake Nicaragua; the Isthmus of Panama; the San Bias and Chepo route; the Caledonian and North routes; the Caledonian and Sucubti route; the Cacarica and Tuyra route; the Atrato and Truando route; and the Atrato-Napip route. The Commission unanimously reported that the Nicaragua route possessed, both for construction and maintenance of a canal, greater advantages, and offered fewer difficulties from engineering, commercial, and economic points of view, than any one of the routes shown by surveys to be practicable. This route, beginning on the Atlantic side, at or near Greytown, would run by canal to the San Juan River, thence following its left bank to the mouth of the San Carlos River, at which point navigation of the San Juan begins, and by the aid of three short canals of an aggregate length of three and a half miles reach Lake Nicaragua. Thence across the lake and through the valleys of the Rio del Medio and the Rio Grande to what is known as the Port of Brito, on the Pacific coast. No doubt exists as to the entire practicability of constructing this canal, the cost of which, with all the necessary adjuncts—locks 400 feet in length and 26 feet depth of water—may be set down as at least twenty million pounds sterling.

The last survey of the several routes has very lately been completed by Lieutenant-Commander Wyse of the French Navy. After an exhaustive survey, he judges that the best route for a canal is what he describes as the Acanti-Tupisa route. This starts from the Gulf of Darien on the Atlantic side, following the Atrato River for a short distance and passing through the valley of the Tupisa to the Tuyra River, which flows into the Gulf of San Miguel. Commander Wyse has proposed that M. de Lesseps should be President of an International Commission that shall assemble before long to examine the different lines that have been surveyed, and to select whichever will be, in their judgment, the easiest and most desirable to construct. It is probable that the choice of routes will rest between the Acanti-Tupisa and that of Nicaragua, but when work will actually be commenced on either is doubtful. Before the Atlantic and Pacific join hands across the Isthmus another century may elapse, and the problem propounded four hundred and fifty years before may still be unsolved.

CHAPTER XXX.

COLON—DEPARTURE—COLUMBUS AND MR. ASPINWALL—RAILWAY ACROSS ISTHMUS—SCENES ON THE ISTHMUS—TELEGRAPH POSTS—HOLY GHOST ORCHID—PANAMA HATS—PARADISE—MOUNT ANCON—PACIFIC MAIL STEAMER—ON THE WHARF AT PANAMA—PANAMA FROM THE SEA—LAST LOOKS.

From the sea Colon had looked pretty and mysterious; gauzy vapours floated over the town, and all we could see were the outlines of palms, a few roofs, and behind the surrounding forest the dim shadows of the distant hills. We landed, and with the vanished mists all romance disappeared. We stepped from the shelter of the roofed wharf, and in the dirty, decayed village that lay before us beheld Colon, or the city of Aspinwall as it is called by the Americans.

The principal street runs along the shore, and its shambling frame-houses with verandahs and balconies are of the most tumble-down description. Drinking saloons predominate, and the various stores and shops are stocked with a miscellaneous assortment of goods, such as shells, calico, coral, toilet articles, parrots, hats, pale ale, boots, oranges, bananas, and ready-made clothing. The untidy tenement houses, the dirty lanes, the swamps, and the apparent effort to make life in the tropics as uncomfortable as possible, give an impression of squalid poverty. Nor are the inhabitants unsuited to their dwellings; from the sallow German Jew who dispenses iced drinks across a dirty counter, to the slippered negro who beats a gong at meal time in front of a wretched eating-house, all are unkempt and unclean. The officials and their houses are too few in number to counteract the general atmosphere of unpicturesque decay, and both they and their well-appointed offices render the native unsightliness more conspicuous by contrast.

After arriving in Colon the principal aim is to get away as soon as possible. "Thank goodness it isn't a full stop," was remarked by a perspiring passenger, whose extreme heat must account for the want of brilliancy in his joke. The Panama Railroad Company facilitates this object by starting a train for Panama as soon as the passengers' luggage has arrived from the steamer. As the main street is the terminus of the railway, the entire population assembles to bid farewell to their only source of income. Then may be seen a motley crowd, each member of which is endeavouring to extract some coin or other from the pockets of their late guests. Black porters appear at the last moment with some trifling article that they have taken care their employer should forget; jet-black Africans, Jamaica negroes, half-castes, yellow Peruvians, naked children, both black and brown, all endeavour to sell some article or other, either cakes, fruit and sweetmeats, or fans, coral, and smoking-caps of palm-fibre. Nor are the passengers themselves of less varied nationalities, as the steamers from New York and St. Thomas have brought emigrants, business men, pleasure-seekers, fortune-hunters, and travellers from all parts of the world.

Here is an entire German family, from the grandmother to the baby in arms, and not one of them can speak other language than their own; there are some Mexicans carrying on a rapid conversation in mixed French, English, and Spanish, with the negro fruit-sellers, and those five ladies, who have paid such a tender adieu to the captain of the American Mail Steamer, are tourists—probably you will learn that they are not travelling *viâ* Panama on account of its cheapness, but for the sake of the sea-voyage. Then there are several commercial travellers, each of whom thinks it correct to wear one of the fibre smoking-caps and chaff the crowd in "h-less" English. Those rosy-cheeked damsels, with flower-decked hats and general gaudy aspect, are Irish servant-girls who have left New York to seek a fortune in San Francisco. On leaving the wharf I had passed two of these maidens, who were looking at the beautiful statue—the only beautiful thing in Colon—of Columbus and the Indian. Said one to the other, "Sure an' its Mr. Aspinwall himself, the man who built the town."

At last, amid a faint cheer, or rather a hoot of derision, the train moves slowly off, and we pass almost at once from the so-called civilization into the primeval forest. Perhaps we were a very ignorant set of passengers, but strange to say none of us—and some had crossed the Isthmus before—knew to whom the railroad or the land belonged. Some said both land and road belonged to England, others to America, and a few that both belonged to Colombia, who leased it to the United States. Afterwards we found out that the Panama Railway is American, by contract with the Government of New Granada,[116] to whom the land belongs.

With the history of the survey, and the building of the road, the world is familiar from the time when in 1850, "two American citizens leapt, axe in hand, from a native canoe upon a wild and desolate island, (Manzanilla), their retinue consisting of half-a-dozen Indians, who clear the path with rude knives," up to the 27th of January, 1855, when, "at midnight in darkness and rain, the last rail was laid, and on the following day a locomotive passed from ocean to ocean." The undertaking was intrepid, the expense enormous, and the loss of life tremendous. Pestilential vapours, reptiles, poisonous insects, fevers, incessant rains, working waist deep in water, insufficient food and shelter, all combined to sweep off thousands of the labourers. Americans, English, Irish, French, Germans, Austrians, natives of India, South America and the West Indies fell victims to the malarious climate, but misery and suffering seems to have fallen most heavily on the Chinese. Of these, one thousand had been brought to the Isthmus by the Company, and though as much care as was possible was taken with their health and comfort, yet before a month had elapsed almost the whole of them became affected with a suicidal tendency, and scores ended their existence by their own hands. The memory of these sad details throws a shadow over the interesting journey of forty-seven miles from ocean to ocean, where each advancing step has only been gained by the sacrifice of a human life.

The traveller will gain some idea of the deadly swamps directly the train has crossed the artificial isthmus—(for Colon is situated on the little island of Manzanilla)—which connects the island with the mainland. Dense mangrove thickets border the waters, both of the sea and swamp, the stems of those near the sea being loaded with clusters of small oysters. White egrets and an occasional roseate spoon-bill grace the banks with their presence, and the black forbidding water of the marshes is redeemed by the starry crinums and aquatic plants which grow in great luxuriance.

After passing Mount Hope, where the cemetery of Colon is situated, we are deep in the forest jungle. Cassias, pleromas, and all kinds of feathery-leaved shrubs mingle with giant cedros, ceibas, and locusts, and all are knitted together by the purple convolvulus, or by the chains of some thick-stemmed liane. Most conspicuous are the palms with their crimson clusters of fruit hanging like tassels below the green crown, and the red and yellow blossoms of the helianthus. Fleet-winged heliconias dart among the shrubs at the forest edge, and in the shady glades, which sometimes break the monotony of the jungle, silver-blue morphos and yellow and orange pieridæ flit heavily along. Now and then a flock of parroquets wheels rapidly in the air, or a black and yellow troupial pipes from a high tree top, but birds are not numerous, with the exception of the ugly "black witches,"[117] that treat the passing train with the utmost contempt. To those who have been accustomed to travel through tropical forests only, after toilsome journeys on foot or on mule-back, it is an agreeable sensation to glide—although there certainly is a good deal of jolting—swiftly through the luxuriant vegetation in a comfortable railway carriage. And yet it was strange, in the trip I have been speaking of, to witness the indifference with which most of the passengers viewed the many pretty scenes. Some did not see them at all, but played whist during the whole journey, others slept, and not a few improved the occasion by deliberately drawing up the wooden blinds, so that nothing outside should disturb their attention whilst they read. "Look at the grave-stones!" screamed one of the passengers, who hitherto had been impervious to the novel scenery. When the information was gently broken to her that the small stone-like columns were not grave-stones, but merely pillars to support the wires of the telegraph,[118] she was quite disappointed.

Near the stream called the Mindee, we saw patches of cultivated ground, and perched on the high knolls were a few picturesque wattled and thatched cottages, with clumps of bananas, mango-trees and palms. Gradually the ground became less swampy, and by the time we reached Gatun Station, situated on the eastern bank of the Chagres River, had given place to dry savanna land that stretched to the hill range. Almost immediately after leaving the station we crossed the Rio Gatun, and again entered a region of swamp and jungle. On the left rose the twin peaks known as the "Lion" and the "Tiger," conical in shape and clad with thick forest. And thus we sped on through an ever-changing scene; from marsh and swamp we passed to plain and forest hills, and from the silence of the wilderness to the life and cheerfulness of the little settlements that dot the road.

Here was a swamp covered with pretty aquatic plants, then a stream almost hidden by overhanging bamboos, then forest trees laden with orchids, and from whose branches the pendent nests of the orioles swayed to and fro, or a narrow country-lane walled in by petrœa and convolvuli so dense and of such shapely growth that they appeared like old ruins over which time had thrown a mantle of verdure. One view of the Chagres River, which we crossed near Barbacoas over a fine wrought iron bridge, was very charming. There were wide stretches of meadow-land with cattle farms, and in the broad stream which curved off to the undulating hills cows stood knee-deep, and under the high banks groups of women wearing flowers in their black hair were hard at work clothes-washing. It formed a pretty picture in the happy blending of wild forest and rural scenery. At a native village, composed of three rows of picturesque huts, standing in an open glade surrounded by palm trees, we found much needed refreshments, as breakfast that morning had been small and early.

All the inhabitants vied with each other in their efforts to secure customers, yet though the competition was great, fixed prices prevailed. There was a rare mixture of home and foreign productions; Bass's ale, claret, sardines, biscuits and potted meats were carried by some, whilst others bore trays of bread, cakes, native sweetmeats, pine-apples, oranges, inga pods, mangoes, and other fruits. Here was a little urchin with a bottle of milk, and there was another with hard-boiled eggs and neat little packets of pepper and salt. The chief trade was in eggs, and though they were not sold "four for a dollar" as in the ante-railroad days, yet the charge was sufficiently remunerative. Probably, the sellers agreed with the dairy-woman who said that a smaller price than that at which she sold her eggs "would not pay for the wear and tear of the hen." Old travellers shook their heads ominously at the quantity of mangoes, starapples, and granadillas that were consumed, and hints of Panama fever were thrown out; but the novel fruits here, and the magnificent Guayaquil white pine-apples that afterwards tempted us at Panama seemed to be irresistible. The latter were not mere consolidated lumps of sugar and water like the West Indian pine, but equalled in flavour, and in size surpassed, those of our hot-houses. It was a miracle that no one was harmed by the fruit-consumption, as everybody appeared to follow the example of Artemus Ward, who "took no thought as to his food; if he liked things he ate them, and then let them fight it out among themselves." Some bulbs of the beautiful orchid[119] known as the "Holy Ghost," on account of the marvellous image of the dove that rests within the exquisite flower-cap, were for sale, but none of the plants were in bloom, as they seldom blossom before July. They are numerous on the Isthmus, and grow luxuriantly on the decayed trunks that abound in the hot, damp, low-lying grounds.

Some of the natives wore straw hats of a crimson tint, which colour is extracted from the leaves of a vine called "china." As yet but little attention has been paid to this dye as an article of commerce, but it must be of considerable value, as neither sun nor rain alters the colour which is said to be permanent. The vine grows abundantly in the hill districts, and sheds its leaves annually. Such a dye would be vastly superior to those so-called "fast" colours, whose only "fastness" consists in their tendency to run. The hats themselves were coarse and very unlike the famed "Panama," specimens of which were only to be seen on the heads of some of the passengers from the West Indies. Although the plant—Carludovica palmata—from whose young unexpanded leaves the "Panama hats"[120] are made, grows on the Isthmus, yet the manufacture is confined to Moyobamba, on the banks of the Amazon, Guayaquil, and the Indian villages of Peru.

After leaving the refreshment-station the grade makes a gentle ascent until the summit—260 feet above sea level—is reached, and then we descend the Pacific slope. Here the scenery is bolder than previously, but the vegetation is as luxuriant as ever. Quickly we rush through cuttings and across rocky spurs, the Rio Grande winding through the forest maze below us; the pretty valley of Paraiso, enclosed in high conical hills, is passed, then once more we enter alternate stretches of swamp and cultivated savanna land.

We see meadows and cottages lying at the base of Mount Ancon, from whose summit Balboa, in 1513, saw the Pacific, and thus proved the fallacy of the belief in which Columbus died, that the New World was part of India and China. Then groups of huts, chiefly composed of flattened tin cans and shingles, came in view, and beyond them rose the Cathedral towers and the red roofs of Panama. Through the groves of cocoa-nut palms we caught sight of the glittering sea, and in a few minutes we entered a commodious station close to the wharf, where a tug lies ready to take passengers to the ocean steamer bound for California.

From Panama I had intended to visit Quito, and to descend the Amazon, but on account of ill-health I was advised to postpone that journey for a time, and to hasten to a colder climate. Of the town I, therefore, saw but little, and after a short ramble went on board the Pacific mail-steamer. Regarding the vessel, I will only say that she was very comfortable, and the food and attendance were very bad, and the ice and liquor supply grossly insufficient. The poor table was ascribed to the cheap rate of passage-money from New York to San Francisco, but when I pointed out that the Company reimbursed themselves by exorbitant coasting charges—a first-class ticket from Colon to San Francisco costing several dollars more than the entire passage money from New York to San Francisco—a shrug of the shoulders was the only answer. It is a misfortune for travellers that the Pacific Mail Steamers have no competitors on this line.

It might be imagined that in the great central hive of commerce, the old features of Panama would have been replaced by those of more modern date. But it is not so. Once leave the bustling wharf and freight-depôt, loaded with coffee, cacao, ivory nuts, pearl shells, india-rubber, ores, hides, woods, balsams, quina bales, sarsaparilla, wool, and other products collected from the two great continents, and pass through the quiet lanes into the narrow streets of the town, and the active life of the present is forgotten in the all-pervading memories of the past. It is like passing from the busy work-shops of the stone-cutters into the quiet shadows of the adjoining cemetery. Convent ruins, voiceless bell-towers, grass-grown walls, broken arches and fallen pillars, all tell of the departed glory of Panama. Mellow time-stains have tinged alike the carved stone-work and the rich mouldings of the plaster façades, and over the crumbling edifices and through the window-piercings, passion-flowers and luxuriant creepers twist and twine in the wildest confusion.

During my short ramble, I rested for a moment on the ancient ramparts with their old-fashioned sentry towers, at whose feet lay the waters of the Pacific; so still and glaring in the intense heat, and reflecting so many colours from the pink-brown walls and high tiled roofs that it resembled a sea of old Bohemian glass. The hot sun had caused the streets and walks to be deserted, and the only signs of life were the swinging hammocks in the heavy balconies, and the turkey-buzzards,[121] which with out-stretched wings sunned themselves on every roof and steeple. The natives of Panama have an odd legend, which accounts for the absence of feathers on the head and neck of these birds—gallinazos, as they call them. It is said that after the deluge,

Noah, when opening the door of the ark, thought it well to give a word of advice to the released animals. "My children," said he, "when you see a man coming towards you and stooping down, go away from him; he is getting a stone to throw at you." "Very good," said the gallinazo, "but what if he has one already in his pocket?" Noah was taken aback at this, but finally decided that in future the gallinazo should be born bald in token of its remarkable sagacity.

And now, before bidding farewell to the reader who may have glanced through these pages, let me record one more scene. Our vessel lay at anchor far out in the bay, as owing to the reef and the great rise and fall of the tide—between twelve and twenty feet—no ships of heavy tonnage can anchor within two miles of the wharf. Close to us were the pretty green islands of Perico and Flamenco, and through a quivering haze, which gave additional charm to the lovely panorama, we saw the bold and rocky promontory on which stands the city of Panama. Behind it rose the volcanic peak Ancon, crowned by a signal-station—La Vigia—forming the centre of the coronet of undulating hills that encircle the land. On either side were glimpses of white beach, palm groves and valleys, and away to the south-east, in a tangled wilderness of forest and brush-work, a solitary tower—at least we were told it was a tower—marked the site of the "ancient city of Panama." In the surrounding silver-green haze the town stood out like a dainty mosaic, whose tints of red, pearl, and brown flashed brightly in the warm sunlight. And in harmony with the tender beauty of the scene was the stillness which rested on all around; save the creaking of the anchor which was being weighed, and the distant notes of a song from some shore-returning boat, no other sound broke the silence.

Suddenly, some startled birds flew shrieking overhead, the water lost its sparkle and the colours faded; a rush of footsteps forward made us look to windward for the cause. Close to us, and rapidly approaching, was a long white line of foam which was driven along under a dense curtain of mist and rain. In a second the squall struck the vessel; the awning which the crew had hurried forward to save was torn to shreds, with a loud crash one of the ship's-boats was dashed against the hurricane deck, and for a moment the ship quivered and careened over from the extraordinary force of the wind. As quickly as it came, so quickly it passed, but the land was hidden from view by the grey mist, and before it had dispersed we had steamed out into the open sea, and Panama was soon left far behind.

APPENDIX.

The tracing of territorial limits has always been considered of the highest importance, not only because it determines and consolidates rights which constitute the welfare of the present, but also because it frees nations from conflicts in the future.

Guided by such considerations, we propose seriously to call the attention of our National Government towards the establishment (fixing) of our boundaries with British Guiana, as we consider that survey of the greatest public interest and of the highest transcendency. The importance of the territory of the State of Guiana, under the diverse phases that it may be considered, is beyond all doubt and discussion. It notably attracted attention since the times of the Spanish Government, and since then by the frequent invasions and controversies about boundaries, between Spaniards, Dutchmen, and Englishmen.

Our Republic began to fix, with marked interest, its consideration upon that territory since 1841, in consequence of the deeds of Schomburgh upon the Barima, always in pursuit of the great mouth of the Orinoco. Those deeds gave rise to the preliminaries of a Boundary Treaty, initiated in London in 1841, and which did not merit the approval of our Government. When in 1857, we found ourselves managing the Government of the Province of Guiana, we had occasion to confront new and more exaggerated pretensions consummated by the Governor of Demerara, at the time when the discovery of the mines of Tupuquen powerfully attracted public attention. It even got to be officially maintained that those auriferous lands were within the limits of British Guiana; and in so false an idea, expeditions were authorized and exploring licenses granted to Engineers, who might carry them out in the name of the Government of Great Britain. We opposed ourselves vigorously to all this in fulfilment of our official duty; we maintained the exclusive right of the Republic over those lands, in controversy with the English Vice-Consul, and we gave a documentary account of everything to our National Government.

Such a number of acts reveals undoubtedly the marked tendency of our neighbours for those regions, to invade progressively our territory, induced to it without doubt by the indecision of our boundary lines, and the easy and frequent communication between both territories. There are later acts of noteworthy significance, and we believe it is our duty to place them clearly before public consideration, and very specially before the National Government, for the purpose of inspiring the profound conviction of the importance of the demarcation about which we are discoursing.

In the vicinity of the river Amacuro—a navigable and important affluent of the Orinoco, which empties to the west of Barima—there exists an Indian village belonging to the district Curiapo, Department of Zea. On taking our last census, in 1874, some British subjects from Demerara, who trade with those Indians, claimed the non-incorporation of that village in the census of the Republic, with the pretext that it is under the jurisdiction of the Government of Demerara. Fortunately our Commissioner for taking the census energetically opposed that design, and the Indian village was incorporated in it. Still further: an Indian (of the tribes of the Moroco, a river which undoubtedly belongs to us, as it rises and empties in our territory) having committed a murder, was taken to Demerara to be judged. The defendant's lawyer demurred on the ground of the incompetency of that tribunal, because the crime had been committed in Venezuelan territory, and to that nation belonged also the indictment. The controversy being carried to the superior tribunals, it was declared that there was competency to continue the suit, because the territory as well as the accused were under the jurisdiction of the English nationality, and this opinion was printed in the official newspaper of Demerara.

The acts which we have already narrated and others still which we omit, not to be prolix, demonstrate the great necessity of fixing definitely on boundary lines with the neighbouring British Guiana. The want of that demarcation, the proximity of the territories, and their easy and frequent communication by diverse ways are the causes why they continue slowly, but progressively, to invade us; an invasion that may be perfected by the great distance of our capital cities, and without the public authorities being able to be warned. For example, by the Yuruari, an affluent of the Cuyuni, which runs navigably close up to Tupuquen. By the Batonamo, an affluent of the same river, and which is situated in the neighbourhood of Tumeremo. By the road of the Palmar seeking the waters of the channels of the Toro, which communicate interiorily with those of the eastern Delta of our Orinoco till they descend to the currents of the Moroco.

Still further and of graver consideration. There exists the tradition of a land communication between the mouths of the Essequibo and the interior of our Guiana—a communication which is not at all unlikely, since it is well known that the sources of the Pumaron and of the Moroco descend from the hill country of Imataca, which penetrates considerably into our Guiana territory. The facility of such communications being allowed, and the proper industrial interests of both territories, the consequences of an unsettled state of boundary are as obvious as grave, and worthy of consideration by the high national powers. It should be known and kept well in remembrance that there exists a constant and frequent commercial traffic between the English establishments of Demerara and the interior of our channels of the eastern

Delta of the Orinoco, that the Indian inhabitants of these districts are found provided with all kinds of goods for their clothing, with powder and arms for their hunting, effects which they obtain either from the English colonists who come to trade with them, or get for themselves when travelling to Demerara; that some of these traders fix their residence among our Indians, and come to establish families. And what will be the result of that proceeding in no distant time? that in lands situated on the banks of our rivers, tributaries of the Orinoco, populations will be formed whose instincts, whose interests will not be those of Venezuela; a prediction that is not exaggerated if we bear in mind the ignorance and simple disposition of those Indians, and the little interest with which past governments have unfortunately regarded the immense advantages and the vast future of that territory.

Grave, very grave conflicts will arise for the Republic the day in which these Indians, ours to day, influenced by whatever suggestions, become inclined to invoke British Nationality. We understand that the English language is no longer unknown to many of those Indians. We do not exaggerate upon vain hypotheses. It is indisputable that our boundaries extend beyond the Essequibo. Such was the insurmountable domination of Spain, such is ours as their legitimate successors. Every occupation from the western bank of the Essequibo towards the mouths of the Orinoco has not been, neither is it in fact, anything but an occupation always opposed by Spain, never accepted by us, and which no legitimate right can consolidate. Well then, if by occupying, in fact, part of the western banks of the Essequibo and of the mouths of the Pumaron, they aspire to the domination of those rivers and the territory which they occupy, will there be no foundation for believing that when that occupation is consummated upon the interior tributaries of the Orinoco, the same pretensions will be unfolded?

Nobody at present disputes with the Republic the exclusive domination over that river which involves the vastest and grandest future. The day in which it must be divided with any other nation, it will decline under all its aspects, principally if we treat with a foreign power with institutions contrary to ours. Its internal and external security will be in a great measure compromised, the first military line of its defence exposed. Under a commercial aspect it seems superfluous, writing in Venezuela, to call to mind the advantages of the navigation of the Orinoco. It will be sufficient to consider it from the western confines of our territory, serving as a base to the future prosperity of these districts, and carrying its waters to the provident Casiquiari to open a way for us to the regions of the Amazon. To descend then in its course to receive from the territory of Granada powerful affluents like the Meta, the Arauca and others that put us in communication with the industrious States of Colombia, so effectually helping to the prosperity of both nations. Later, by its right bank to promote with astonishing facility the industrial and mercantile development of the extensive State Guiana—one might say maritime at the same time as continental—very fecund in natural wealth. By the left bank, and by numerous affluents that form an immense network of water communications, to foment the agricultural and commercial growth of important States to the South and West of the Republic—Apure, Guárico, Zamora, Portuguesa Cojedes y Záchira. Afterwards to run over the Eastern States where all its banks have easy and secure ports, with navigable tributaries that penetrate extensively into those same States running over immense belts as suitable for agriculture as for stock-raising. Then to descend majestically to the ocean by an infinity of canals that fertilize the fruitful lands of its beautiful Delta.

Such is in a general way the course of the Orinoco, such is that immense water-way of four hundred leagues of navigation, whose exclusive domination the Republic must never share with any other nation. And it is not that we are partisans of that selfish and retrograde policy that Rosas maintained in Buenos Ayres, nor that we aspire for our Orinoco, to the restrictions which Brazil maintains over the Amazon. No, ours are other designs. What we do not want, is that our territory upon that river should be invaded as by alluvion, slowly but surely, for the want of a settlement by boundaries.

What we do not want is that on those banks populations should be encouraged that may have another spirit, other interests and other tendencies that are not essentially Venezuelan. What we do want is that no nation may be able to allege any right, of whatsoever nature it may be, over the banks of that river that may disturb our exclusive domination, and give rise sooner or later to questions about territorial limits, nor about any regulations restrictive of our free traffic and commerce like those which disturbed Paraguay and the Argentine Republic—whose inhabitants live on the banks of the La Plata—and which served as a pretext for a prolonged as well as a disastrous and bloody war. We wish that our maritime ports, like our interior rivers, may be open as they are to all the nations of the world, as becomes a civilized people; but we wish also above all that the territory of the Republic may remain integral, and that its rights may be properly respected.

Entering now into the question of boundaries, we maintain the following conclusions:—First: Our limits extend beyond the Essequibo up to the limits of French Guiana. Second: Spain, as the first discoverer and first occupier, and of whose rights we are the legitimate successors, always maintained her boundary lines beyond that river. Third: The occupation in fact, first by the Dutch and afterwards by the English does not give a right to the exclusive domination of the Essequibo. Fourth: The Dutch possessions never went beyond Cape Nassau. Fifth: The boundaries proposed by the British Minister must be rejected as invasory of our Guiana territory.

For greater clearness let us invert the order of these propositions. That Spain, as the first occupant, always maintained her boundaries beyond the Essequibo, in spite of the Dutch possession, which it always considered but as an occupation in fact, different documents of indisputable authority evidently prove. In the general map of the province of Cumaná sent to Spain by the Governor Don José Dibuja in 1761, and which was properly approved, it said that the province of Guiana is bounded on the East by all the coast in which are found situated the Dutch colonies of Essequibo, Berbice, Demerara, Corentin and Surinam; from which it is clearly deduced that Spain considered these possessions as Dutch colonies established on territory belonging to her. So certain is this, that on tracing in the same map the Southern boundaries, it says: by the South the dominions of the very faithful King of Brazil. Here exists a true acknowledgment of territorial domination which does not occur with the Dutch possessions.

With such boundaries was erected the province of Guiana by Royal Decree, June 4, 1762, under the command of Don Joaquin Moreno de Mendoza. In proof of this right, always maintained by Spain, may be cited the Royal Decree of May 5, 1768, confirming the arrangement that the Upper and Lower Orinoco and Rio Negro should remain in charge of the Governor of the province of Guiana, in which is given, as the Eastern boundary of this province, the Atlantic Ocean. It may also be adduced, in proof of the assertion, that we are maintaining the Royal Decree of September 19, 1777, describing the boundaries of the province of Guiana incorporated already, as was also Upper and Lower Orinoco. In it is also given as the Eastern limit, the Atlantic Ocean. From these antecedents, deduced from official and authentic documents, the truth of what we have stated is evidenced, that Spain, as discoverer and first occupant, maintained her boundaries beyond the Essequibo, and did not consider the Dutch possessions but as an occupation in fact. Such was undoubtedly the character of the Dutch colonies to which we are referring.

Two acts came afterwards to modify that occupation. The Treaty of Munster, ratified in 1648, and that of Aranjuez in 1791. By the first, Philip IV. recognised the sovereignty and independence of the Netherlands, and agreed that the high contracting parties should remain in possession of the countries, forts and factories which they occupied in the East and West Indies. By the second, bases and conditions were established for the extradition of the deserters and fugitives in the American colonies. These agreements considered in the light of the principles of the Law of Nations, it cannot be put in doubt that Spain recognised the possession of the Dutch colonies, since, in regard to them, she undertook to treat with Holland as one power with another. However, if this is true, if that possession was recognized, it is also true that Holland, by virtue of those very treaties, was subject to the common condition of conterminous and subordinate nations, in consequence of the established rules and prescriptions of the Law of Nations for the territorial division between bordering nations.

It is not in accordance with the principles of that Law, neither has it ever been so, nor will it ever be, that the occupation of the mouth of rivers in undivided territories between conterminous nations, should confer any right for acquiring the exclusive domination of those rivers, or of the territories which surround them. Such a principle would be equivalent to a justification of the invasions, and to proclaiming the right of force as a legitimate title to territorial property. The Law of Nations prescribes the contrary. It establishes that for the demarcation of boundaries between nations who are joint holders, natural boundaries are to be preferred, such as rivers, mountain chains, &c., and that if those rivers have great volumes of water, each one of the contiguous nations has the domination over the half of the breadth of the river, or all the bank which it occupies. Such are the conditions of the Essequibo.

The territories of our Guiana and of British Guiana are naturally of curved boundaries. So that even raising the right of Holland to the height of that of Spain, which is ours, there is no kind of reason whatever for the supremacy which is claimed over the Essequibo. In almost all its course we dwell on the bank, and it may be said to rise in our territory. We have then, at least, an indisputable right to the domination of one half of its width and to its free navigation. The doctrine that we have explained is so generally acknowledged and accepted that we think ourselves that we can dispense with the production of the authorities on which it is supported. It is among those points on which there is no divergence in the Law of Nations. The occupation in fact, then, first by the Dutch, and lately by the English, does not give any right to the exclusive domination which is claimed over the Essequibo. That the Dutch possessions never passed beyond Cape Nassau, and that Spain repulsed with force every invasion toward the Orinoco, among other and conclusive proofs, the Royal Order of October 1st, 1780, clearly demonstrates. In it instructions are given to Don José F. Inciarte to destroy a fort which the Dutch had constructed on the right bank of the Moroco. Incontrovertible as is the right of the Republic to maintain its boundary beyond the Essequibo, it cannot forego that line without exposing itself to grave perturbations in future. Every other demarcation compromises the integrity of our territory which should be defended on its Eastern flank with the basin of that river. The demarcation proposed by the British Minister since 1841, offers the gravest difficulties besides injustice.

First.—Leaving out the Essequibo, it begins in the Moroco, and comes to compromise, in great part, the course of the Cuyuni. It should be borne in mind, as of the highest importance in the fixing of our boundaries with British Guiana, to preserve entire the course of the Moroco and of the Cuyuni, which belong to us exclusively, as they rise and empty in our territory. The first serves as boundary to our Eastern Delta of the Orinoco, it communicates with all its channels, is of extraordinary importance to the internal security of the Republic, and may serve as a vehicle of clandestine commerce. The second runs extensively into the mainland of our Guiana, and navigable rivers that encircle its interior are tributaries to it. To permit part of its course as a boundary would be the same as to permit foreign navigation in our Guiana territory.

Second.—The mountain ranges and the rivers to which the alluded demarcation refers not being fixed astronomically, it is exposed to further invasions and exaggerated pretensions that may compromise the tranquillity of the Republic.

Third.—The English possessions which may be established on this side of the Essequibo will open a passage to the North in order to be on the banks of the Orinoco, and then will arise complications of immeasurable magnitude. They must then reject the limits proposed by the British Ministry as invasive of our territory. Our general conclusion then may be formulated in the following terms: The question of boundaries between ourselves and Great Britain is reduced purely to a question of fact, viz. Up to where did the Dutch establishments, recognized by Spain, extend? and whose domination was transmitted to Great Britain by her treaty with the Sovereign of the Netherlands in 1814; setting out from the principle that our interior limits, founded on authentic documents, extended beyond the Essequibo up to the borders of French Guiana.

Some will say that we have lost time, that England is a powerful nation, of eminent rank among the Powers of Europe, and will not abdicate her claims upon the Essequibo, and on the territory of Guiana to which she aspires. No, we reply, the question is not of cannons or of squadrons; it is of International Right, of principles consecrated by eyes before which all civilized peoples of the world bow respectfully. Nor do we believe that Great Britain, whose historical precedents in the splendours of our Independence, give her titles to our consideration and high esteem, and who boasts of her respect and importance to the other nations, would found the solution of her boundaries with us on the preponderance of her force. But if, unfortunately, it should be so, we are in possession of indirect and legitimate means to make the rights which with such evident justice we maintain, be respected.

The importance of the demarcation of our limits with British Guiana brings us again to the arena of discussion. Supported by official documents of absolute authenticity, we have proved the most important of our conclusions in our former explanation; that Spain, as the discoverer and first occupier, had always maintained her boundaries beyond the Essequibo, that she had repelled with force every invasion from the banks of that river toward the Orinoco. We reproduce now those documents entire, no longer to prove an argument, but to demonstrate that the question of our boundaries with Great Britain is not situated—nor ought to be—in the region of controversies, but in that of consummated acts.

Let us enter into the matter. Among those authentic documents, two, above others, surpass, and are of the highest transcendency, if they be not decisive. The instruction of the Intendente-General of Venezuela to people the province of Guiana, and the exploration of the Eastern Delta of the Orinoco by virtue of that very instruction; documents corroborated by the authority of the Sovereign of Spain, who was then the Sovereign of that territory; documents that are in the fullest harmony and consequence, and are completed the one by the other.

Respecting the first, it is to be observed that, with indisputable right, Spain made her limits beyond the Essequibo up to the frontier of French Guiana. As regards the second, it is evidently proved that the Dutch possessions occupied, in that epoch, only the banks of the rivers near the sea, without penetrating far into the interior of the country. We will occupy ourselves later, in this same writing, with the legitimate consequences that emanate from those acts authentically proved. We think also of the highest importance the exploration of the Eastern part of the Lower Orinoco, carried out by the Spanish engineer, Felipe de Inciarte, and more important still the Royal approbation of March 9th, 1780, which gives to that instruction, to those traced boundaries, to that exploration, the seal of the national sovereignty which indisputably Spain was competent to do in those times in which those acts were consummated, and it conferred on them irrevocable authority within and without the Peninsular dominions.

One of the most important results of the commission confided to Inciarte is that exploration of the Eastern Delta of the Orinoco in which were comprehended the Barima, the Guaima, the Moroco, and the Pumaron the latter is designed under the authority of Bauruma. The exploration of the rivers is an act of authority of national sovereignty; so the Law of Nations has recognized it. Spain exercised that right exclusively over that territory and over those rivers without any kind of obstacle, and without the participation of any other nationality. We may then allege in all time the exercise of that right with certain and indubitable success in the question of boundaries, with Great Britain principally, as she has not desisted in her claims over the

Barima. However, let us raise the question to its true height. Let us fix it in its proper place, analyzing at length the documents adduced, in order to give it its genuine significance. From this analysis will result, undoubtedly constituted on a solid foundation, the right of Spain, which is our own.

The instruction of the Intendente-General of Venezuela—in order to occupy in the province of Guiana, for its object, for the genius and character of its dispositions by the faculties with which that functionary was invested, and by the Royal approbation which it received in 1780—is not after all anything else than a Government order to occupy a territory in the possession of Spain; and as a consequence of the occupation which was ordered, the boundaries of that territory were traced. Let us demonstrate this. The instruction says: "The commissioners shall try to occupy said lands, as belonging to Spain, their first discoverer, and not ceded afterwards nor occupied at the time by any other Power, nor have they any title for it—advancing in the occupation by the eastern side as much as may be possible until they reach French Guiana." And what were those lands which the Intendente of Venezuela was commanded to occupy as belonging to Spain? The Intendente had surveyed them before. "At the back of the Essequibo and other Dutch possessions, running east up to French Guiana and south up to the river Amazon is situated the territory, unoccupied on this part, and only occupied by Pagan Indians and a large number of fugitive negroes, slaves of the Dutch, and also from the plantations of Guiana."

The Intendente of Venezuela speaking from Carácas, says that the phrase, "at the back of the Essequibo" means "beyond the Essequibo." Here then in the clearest manner, in the most explicit way, is the authority of the Spanish sovereign fixing his national limits, with just and unimpeachable titles, in land of his own. Every nation has a right to trace the boundaries of the territory which it occupies, and it is the duty of the other nations to respect these boundaries, as long as they are not disputed by others with better titles. That Spain was sovereign of the territory which now belongs to us in Guiana, and that she had the right to trace its boundary lines, are asseverations placed beyond all doubt and controversy. We should rather say they are true acts consummated. And in truth, it would be superfluous, except for the claims of Great Britain, to open a discussion to sustain the titles of Spain in the disputed territory, after that for more than three centuries they were recognized by all the Powers of Europe; after having been recognized by Holland—the very one from whom England derived her right—in public treaties like those of Munster and Aranjuez; after having been recognized also in public treaties by Portugal, the only Power of Europe that could have been able, as discoverer, to compete with Spain in the regions of Guiana, but that never dared, respecting those agreements, to overpass the boundaries of what now constitutes French Guiana.

To discuss the titles of Spain after they have been solemnly recognised by England herself in the Treaty of Utrecht! And no one less than Great Britain has a right to dispute territories acquired by Spain with the title of discoverer and first occupant, she that has made use of these same titles and same rights. If not, what right had she—Great Britain—to cede to the North Americans by the Treaty of 1783, in which she recognised their independence, the territory which constituted the primitive Confederation of the North? No other right except that of discoverer and first occupier. And why deny to Spain, and to us now, her legitimate successors, equal rights to those which Great Britain has exercised by public treaties.

Returning again to the document which we are analyzing, we find in it, by explicit acts, the exercise of the public power, by means of a magistrate, who, with full conscience of the rights of the Sovereign whom he represents, orders the occupation of Spanish Guiana, and traces its boundary lines.

Paragraph II.—"The Commissioners shall endeavour to occupy said lands, as belonging to Spain, their first discoverer, and not ceded afterwards, nor occupied at this time by any power, neither have they any title for it."

Paragraph I.—"The principal and greatest importance of this business being, not to work uselessly the securing the said boundaries of the said Province of Guiana, that begins on the Eastern part of it at a point where the Orinoco empties into the sea, called Barlovento, on the border of the Dutch colony of Essequibo."

Paragraph XXX.—"The principal object is the occupation and security of the boundaries of the Province of Guiana, on the East of Essequibo and French Guiana."

Such Government acts, sanctioned by the authority of the Sovereign of Spain, give to this document the character of a direct and unimpeachable proof in the question of boundaries that we are elucidating. And will Great Britain be able to present documents of equal nature and with equal titles? Has she presented them up to now?

As a result of the preparations of the Intendente-General of Venezuela, they proceeded to the exploration of the lower Delta of the Orinoco. The official Report of Inciarte which contains it, is an important document of high significance under various aspects. In the first place, it confirms the idea which the instructions of the Intendente give in respect to the nature and true position of the Dutch colonies in the times to which it refers—1779— situated on the banks of the rivers near the sea, and without penetrating far into the interior of the country. Inciarte explored all the territory embraced between the Orinoco and the Essequibo, and finds no establishments, nor buildings of any kind with the exception of the small fort of Moroco, whose insignificant nature he describes, and that he was ordered to destroy it by express order of the King of Spain.

And where is the act of our national sovereignty in virtue of which we may have abdicated the right that we have to the immense extent of territory which extends from the Essequibo to French Guiana? Who has marked for us the limits of those possessions? Who has marked those boundaries? Great Britain, intercepting us by means of the Essequibo. And still more is claimed; they deny us all share in that river, and limits are proposed invasive of our territory. And we must not cede any more. It is not just, neither politic nor convenient. Every foreign invasion on this side of the Essequibo ruins our territory. The British possessions which might commence on that flank, increasing themselves towards the North, would become part of the banks of the Orinoco; while advancing towards the south, they have a speedy way to the auriferous zone of our interior. Lord Aberdeen well understood this when he proposed to our Minister in London—Fortique—according to official data that we have before us, that the English Government would cede territory in Barima, provided that of Venezuela would yield on the Cuyuni. That Great Britain ought not to consider herself exclusive mistress of the Essequibo, she herself has said in the most solemn and explicit manner.

There exists in our Ministry of Foreign Relations a communication which she made by means of the public Minister, in 1840, of the commission which she had given to Schomburgh to explore the Essequibo, and mark its limits. Certainly Great Britain would not have made such a communication if she had considered herself possessed of the exclusive predominance which she now claims over the Essequibo. Neither is the object conceived of informing our Government of the establishment of their boundaries on that river, if they did not consider the Republic joint possessors of its waters. That communication involves an explicit acknowledgment of our right. The vacillation of Great Britain certainly contradicts her claims over Guiana. Before the exploration of Schomburgh, she communicates officially to our Government, giving public testimony that she considered the Republic joint holder in the waters of the Essequibo. But after the exploration, and when the intelligent English engineer had, without doubt, revealed the immense advantages of that water-way, by its prolonged extension, by its numerous affluents, by its ramifications that extend to the Amazon, then they deny us all right in the Essequibo, and they propose to us boundaries which extravagantly invade our Guiana territory.

We wish now to enter into a new kind of argument, either for greater clearness of our right, or to reply to some observations which have already been made on the part of the Government of Great Britain, and others that may be made in future. The explanation of our Plenipotentiary Fortique in

London; the demarcations of Codazzi; the records of those eminent men, Messrs. Yones and Baralt; the diplomatic notes addressed to the British Government by our Minister of Foreign Relations in November 1876, so full of abundant reasoning on behalf of our right; the statistics of Guiana published in 1876, and the annual statistics of 1877; in all these explanations and official data, the Essequibo is presented as the absolute Eastern limit of our territory with British Guiana. We believe that that boundary, so expressed, diminishes the territorial right of the Republic, and we are going to explain ourselves. The records of Messrs. Yones and Baralt, like the observations of Codazzi, which served as a base to our Plenipotentiary Fortique, for his explanation before the British Cabinet, and the said official data, rest on two foundations to which we do not lend the merit or the force which have been attributed to them. The opinions of geographers and historians, and the demarcation of the Missions were made by the Government of Spain. However valuable may be the opinions of wise men, of historians and geographers, they have no authority whatever where national boundaries are treated of, which are but legitimate acts of the Sovereigns in use of their natural prerogatives; so that in the present question, every opinion, however authorised it may be considered, is ineffectual and unable to exist before the Royal decrees of the King of Spain, which, drawing the boundary lines in Guiana places them beyond the Essequibo up to the borders of French Guiana. No asseveration, whatever its nature may be, can oppose itself to the authority of the official documents that we have analyzed.

The demarcation of the Missions has no more strength. Guided by its intentions of occupying their dominions, and of widening the civilization and culture of the Indians, Spain continued, in the course of time, to mark out Mission districts which it subordinated to the different religious orders; but such demarcation was made within its territory and national boundaries, it was an eternal economic act, purely administrative, and had no other object but order and regularity in the service of the Missions. And it is certain that the demarcation carried out in Venezuela was ordered by the Governor of Cumaná, in agreement with the "padres" in charge of the Mission, who had to make their residence in Guiana. There is then no truth, no reason for confounding the demarcation of Missions with the national boundaries of Spain. From that confusion of boundaries, which we oppose, it would be reasonably deduced that Spain did not possess in Venezuela any other territory than that marked out by its Missions; an assertion very far from the truth, and which fails in every legal and rational foundation. Such an assertion leads us evidently to the maintenance of the theory which establishes that the material occupation of the whole of the territory of a nation is necessary in order to found exclusive domination over it, or it may be right of property. Such a theory that recognises, as a principle, only an erroneous idea about the nature of the possession which serves as a title to acquire, by the Law of

Nations, cannot be sustained, cannot be accepted, without confusing and shaking the territorial domination of all nations, because none of them occupies materially all the territory which they have declared in their possession. That theory, inadmissible under all aspects, would be extremely disastrous to all the nationalities of South America.

More than this—Great Britain can produce no argument favourable to her right as emanating from the explanations and data to which we have referred. Of whatsoever nature may have been the asseverations of our Minister-Plenipotentiary Fortique in London, they are null, and of no value, since our Government denied its approbation to the preliminaries of the boundary treaty initiated by him, and they cannot be the object of any reasonable pretension. As regards Codazzi, it is certain that Lord Aberdeen replied to Señor Fortique, in a diplomatic note, denying the Essequibo for the dividing line, and supporting himself on the demarcation of Codazzi, that presents the Moroco. Such an agreement has no value whatever. The map of Codazzi is not an official map. There is no act of competent authority which declares it such; on the contrary, our Government has lately rejected claims from the Government of New Granada for possessions on the bank of the Orinoco, founded on his demarcation. Great Britain cannot constitute an exception.

The records and official data to which reference has been made, are opinions of citizens and public functionaries which in nowise compromise, or diminish, the rights of the Republic. It is certainly strange that our Government, being in possession of the documents that we have analyzed— the Instruction of the Intendente of Venezuela, and the Exploration of the Delta—it being allowed that Messrs. Baralt and Fortique refer to them, they should have been presented to demonstrate our boundaries by the Essequibo, when they prove most abundantly that they extended beyond that river. There not existing then any act of our National Sovereignty which defines our boundaries with Great Britain in detriment of what we are sustaining, the rights of the Republic continue to have unalterable force.

We have demonstrated that since 1810, we find ourselves in legal possession of the territory which constituted the ancient Captaincy-General of Venezuela with its legitimate boundaries, and it was only in 1814 that Great Britain obtained possession of some Dutch colonies which the Sovereign of the Netherlands transmitted. Well, what were the boundaries of that transmission? What the boundary lines traced by Holland in the ceded territory? None, because Holland herself was without them. Her possession was only in fact. She only held in Guiana what Spain, the discoverer and first occupier, had seen fit to permit her. And for that reason, with the good faith which ought to distinguish nations in their treaties, in the Third Article in which she ceded to Great Britain some of her colonies in Guiana, she does not mark out any kind of boundaries whatever. It is to be noticed that that treaty was an agreement between Holland and Great Britain, without the intervention of Spain; that it establishes bonds and obligations between the contracting parties, but in no way can it bind Spain, that no longer legally possessed that territory, nor her legitimate successors, in all that may prejudice them.

We have founded our right to the territory which constituted the ancient Captaincy-General of Venezuela on the "*uti possidetis*" of 1810. We are going to make clear that right beyond all controversy. Nobody has ever put in doubt, not only in Venezuela, but in all the sections of South America, that by virtue of the political transformation that gave rise to our new nationalities, these were substituted respectively for the territorial Seignory of Spain in all her former dominions. Brazil herself, in spite of the diversity of her institutions, has recognized that principle, and could not proceed differently without grave inconsequence, because, in short, what other right did the new empire represent but the one proceeding from the old kingdom of Portugal? If she has maintained controversies about boundaries with adjacent nations, it has not been in denial of the principle cited, but rather confirming it, for having believed herself helped to rights which she could enforce before Spain herself by virtue of old treaties. Our succession to the seignorial rights of Spain in all the territory of the ancient Captaincy-General of Venezuela was constant prescription, and an infallible arrangement of all our constituent bodies-politic, even in the midst of our great struggle for independence.

The Liberator, in incorporating the Province of Guiana in 1817 with the territory conquered by the Republican arms, traced its boundaries after the tenor of the Royal Decrees of Spain which he expressly mentions. The first Congress assembled in Angostura, which sanctioned the Fundamental Law of Colombia, established in its Second Article: "Its territory shall be that embraced in the old Captaincy-General of Venezuela and the Vice-royalty of the new kingdom of Granada." The "Constituyente" of Cúcuta in 1821, ratifies the former Fundamental Law by that of July 12th, whose Fifth Article reads: "The territory of the Republic of Colombia will be comprehended within the limits of the old Captaincy-General of Venezuela and the Vice-royalty and Captaincy-General of the new kingdom of Granada, but the assignment of its exact boundaries will be reserved for a more opportune occasion."

The same "Constituyente" sanctioned, at last, the Constitution of the New Colombian nationality, and ratified the former prescriptions in its Articles 6th and 7th.—7th. "The towns of the said extension still under the Spanish yoke, at whatever time they may free themselves, will form part of the

Republic with rights and representation equal to all the others that compose it."

6th.—"The territory of Colombia is the same that comprised the old Vice-royalty of New Granada and the Captaincy-General of Venezuela." As is seen from Article 7, the right sanctioned by the "Constituyente" of Colombia referred not only to the towns that had already gained their independence and liberty, but also to all those that remained under the rule of the Spanish Government. It was not only to the territory of which the founders of our nationality were already in possession, but also to all that which they believed themselves to have the right to possess.

Venezuela, which separated from the Colombian Union, and constituted her nationality independently, in 1830, sanctioned the same right in her fundamental agreement. Article 5th. "The territory of Venezuela comprehends that which, before the political transformation of 1810, was denominated the Captaincy-General of Venezuela." And this canon has been essentially reproduced in all the Constitutions that afterwards have been given to the Republic. In that of 1857, 1858 and 1864. "Article 3rd. The territory of Venezuela comprises all that before the political transformation of 1810, was denominated the Captaincy, &c., &c."

Such is the canon which has reproduced itself in all our fundamental institutions since the birth of our nationality, in the glorious splendours of Colombia; the same which is found sanctioned in all the Constitutions of our sister Republics. Its appearance as constant as universal has elevated it to a dogma of the Public International Law of South America. It could not happen in any other way, because the existence of such a precept is not a creation of that public right, but a natural and legitimate consequence of the political transformation which the different sections that constitute the dominion of Spain have experienced. In truth, political forms are variable, are purely accidental, in conformity with the times; at the wish of the radical sovereignty of the people; yet those same people, in society congregated, have by the Law of Nations the eminent domination of the territory which they occupy with the demarcations which they have assigned to them for their special use.

Such is, in short, the radical foundation of the "*uti possidetis*" of 1810. The existence of that right, as far as we are concerned, is solemnly sanctioned by the public treaty with Spain upon recognition of our Independence.

"Article I. In consequence of this renouncement and cession, His Christian Majesty recognizes as a free Sovereign and Independent Nation, the Republic of Venezuela, composed of the provinces and territories expressed in its

Constitution, and other later laws, viz.: Margarita, Guiana, Cumará, Barcelona, Carácas."

Separation being made of the renouncement and transfer of rights on the part of Spain, which are but diplomatic formulæ that do not embody any modification of the treaty, the truths which in it appear as a relief, are, the recognition of our Independence, the legitimate succession of our right in the right of Spain, and that the territory of the old Captaincy-General of Venezuela came to constitute that of the Republic of the same name, traced out in its Constitution and in its laws. Such understanding Spain has lately confirmed by an act of her own, extremely solemn. A controversy being raised by the Netherlands about the ownership of the island of Aves, the Court of Spain was designated as arbitrator by the contending parties, and in 1865 declared that the said island belonged to Venezuela in right and possession, basing its decision especially on the fact that all the islands of the Caribbean sea, among which is found the aforesaid—were discovered by Spain, and on Venezuela being established with the territory of the old Captaincy-General of Carácas, she had succeeded to Spain in all her territorial rights.

There exists a public act emanating from our Government which we judge worthy of being commemorated in this writing, because it strikes the heart of the question which we are sustaining. About the middle of 1822, Señor J. Rafael Ravenga was accredited as Plenipotentiary to His Britannic Majesty, and in the instructions sent by the Secretary of Foreign Relations is found the following paragraph:—

"May I be permitted, however, to call your attention particularly to Article 2nd of the projected treaty about boundaries. Agree as exactly as may be possible about fixing the dividing line of both territories, according to the last treaties with Spain and Holland. The colonists of Demerara and Berbice have usurped a great portion of land, which according to them belongs to us, from the side of the river Essequibo. It is absolutely necessary that said colonists either put themselves under the protection and obedience of our laws, or that they retire to their former possessions. In short, the necessary time will be given them, as is set forth in the project."[122]

The conscientiousness of the Government of Colombia—which was ours then—expressed in the preceding instructions, has two important phases; the usurpation of our territory on the Essequibo by English colonists, such as exists now, and the possession of the *uti possidetis* of 1810, which is nothing else than the guaranteeing of our rights in the treaties celebrated between Holland and Spain, and to which the Colombian minutes refer.

Again, in order to carry to the highest evidence the demonstration of our right in the present question we will say that Great Britain has virtually recognized the *uti possidetis* of 1810, in public Convention in the Treaty of 1783, in which it recognized the independence of the United States of the North. Let us prove it. The Articles 1st and 2nd of that Treaty are the following:

"Article 1st.—His Britannic Majesty recognizes as free, sovereign, and independent the States of New Hampshire, Massachusetts, Rhode Island, &c., agreeing to recognize them as such, and renouncing for himself, his heirs, and successors all claim against the rights of their government and territory.

"Article 2nd.—In order to avoid all discussions and differences that may arise in future about the question of the boundaries of the said United States, it is declared and agreed that those shall be the following, namely, from the North-west angle of Nova Scotia, &c."

Well then; what difference exists between those articles and those of our treaty with Spain upon the identical object of recognizing our independence, which we have reproduced? Essentially none. In one, as much as in the other, the national sovereignty of a people is recognized that proclaims its independence and effects it. In the one, as much as in the other, the right which it has as a sovereign nation to all the territory which they occupied as colonies is recognized. And what else is the *uti possidetis* of 1810? On what principle of the Law of Nations, on what practice of civilized nations will Great Britain be able to found the difference which she claims, between the national sovereignty of the United States and the national sovereignty of the people of Venezuela? No difference exists which can be founded on reason, and if any could be adduced it would undoubtedly be in our favour, because no chain of former subordination linked us to the government of Great Britain.

From the mass of reasoning which we have brought forward, we can deduce the following conclusions. 1st.—Spain, as a sovereign nation, traced the boundaries which belonged to her in Guiana. 2nd.—On establishing herself, the Republic of Venezuela succeeded Spain in the domination and ownership of that territory, under its legitimate boundaries, either by virtue of the *uti possidetis* of 1810—recognized by all the nationalities of South America—or as a national prerogative of its national sovereignty. 3rd.—Great Britain has no right to annul the legitimate exercise of two national sovereignties. 4th.— As a European Power, possessor of territory on our continent, she is incorporated in the great family of nationalities of South America, and has no right to violate a principle recognized and sanctioned by all other nationalities, as that of the *uti possidetis* of 1810.

From these affirmations that we have deduced from authentic official documents, and from indisputable principles of the Law of Nations, we may conclude definitely that the question of our boundaries with Great Britain does not present, in its solution, such grave difficulties as we supposed. That it should not be placed in the region of controversies but in the district of accomplished facts, allowing that Spain of whom we are the legitimate successors, traced its boundaries. That by the priority of our right, and the nature and origin of the titles that confirm it, we are rather in the position to grant concessions than under the necessity of accepting conditions which it may be wished to impose upon us. Above all, we wish to inspire the profound conviction, as a result of this writing, which is extremely important to the Republic, *viz.*, the necessity of a speedy solution of this controversy, that its delay prejudices immensely its gravest and most transcendental interests in various respects. Thus, it betters the conditions of Great Britain; time, our silence and indifference give margin that they may effect invasions, which are afterwards alleged as accomplished facts, as bases of acquired rights, which is the formula hitherto adopted. Lord Aberdeen well judged it so, when in a diplomatic note he said to our Plenipotentiary Fortique, in London, that he did not understand the interest of Venezuela in the urgency of the question of boundaries, and that he should be satisfied that things should remain as before.

Our Government has officially addressed that of Great Britain proposing a speedy solution of the controversy. We understand that no satisfactory answer has been given, and it is probable that it will not be given, because, thus, it suits the interests of Great Britain. We think that it would be convenient to reiterate that effort in explicit and peremptory terms, by proposing the arbitration of a third Power, in case of negation to a direct convention. We have all the data sufficient to accept, without any kind of fear, an absolute decision; and as far as principles are concerned, all of them are also in favour of our right.

Lifting the question to its highest, it will be understood easily that these interests are not purely Venezuelan. The position of the Orinoco in the hands of a friendly power, that fraternizes in institutions, is a question eminently American and of the highest transcendency. The day in which this is not so, the day in which a European Power of political institutions adverse to ours dominates on the Orinoco, or makes its influence felt as a possessor on its banks, and in any other respect with the water communication of that river, with the Amazon, or the numerous navigable affluents of either, then not only the political and commercial interests of Venezuela would be in a great measure compromised, but also those of New Granada, Ecuador, Peru, and Bolivia, and even those of Brazil herself. Under these circumstances, the navigation of the Orinoco may become a grave international question of South America. (Here, follow a few paragraphs relating to the ruptured intercourse between Colombia and Venezuela, which I omit.)

In continuation:—We offered to discuss the demarcation proposed by the British Government. We are going to comply with that promise as a summary of our former observations. At once we maintain that that demarcation is inadmissible, because it compromises and prejudices in the highest degree the interests of the Republic, in the present and in the future. In short, every dividing line between us and British Guiana that is not in the Essequibo, ruins the territory of the Republic. In the first place it is extremely difficult to fix that dividing line, making it correspond with mountain chains and rivers of the second class, geographically unknown; to trace meridians in unexplored and perhaps unexplorable lands without exposing our territory to new invasions and dangerous controversies, and of uncertain success, which have always to be sustained with powerful nations accustomed to impose their will by using force. The Essequibo being free and only under British domination, our territory may be invaded and dominated with impunity. It being allowed that that river communicates by means of the channels of the Orinoco, which are difficult to be watched and guarded, so also it communicates with our territory of the Amazon by its upper part. These ways of communication would be free, rapid, and without power of being restricted, as long as the Essequibo remains under the exclusive domination of Great Britain. The demarcation proposed by the British Minister is the following:—

"A line that should go from the mouth of the Moroco to the point at which the river Barama unites with the Guaima; thence by the Barama up the stream as far as the Aunama, which would be ascended up to the place where this stream approaches nearest to the Acarabici, and following this river to its confluence with the Cuyuni; then continuing by this last up stream till it arrives at the high lands in contact with the Roraima range, in which are divided the waters that flow into the Essequibo from those which run into the Rio Blanco."

This line has inconveniences and most prejudicial disadvantages for the Republic. As is seen, it begins at the mouth of the Moroco, it runs by insignificant rivers, almost geographically unknown, and mountain-chains of the same kind, till it arrives at the waters of the Cuyuni; it follows then the course of this river up to the Roraima range.[123] The explanation of that line is the following; as a point of departure and continuation it takes the secondary mountain ranges and rivers of our continent, subject to controversies and invasions, till it arrives at the Cuyuni, an affluent of the Essequibo, which belongs to us integrally: it runs all its course, attaching great part of the territory of our State Guiana, up to the Roraima range, where rises our Caroni. That is to say, England marks herself boundaries within our territory, imprisoning us within a line of circumvallation from the ocean up to the sources of one of our most important interior rivers. And with what right can Great Britain claim from us the abrogation of incontrovertible principles of the universal Law of Nations? Even laying aside our original titles from Spain, which prove, evidently, that our interior boundaries passed beyond the Essequibo up to the borders of French Guiana, even laying aside, we say, those titles which we have analyzed over-abundantly, England has no right to take possession of the Essequibo and to declare it her exclusive property.

It is an invariable law and constant practice of the Law of Nations that in order to divide nations, possessors of common territories, the rivers and mountain ranges of consideration and importance are preferred as boundaries. In these conditions is found the Essequibo, which is a natural curved boundary between us and British Guiana. And what right has Great Britain not only to declare that the Essequibo is her exclusive property, but also to pass beyond its banks and penetrate into our territory and leave her boundaries? It is also an invariable law of the Law of Nations that when a broad river divides the territories of two conterminous nations, each one of them has a right to the domination of the half of that river in all the bank which it occupies. And with what right can Great Britain claim from us the abrogation of that incontrovertible prescription of the Universal Law of Nations? Besides the line which we have traced and which was proposed by Great Britain, there was also the dishonourable condition that Venezuela should engage herself not to alienate that territory to any other foreign power.

The Government of Great Britain well understood the importance of that territory under diverse phases, and that it would not suit for it to pass into the power of a nation that might be able to repel force by force with equal advantages and conditions. Guided by the design of putting an end to this question of boundaries, our Government Council, in 1844, submitted for discussion a proposal for a dividing line that should be offered to Great Britain. It humoured sufficiently the exactions of Great Britain, but that dividing line was not so onerous as that which had been proposed by that nation. It began at the mouth of Moroco, following the course of that river up to its source. Thence it drew a meridian, which crossing the Cuyuni went up to the Pacaraima range, which divides the waters of the Essequibo from those of the Rio Blanco. If not so prejudicial as that proposed by Great Britain, it compromises, in a great measure, the gravest transcendental interests of the Republic in the present as much as in the future. All that may be cut off from the Essequibo, as our eastern boundary with British Guiana, is to ruin the territory of the Republic; it is to cause that British subjects, that the foreigner may travel and navigate through our territory without our being able to impede it. Having the exclusive domination of the Essequibo, they have the free navigation of that river and of its most important affluents, which penetrate extensively into our territory, and among others the Cuyuni and the Mazaruni.

Besides this, the nation has already given forth its judgment, has already expressed its will respecting the territorial rights by that flank in the most solemn manner, and it is not possible to contradict itself without great indignity, besides grave prejudices, under different respects and considerations.

The 1st Article of our Boundary Treaty with Brazil, in its 3rd division, speaks thus:—"The line will continue through the most elevated points of the Pacaraima range, so that the waters which go to the Rio Blanco may remain belonging to Brazil, and those which run to the Essequibo, Cuyuni, and Caroni to Venezuela, up to where the territories of the two States reach on their eastern part." From this boundary convention with Brazil, the only nation that could dispute with us original titles in Guiana, is deduced that the Republic stretches its territorial dominion on the south as far as the Pacaraima range, a continuation of the Parima and which divides the waters of the Rio Blanco from those which run to the Essequibo; that it has declared and maintained its dominion over that territory, and over the Essequibo and its affluents in those regions, and, what is more important, that it is bounded on the east by Brazil. Comparing this demarcation with Brazil with the line proposed by the English Government, it results that the latter is going to terminate in the Roraima range, which is in the interior of our State Guiana, and which is a ramification of that of Pacaraima. In short this line with our Brazilian division comes to form an immense angle in our Guiana territory. If it is cut off then from the Essequibo the following absurdities result, in which grave prejudice and national indignity dispute the palm.

1st.—That we lose not only the territory that belongs to us, from the Essequibo to the boundaries of French Guiana, but that comprehended to the east between that river and the line proposed by Great Britain, which amounts to a multitude of square leagues.

2nd.—This nation taking possession of the Essequibo, she bounds herself in fact and divides us from Brazil, by which we are bounded on the east according to the public treaty with that nation.

There is then in the usurpation of the Essequibo, a usurpation of territory and a usurpation of national sovereignty.

We terminate these articles, recommending as we have already done in several places, the importance of putting, as soon as possible, an end to the question of our boundaries with Great Britain, and the necessity and justice of maintaining the Essequibo as the limit of our concessions, as the natural boundary of our territory, as much by the original authentic titles which we have from Spain as by the principles of the Law of Nations, which we have discussed and analyzed in these writings.

FRANCISCO J. MARMOL.

Carácas, February 18th, 1878.

(Here follow copies of the original documents from which these arguments have been deduced, but it is unnecessary to reproduce them, as their substance is contained in the above writings.—J.W.B.W.)

THE END.

FOOTNOTES

[1] Some magnificent roses are grown near Hamilton, and one gentleman informed me that he had over two hundred varieties thriving luxuriantly; not the over-blooming, straggling plants, whose blossoms are coarse, ill-shaped, and of faded colour, so often seen in hot climates, but beautiful bright roses with thick petals and rare symmetry of outline.

[2] A curious circumstance about these creatures is that nearly every individual harbours in his stomach a large parasitical fish, that lies at ease and feeds upon whatever comes in its way.

[3] In appearance these gigantic pots and cauldrons are similar to the large basin-shaped, or funnel-like holes made ages ago by the glacier on the sandstone ridge in the "Glacier garden of Lucerne," Switzerland. But there, lying at the bottom of the basins are the colossal balls, which once as hard blocks of stone had slipped through the icy fissures, and had then been rolled and twisted about by the action of water rushing down upon them until the deep holes were made. The Bermudian boilers appear rather to have been built up than hollowed out.

[4] Crescentia cujete.

[5] Just before our arrival a case occurred in which a little urchin was sent on a similar expedition, his only offence apparently being that of running about the streets in a shirt which only extended as far as his breast-bone, and consequently was not regulation.

[6] The bread-fruit naturally recalls the "Mutiny of the Bounty," as it was for the purpose of introducing that tree into the West Indies that Bligh was sent to Tahiti in 1788. On the failure of that expedition he again set out for Tahiti in 1792, obtained his trees, and landed a number safely at St. Vincent. But in these islands it is not the grand tree which in the South Seas affords the chief sustenance of life, and the degenerated fruit is left untouched even by the negro.

[7] The Moravians here, as elsewhere, have schools judiciously administered, and these zealous people are still worthy of Cowper's eulogy when he said,

"Fir'd with a zeal peculiar, they defy

The rage and rigour of a polar sky,

And plant successfully sweet Sharon's rose

On burning plains, and in eternal snows."

[8] Among the important improvements, the factory intended to burn coal for fuel, thus saving the waste cane which it was customary to use for that purpose, for manure.

[9] Since the above was written news has arrived of a negro insurrection, and the destruction of nearly every sugar plantation on the island.

[10] A favourite amusement in St. Thomas; a dead horse is towed out behind a boat, and the greedy monsters, eagerly fastening on it, are then harpooned.

[11] Leeward Islands consist of Dominica, Antigua, Montserrat, Nevis, and St. Kitt's. Windward Islands consist of Barbadoes, St. Vincent, St. Lucia, Grenada, and Tobago.

[12] Erythrina umbrosa.

[13] Oreodoxa oleracea; called the mountain-cabbage because within the central spike lies concealed the cabbage, composed of white longitudinal flakes forming a crisp compact body. When cut up into thin ribands and boiled, it is served as a vegetable with meat. As all palm trees possess this eatable spike, it is hard to tell why this species should in particular be called the "cabbage."

[14] Carolinea.

[15] Brownea.

[16] Eugenia Michellii.

[17] Swinburne.

[18] Abrus precatoria.

[19] Jatropha manihot.

[20] Eulampis Jugularis.

[21] Chrysotis Augusta.

[22] Cathartes aura.

[23] Trochilus moschitus.

[24] Chlorostilbon atala.

[25] Thaumatias chronopectus.

[26] Mauritia flexuosa.

[27] This, the largest of our colonies in the West Indies, and the only one in South America, comprises the three counties of Demerara, Essequibo and Berbice, which derive their names from the three principal rivers which border them. Georgetown, the capital, and seat of Government, has a

population of 37,000 inhabitants, whilst the total population of the colony approaches 240,000. The coast line of British Guiana on the Atlantic is about 280 miles in length, and in breadth the country varies from 200 to 450 miles, the total area being estimated at 76,000 square miles. Its boundaries inland may be said to be Venezuela, Brazil, and Dutch Guiana, but the precise limits of the two former are still undetermined. Cultivation is restricted to a long narrow strip of the coast and along the banks of the rivers for a few miles. The whole of the cultivated area is under 80,000 acres, and the greater part of that is in sugar cane alone.

[28] As there is no natural fall of water, these open trenches, which are seen everywhere in the country as well as town, are necessary to carry off surface water to prevent flooding in the wet season. By sluice-gates the town trenches can be flooded when required.

[29] Couroupita Guianensis.

[30] Gelasimus vocans.

[31] Anablaps tetraophthalmus.

[32] Phœnicircus carnifex.

[33] Centrifugals are open round boxes of metal, pierced like gauze. These are whisked round and round at a tremendous speed, and the molasses flying out through the gauze leave the sugar white and dry.

[34] Physalia atlantica.

[35] Avicenna nitida.

[36] Coryphœ cerifera.

[37] Provisions intended to last for three months. Six barrels of flour, one and a half boxes of cod fish; three bags of brown rice; three barrels of ship's biscuit; one hundred and forty pounds of bacon; seventy-five pounds of coffee; one barrel of sugar; one case of brandy; fifty pounds of onions; twelve gallons of split peas. Also a small quantity of canned provisions.

[38] Chaconia Calycophyllum.

[39] Mora excelsa.

[40] Nectandra Rodiei.

[41] Oreodaphne sp.

[42] Hybiscus elatus.

[43] Eperua falcata.

[44] Topaza pella.

[45] Cacicus citrius.

[46] Mycteria Americana.

[47] Gynericum.

[48] Myletes pacu.

[49] Paiworie is a drink made from cassava bread, which is prepared in the same disgusting way, viz.: by chewing, as is the "kava" of the islanders of the South Seas. When a drinking feast is at hand the women are occupied for several days in chewing cassava, which with the addition of hot water gradually fills an enormous wooden trough, shaped like a canoe, and capable of containing a hundred and fifty gallons. On the appointed day, the invited guests dressed in their best feathers and decorated with teeth and beads in the latest styles, assemble round the trough. A preliminary song and dance are indulged in, then the calabashes are dipped into the intoxicating beverage, and the orgie commences. It does not finish until the paiworie is exhausted, or not a soul is left with a leg to stand upon. The scenes incident to such a performance need no description.

[50] Crax alector.

[51] Plotius anhinga.

[52] Ibis infuscata.

[53] Lachesis rhombeata.

[54] Trigonocephalus.

[55] Eunectes murinus.

[56] Anacardium occidentale.

[57] A woodskin is constructed out of a single piece of bark of a tree—generally the purple-heart. After the bark has been removed from the wood it is kept open by cross sticks, and the extremities are supported on beams so as to raise those parts. A more cranky affair cannot be imagined, and even to step into one required the greatest care; and if upset it sinks instantly, owing to the great specific gravity of the bark, which is hardly one-eighth of an inch in thickness. Its great advantage is that it can float where no boat or canoe could possibly pass. Some of the large ones will carry six or seven persons and their effects.

[58] Serra salmo.

[59] Bixa Orellana.

[60] Genipa Americana.

[61] We found it very difficult to determine with any exactness the names of mountains and falls, not only on account of the names themselves, but also from the Indian habit of slurring over the last syllables. Then again different tribes have different names for localities, and not unfrequently the various parts of mountains and even of rapids are called by various denominations. By constant repetition we approached as nearly as we could to the names uttered.

[62] Dasyprocta agouti.

[63] The Indians to the present day do not recognise in the alligator that shapeless fleshy mass, which is incapable of extension, as a tongue. Herodotus, too, who was a keen observer of the crocodile, repeats the idea that it is tongueless, and for that reason was regarded by the Egyptians as an emblem of mystery.

[64] Paca caligenis.

[65] Capybara.

[66] Caladium arborescens.

[67] In speaking of the course of the Mazaruni, Mr. Barrington Brown in his "Geology of British Guiana," says that it rises in the "Merumé mountains, part of the Pacaraima group, at a height of 2,400 feet above the sea, near the 60th degree of west longitude; it runs eastward for some miles, curving round to the south in 68° 8′ 30″ west longitude, and 5° 34′ 23″ north latitude, and descends to a level of 2,000 feet. From this it flows in a tortuous course in a west-north-west direction to the Cako river mouth, in 60° 44′ west and 5° 47′ 11″ north, being joined on the way by numerous large tributaries, and descending by a set of high falls at Chi-chi to a level of 1,400 feet above the sea. Flowing smoothly along at this altitude in a north-north-west direction to Sericoeng, it is precipitated down a succession of lofty falls, occupying a distance of eight miles to a level of 500 feet. Passing along at this level with a north-north-east course, it plunges over two more sets of falls to a height of 150 feet, and, emerging from the sandstone mountains in 6° 26′ 14″ north latitude, turns suddenly to the east-north-east for a distance of 105 miles to Teboco cataract, passing on the way near the foot of the Merumé mountains, 20 miles to the northward of its source."

[68] The "lucanani," or sun-fish, so called from a golden ring in its tail, weighs five or six pounds, and its flesh is by many preferred to that of the pacu. A peculiarity in the habits of this fish is that, when the young—which always swim near the mother—are in danger, the mother opens her mouth and they all rush in.

[69] During our journey the principal butterflies that we noticed were as follows:—

"Morpho Adonis," of the most brilliant azure blue.

"Urania Leilus," with black velvet ground and golden green bands of a silky lustre, and black tail.

"Marius Thetis," tawny, with narrow black lines.

"Erycina Octavius," dark bands and crimson spots, long black tail with crimson patch.

"Papilio Æneas," velvet black wings, with red patch in middle of hinder wing, upper wings with large green spot.

"Papilio Sinon," black wings with pale green bands.

"Callidryas Eubule," surface of wings a fine yellow.

"Vanessa Amathea," dark brown surface, with broad band of deep red across centre of wings, which are edged with white spots.

"Heliconia Cynisca," surface deep black, red at base of upper wings, under wings with red stripes.

[70] Buprestis gigas.

[71] The "kanaima" is a secret murderer who performs his work generally by poison.

[72] The "peaiman" is the sorcerer and doctor of the tribe.

[73] The "didi" is supposed to be a wild man of the woods, possessed of immense strength and covered with hair.

[74] Tinamus Brasiliensis.

[75] Odontophorus Guianensis.

[76] Brownea racemosa.

[77] Ardea cocoi.

[78] Ardea myrticorax.

[79] Procnias carunculata.

[80] "Amblyornis inornata." Dr. Beccari, the well-known Italian naturalist, in describing the home of this species of paradise-bird says: "Directly in front of its cabin is a level space occupying a superficies about as large as that of the structure itself, which has a diameter of about a metre. It is a small lawn of soft moss, all transported thither, kept smooth and clean and free from

grass, weeds, stones, and other objects not in harmony with its design. Over this graceful green carpet are scattered flowers and fruit of brilliant colours in such a manner that they really present the appearance of an elegant little garden. After these objects have been exposed for some time, and have lost their freshness, they are taken from their abode and thrown away, and are replaced by others."

[81] Felis onca.

[82] The hammocks of Indians are invariably of a greasy red colour from contact with their painted bodies.

[83] Icica heptaphylla.

[84] I use the expression "Venezuelan side" because of our own idea of the national boundaries, but the Venezuelans claim as theirs the territory stretching east as far as the Essequibo river, and south to Brazil almost to the River Parima.

[85] Janipha Coeflingo.

[86] Psophia crepitans.

[87] Anas moschata.

[88] Ampelis cotinga.

[89] Cyperus alternifolius.

[90] Lacythis ollaris.

[91] Carapa Guianensis.

[92] Cyphorinus cantans.

[93] I have adhered to the spelling of Roraima as laid down by Sir R. Schomburgh and Mr. Barrington Brown, but the natives certainly pronounce the "ai" in the same way that they pronounce the i in Marima, i.e. Mareema. It may be, as in other cases, that different tribes have different pronunciations of the same name.

[94] Most of these so-called mountains are little more than high hill ranges, but their excessive steepness and the difficult nature of the ascent render them far from despicable.

[95] Cladonia reticulata.

[96] The height of Roraima above the sea is about 8000 feet; the table-land from which it rises being about 3,500 feet above sea level.

[97] Ladenbergia densiflora.

[98] Milvulus forficatus.

[99] Sturnella magna.

[100] Myrmecophaga jubata.

[101] Cleistes rosea.

[102] Stanhopea oculata.

[103] Tillandsia lingulata.

[104] Sobralia Elizabetha.

[105] Thibaudia Pichinchensis.

[106] Waterton, in speaking of the blow-pipe says that this extraordinary tube of death is, perhaps, one of the greatest natural curiosities of Guiana. The amazingly long reed of which it is composed grows hollow without knot or joint. This is called the Ourah. Being of itself too slender to answer the end of a blow-pipe, a species of Palma is used as a case in which they put the Ourah. This outer case is called Samourah. The arrow—poisoned—is from nine to ten inches in length.

[107] Nasua.

[108] The "ha-ha" is a wicker shield, with which the opponents try to push each other down.

[109] The Monouri ant is used by the Indians as one of the ingredients in preparing the deadly Wourali poison.

[110] The names of these and the other falls marked in the map were given to us by Lanceman, who claimed familiarity with all of them.

[111] In the mountainous district of Mérida—another of the States of Venezuela—the Sierra Nevada peak attains an altitude of nearly 14,000 feet above the sea.

[112] Amongst the few coleoptera that I recognised were those of the curious genus Brentus and the giant Prionus. There were also brilliant silver green Curculios, golden green and coppery Buprestidæ, steel blue Scarabœi glossed with purple, and a few specimens of Phaucus lancifer, whose golden body was tinged with green and violet.

[113] Tanagra septicolor.

[114] "Amais la libertad? pues—vivais en la campagna."

[115] Bersimum glactodendron.

[116] Mr. Otis says: "Among the most important concessions by the terms of this contract was one guaranteeing that all public lands lying on the line of the road were to be used gratuitously by the Company, also a gift of 250,000 acres of land, to be selected by the grantees from any public lands on the Isthmus. Two ports, one on the Atlantic and the other on the Pacific (which were to be the termini of the road) were to be free ports; and the privilege was granted of establishing such tolls as the Company might think proper. The contract was to continue in force for forty-nine years, subject to the right of New Granada to take possession of the road at the expiration of twenty years after its completion, on payment of five millions of dollars; on the expiration of thirty years on payment of four millions; and at the expiration of forty years on payment of two millions. Three per cent was to be paid to the New Granada government upon all dividends declared. The entire work was to be completed within eight years."

[117] Crotophaga.

[118] Owing to the rapid decay of the wooden poles which were formerly used, the chief engineer (Colonel Totten) conceived the idea of moulding a support of concrete. A small scantling of pitch pine was placed upright and surrounded by a jointed wooden mould, fifteen inches in diameter at base, tapering to about eight inches at the top and sunk into the earth sufficiently for support; this was filled with concrete. When the mould was removed, it was found firm and strong and well adapted to the purpose, being perfectly weather and insect proof. These posts have the appearance of hewn stone.

[119] Peristeria elata.

[120] The author of "Three Years in Chili," says, "The grass of which they—Panama hats—are made is found chiefly in the neighbouring province of San Cristoval. They can be braided only in the night or early in the morning, as the heat in the day-time renders the grass brittle. It takes a native about three months to braid one of the finest quality, and I saw some hats which looked like fine linen, and are valued at fifty dollars apiece even here."

[121] Cathartes aura.

[122] "Historical Record upon the Boundaries between the Republic of Colombia and the Empire of Brazil," By José M. Quijano Otero.

[123] It seems to have slipped the notice both of the proposers and those to whom it was proposed, that by no possible means could a line following the Cuyuni river reach the Roraima range or anywhere near it.—J.W.B.W.

Booksophile
Your Local Online Bookstore

Buy Books Online from
www.Booksophile.com

Explore our collection of books written in various languages and uncommon topics from different parts of the world, including history, art and culture, poems, autobiography and bibliographies, cooking, action & adventure, world war, fiction, science, and law.

Add to your bookshelf or gift to another lover of books - first editions of some of the most celebrated books ever published. From classic literature to bestsellers, you will find many first editions that were presumed to be out-of-print.

Free shipping globally for orders worth US$ 100.00.

Use code "Shop_10" to avail additional 10% on first order.

Visit today
www.booksophile.com

Milton Keynes UK
Ingram Content Group UK Ltd.
UKHW010426131223
434231UK00004B/339